◇ "南京师范大学研究生课程案例库"建设项目

商务英语翻译案例教程

A Case Coursebook for Business English Translation

主　编　董晓波
副主编　唐　瑭
编　者　裴　鸣　李倩雯
　　　　黄　颖　孙苓玉

清华大学出版社
北京交通大学出版社
·北京·

内 容 简 介

本书从语言学、商学、翻译学三个角度对商务英语翻译进行较为全面、系统的诠释,立足于高素质、专门化翻译人才之培养创新,着重于专业化与学术化之高度结合,理论与实践相得益彰,策略与技巧有机融合,内容丰富、系统,视野宽阔,素材新颖、典型、应有尽有。

本书主要供高等院校英语专业(经贸、法律、翻译等方向)的本科生和研究生,商学、经济学等相关专业的本科生和研究生,以及英语教师、商务英语研究人员作为教材或参考书使用。

本书封面贴有清华大学出版社防伪标签,无标签者不得销售。
版权所有,侵权必究。侵权举报电话:010-62782989 13501256678 13801310933

图书在版编目(CIP)数据

商务英语翻译案例教程 / 董晓波主编. —北京:北京交通大学出版社:清华大学出版社,2018.11(2021.12 重印)

ISBN 978-7-5121-3765-3

Ⅰ. ① 商⋯ Ⅱ. ① 董⋯ Ⅲ. ① 商务–英语–翻译–教材 Ⅳ. ① F7

中国版本图书馆 CIP 数据核字(2018)第 250555 号

商务英语翻译案例教程
SHANGWU YINGYU FANYI ANLI JIAOCHENG

责任编辑:	景小卫
出版发行:	清 华 大 学 出 版 社　邮编:100084　电话:010-62776969　http://www.tup.com.cn
	北京交通大学出版社　邮编:100044　电话:010-51686414　http://www.bjtup.com.cn
印 刷 者:	北京鑫海金澳胶印有限公司
经　　销:	全国新华书店
开　　本:	185 mm×260 mm　印张:15　字数:384 千字
版　　次:	2018 年 11 月第 1 版　2021 年 12 月第 2 次印刷
定　　价:	39.00 元

本书如有质量问题,请向北京交通大学出版社质监组反映。对您的意见和批评,我们表示欢迎和感谢。
投诉电话:010-51686043,51686008;传真:010-62225406;E-mail:press@bjtu.edu.cn。

前言 Preface

　　随着中国经济规模的不断扩大，在"一带一路"伟大倡议的推动下，在"构建人类命运共同体"的新时代，我国与世界各国的国际商务活动日益频繁，国际商务英语的应用也越来越广泛，作用也越来越显著。在此背景下，应用性复合型商务英语翻译人才就必然成为国家急需的重要战略资源和储备。本书的目的是通过介绍国际主要商务活动的翻译实践，帮助学习者掌握有关商贸领域和国际商务翻译的基本理论知识，进而提升学习者对各类商务语篇进行翻译实践的能力。

　　我们知道，实践能力原则是案例教学的第一原则，实践能力是案例教学的出发点和立足点，案例教学注重培养学生的思维能力、分析能力、判断能力及运用所学知识处理复杂问题的能力。案例教学为理论与实践的整合提供了一条独特的路径，在理论与实践的沟壑之间架设了一座桥梁。本书的特点是以案例为媒介、以问题为起点，结合翻译理论及其技巧点拨，从商务专业知识、翻译及语言三方面综合探讨商务英语翻译，着重专业化与学术化之高度结合，理论与实践相得益彰。全书共分为12章，第1章至第4章系统地介绍了企业在产品推广及宣传方面的翻译知识，包括商务广告、产品说明书、企业宣传资料和商务报告；第5章至第12章为商务专业领域翻译章节，包括商务谈判、代理合同、国际贸易合同、国际贸易单证、信用证、商务索赔、商务仲裁和国际商法。

　　本书作为《法律英语翻译案例教程》的姊妹篇，同样是"南京师范大学研究生课程案例库"建设项目的研究成果。该书的许多内容在南京师范大学翻译硕士专业学位课程"商务文本翻译"的课堂上讲授过，取得了良好的效果。现将内容整理、完善成书，以飨读者。在整个编写过程中，我们力求完美，但是限于水平和资料等原因，不乏偏颇和疏漏之处，恳请广大同仁和读者不吝指正，以便将来进一步充实与完善。

董晓波
2018年10月

目录

Chapter 1 商务广告 ·· 1
    Section 1   概述 ·· 1
    Section 2   译例分析 ·· 3
    Section 3   实践总结 ·· 5
    Section 4   巩固练习 ·· 11

Chapter 2 产品说明书 ·· 13
    Section 1   概述 ·· 13
    Section 2   译例分析 ·· 15
    Section 3   实践总结 ·· 20
    Section 4   巩固练习 ·· 24

Chapter 3 企业宣传资料 ·· 26
    Section 1   概述 ·· 26
    Section 2   译例分析 ·· 28
    Section 3   实践总结 ·· 34
    Section 4   巩固练习 ·· 39

Chapter 4 商务报告 ·· 41
    Section 1   概述 ·· 41
    Section 2   译例分析 ·· 42
    Section 3   实践总结 ·· 45
    Section 4   巩固练习 ·· 51

Chapter 5 商务谈判 ·· 53
    Section 1   概述 ·· 53
    Section 2   译例分析 ·· 55
    Section 3   实践总结 ·· 59
    Section 4   巩固练习 ·· 63

Chapter 6 代理合同 ·· 64
    Section 1   概述 ·· 64

  Section 2 译例分析 ··· 66
  Section 3 实践总结 ··· 75
  Section 4 巩固练习 ··· 81

Chapter 7 国际贸易合同 ··· 88

  Section 1 概述 ··· 88
  Section 2 译例分析 ··· 94
  Section 3 实践总结 ··· 105
  Section 4 巩固练习 ··· 110

Chapter 8 国际贸易单证 ··· 117

  Section 1 概述 ··· 117
  Section 2 译例分析 ··· 118
  Section 3 实践总结 ··· 131
  Section 4 巩固练习 ··· 136

Chapter 9 信用证 ·· 137

  Section 1 概述 ··· 137
  Section 2 译例分析 ··· 143
  Section 3 实践总结 ··· 153
  Section 4 巩固练习 ··· 160

Chapter 10 商务索赔 ··· 162

  Section 1 概述 ··· 162
  Section 2 译例分析 ··· 165
  Section 3 实践总结 ··· 168
  Section 4 巩固练习 ··· 175

Chapter 11 商务仲裁 ··· 177

  Section 1 概述 ··· 177
  Section 2 译例分析 ··· 178
  Section 3 实践总结 ··· 185
  Section 4 巩固练习 ··· 189

Chapter 12 国际商法 ··· 191

  Section 1 概述 ··· 191
  Section 2 译例分析 ··· 192
  Section 3 实践总结 ··· 199
  Section 4 巩固练习 ··· 205

Keys to Exercises ·· 207

参考文献 ·· 231

Chapter 1

商 务 广 告

Section 1 概 述

一、商务广告的定义

商务广告是指商品经营者或服务提供者承担费用并通过一定的媒介和形式直接或间接介绍所推销的商品或提供的服务的广告。商务广告是人们为了利益而制作的广告,目的是宣传某种产品而让人们去购买它。

二、商务广告的分类

(1) 根据宣传目的的不同,可分为商业广告(commercial advertising)和公益广告(public welfare advertising)。

(2) 根据目标顾客群的不同,可分为消费者广告(consumer advertising)和企业广告(business advertising)。

(3) 根据覆盖地域的不同,可分为国际广告(international advertising)、国内广告(national advertising)、区域广告(regional advertising)和地方广告(local advertising)。

(4) 根据广告媒介的不同,可分为印刷广告(printing advertising)、电子广告(electric advertising)和网络广告(network advertising)。

(5) 根据广告内容的不同,可分为产品广告(product advertising)和非产品广告(non-product advertising);非产品广告则包括劳务广告(service advertising)、招聘广告(employment advertising)、旅游广告(tourism advertising)和征婚广告(dating advertising)。

三、商务广告的功能

商务广告既是一种经济现象,具有功利性;也是一种文化现象,具有思想性。因此,商务广告具有社会功能和文化功能两大功能。

(一) 商务广告的社会功能

商务广告的社会功能会对社会造成广泛而深远的影响。这是因为,不管是有意还是无意,很多广告都表达、折射了某种思想观念，体现出某种价值评判和价值追求。人们接受广告的过程就是一个被诉求、被感染、被影响的过程。广告的传播速度快、传播范围广、重复频次高，每天充斥于广大受众的生活时空，日积月累，潜移默化。可见，广告的确可以影响受众的文化心理，改变受众的思维方式和价值取向。事实上，我国社会风气的变化、思想观念的解放、生活方式的改变，无不与广告息息相关。

（二）商务广告的文化功能

商务广告是商品促销的重要手段，具有鲜明的功利特征和强大的经济功能。商务广告也是一种社会文化现象，是社会文化的组成部分，因而也具有文化的特征和功能。我们在利用商务广告经济功能的同时，还应当把广告纳入社会文化的系统中加以考察，充分认识商业广告的文化功能及其所担负的文化责任，以便更好地利用它，使之在社会精神文明建设中也能发挥积极的作用。

广告向人们所传递的有关商品、服务、企业等经济、科技、文化诸多方面的信息，是人类所创造的物质文化和精神文化的反映。我们可以看到，现代商务广告不仅介绍各种商品和各类服务项目，说明其特点、功能、作用，向消费者作出承诺，而且传播各种文化意识，展示异彩纷呈的文化景观，说明广告商品与文化的关系。这为广告商品增加了文化附加值，增添了文化吸引力，商务广告因此成为一种社会文化现象，既代表一定的物质文化、行为文化，又代表一定的观念文化、精神文化。在商品无差异、同质化造成市场竞争异常激烈的今天，广告文化的影响力往往大于广告商品自身的竞争力。如果受众认同了一种广告文化，那么也就可能会接受该广告商品或服务，成为商品的消费者和服务的利用者。

四、商务广告的特征

（1）以营利为目的。这是商务广告的根本属性。

（2）有明确的广告主并支付费用。广告主通常通过付费来宣传其产品。在现代广告活动中，广告主是指那些为发布广告信息付钱的机构或个人。

（3）商务广告是说服的艺术，目的在于影响消费者的行动。

（4）商务广告是有目的的、有计划的、连续性的。

（5）商务广告通过一定的传播媒介进行。

（6）商务广告的对象是有选择的，即有目标市场和目标受众。

五、商务广告的原则

（1）真实性。真实性是商务广告最基本的原则。

（2）思想性。商务广告既是一种经济现象，也是一种社会宣传活动。

（3）规范性。商务广告必须遵守国家法律法规。

（4）目的性。商务广告有明确的目标受众和目标市场，有的放矢。

（5）科学性。商务广告的制作、使用、管理都与现代化科学技术手段相结合，从宏观、微观上进行定量、定性的科学研究。

（6）艺术性。商务广告也是一门艺术。艺术性越强，广告越有吸引力、表现力、感染力。

Section 2 译例分析

>> *Passage On*[1]

In the ocean wildness[2], a tower of rock crowns a very private cove, a cove untouched by the world, yet replete with world luxuries, with only the murmur of waves to break the solitude[3].

Exotic blooms…quiet strolls…feasts of fresh-caught seafood[4], create an experience of pure magic.

Let Dakak in Dapitan city charm you…the way you will go on board Philippine Airlines.

▸ Key Words

ocean wildness	一望无垠的海洋深处
untouched by the world	人迹罕至
the murmur of waves	海浪的喃喃细语
break the solitude	打破无边的静寂
pure magic	奇妙的仙境

▸ Notes

1. 这是一篇描述性极强的广告，符合广告的祈使功能和美感功能。由于汉语的描述性更强，所以译文应该把原文的韵味传达出来。

2. 这里的 wildness 没有取其"荒野"之意，而是译成"一望无垠的海洋深处"，以达到广告的美感。

3. 原文使用了拟人的手法，译文也应使用拟人的手法，murmur 一词可以译成"喃喃细语"，这样便非常生动形象。

4. 原文多用形容词，译文为突出广告语的特点，可以使用四字的修饰语，如可以译成"异国情调""悠闲漫步""海鲜盛宴"等，进一步生动形象地展现原文的意境。

参考译文

在一望无垠的海洋深处，一座石塔高高地耸立在静静的海湾之上。

这是一个人迹罕至的海湾，却充满了人世间的奢华，只有海浪的喃喃细语打破无边的静寂。

充满异国情调的鲜花，悠闲漫步的游客，美味的海鲜盛宴……使人仿佛置身于奇妙的仙境。

达皮丹市的达卡令您如此痴迷……就如同您登上菲律宾航班一样。

Passage Two

"金猪玉璧"——和谐盛世的收藏极品[1]

古有"和氏璧"，今有"金猪玉璧"[2]。"和氏璧"，价值连城，玉中至尊；"金猪玉璧"，升值无限，收藏极品[3]。"金猪玉璧"是由中国印钞造币总公司发行的"金玉良缘"系列生肖藏品之首款藏品。它金相玉映，品质卓越，格调不凡，身价不菲。宜馈赠，永志良缘；宜珍藏，金吉玉瑞。[4]"金猪玉璧"一相逢，便胜却人间无数。[5]"金猪玉璧"是作为情缘礼品、亲情赠品和艺术藏品的理想选择。

Key Words

收藏极品	superb treasure for collection
价值连城	precious
品质卓越，格调不凡	with excellent quality and exceptional style
金吉玉瑞	indicating auspiciousness
理想选择	an ideal present

Notes

1. 原文是一篇文言味极强的广告，体现出"金猪玉璧"的中国文化传统和韵味。所以，要翻译此篇广告并非易事。由于英文的描述性不如汉语的描述性强，英文读者对英译文的文化预期也会不同于中文读者对中文的文化预期，所以有些地方可以进行归化处理，这样还可以照顾到英文读者的文化心理结构。

2. 这里使用了对仗，但是应考虑到英文读者可能不太清楚何为"和氏璧"，所以在翻译时，可以使用较短的同位语 a precious emerald 进行解释。

3. 这里又使用了对仗。而且，汉语喜欢使用重复，即重复前文所述的"和氏璧"和"金猪玉璧"，而英文喜欢用指代以避免重复，所以译文可以分别将之译成 the former 和 the latter。同时，译文可以将原文的并列结构转化成英文的从属结构，但两个分句应基本保持对应和平行。

4. 原文中的"金相玉映""永志良缘""金吉玉瑞"有着深刻的中国文化内涵，但如前文所述，英文读者不一定理解其中的内涵，所以可以将之简单化。同样，"品质卓越，格调不凡，身价不菲"也可以作简化处理，两句合译成："With excellent quality and exceptional style, it can be both a present suggesting good luck and a treasure indicating auspiciousness."。

5. 本句套用了中国的一句古诗："金风玉露一相逢，便胜却人间无数。"这实际上是一种双关表达法,但是由于两种文化的差异,双关语很难进行翻译,所以依然可以作简化处理:"Gold Pig & Crystal Emerald, distinctive and priceless, a perfect match of gold with emerald"。英文使用的是句子片断而非完整的句子,显得短促明了,符合英文广告语的特点。

 参考译文

Gold Pig & Crystal Emerald
—Superb treasure for collection in an age of harmony prosperity

In ancient China, our forefathers already crafted "He Shi Bi", a precious emerald, and today, we are proud to present Gold Pig & Crystal Emerald. The former was invaluable and second to none, while the latter is superb treasure for collection. Gold Pig & Crystal Emerald, issued by China Banknote Printing and Minting Corporation, is its first of Gold-Emerald-Match series. With excellent quality and exceptional style, it can be both a present suggesting good luck and a treasure indicating auspiciousness. Gold Pig & Crystal Emerald, distinctive and priceless, a perfect match of gold with emerald, is an ideal present for lovers and families as well as ideal treasure for collection.

Section 3 实 践 总 结

一、翻译技巧

(一)商务广告的词汇特点

1. 简明、通俗、易记

为吸引消费者并给他们留下深刻印象,广告文字必须具备简单通俗、易懂易记的特点。具体来说,就是注重运用频率较高的词语,多用大众化的口语词语、简单动词、常用形容词和俚语,并使之附上时代感和引申义,尽可能少用晦涩难懂、有歧义的词语,并删去可有可无的词语。例如:

① 原文:Mosquito Bye Bye Bye.

　　译文:蚊虫杀杀杀。

　　解析:Bye 是非常口语化的词语,大家每天都在用,而在这里对蚊子连道三声再见,既形象又俏皮,让消费者过耳不忘,可以达到非常好的广告宣传效果。

② 原文:Minolta, finest to put you finest.

　　译文:第一流的美能达,第一流的你。

解析：形容词最高级 finest 富于感情色彩和渲染力，重复使用含有褒义色彩的评价性词汇为广告语增添了极大的魅力。

2. 新奇与创意

商务广告文字要有创新性，使文字富有个性和新意，因为独具一格的广告语是使消费者"倾心"的秘诀。广告语言新奇感的创造，一般从微观入手，注重词语的选择和锤炼，还要善于创造新词、新字、新表达，并加以巧妙运用。例如：

① 原文：Give a Timex to all, and to all a good time.

译文：拥有一块天美时表，拥有一段美好时光。

解析：这是天美时表的广告标题。Timex 由 Time+Excellent 构成，合成的新词 Timex 在构词上可以让读者联想到"时间"和"优秀"，充分强调了此表计时准确的优点。

② 原文：We know eggsactly how to sell eggs.

译文：我们怎不知如何卖蛋。

解析：这是一则销售禽蛋的广告，原文的 eggsactly 来自 exactly。由于该广告与禽蛋有关，所以故意将 exactly 拼写成有 egg（蛋）的 eggsactly，以增强 egg 给人留下的印象。

3. 强烈的针对性

商务广告理想的效果是让目标客户群尽可能多地了解该产品或服务，因此要抓住产品最主要的特点，根据消费者的特殊心理，有的放矢，打动听众。例如：

① 原文：汰渍放进去，污垢洗出来。

译文：Tide's in, dirt's out.

解析：该广告抓住了洗衣粉的最大特点和消费者的心理，然后用最形象、最生动的对称性语言表达出来，针对性极强。

② 原文：Not all cars are created equal.

译文1：并非所有的车都是一样的。（美国版）

译文2：古有千里马，今有三菱车。（中国版）

解析：三菱汽车公司向美国市场推销产品时，创造了广告标语 "Not all cars are created equal."。熟悉美国历史的人一见这则广告，立即会想起《美国独立宣言》中的 "All men are created equal."。日本广告商将原句中的 men 改为 cars 来突出广告目标，将原来的肯定句式改为否定句式，道出了该车的优越性能。而三菱公司面向中国市场时则将其广告标语改为"古有千里马，今有三菱车"，巧妙地运用对偶这种中国人喜爱的修辞手法，使中国消费者读起来既亲切熟悉又生动形象。同一广告语的不同翻译，体现了该广告对于不同市场和不同消费群体的极强的针对性。

（二）商务广告的句法特点

1. 句式简单

英汉两种语言中的广告语都倾向于使用言简意赅的表达方法，贴切自然地表达所宣传的产品，所以商务广告多用短句、简单句、不完整句和省略句，这些句子简单明了，目的就是引人注意。例如：

① 原文：For next generation.

译文：新一代的选择。（百事可乐）

② 原文：A work of art.
　　译文：艺术精品。（苏格兰威士忌）

2. 多用祈使句

广告语使用祈使句能引导消费者走进产品，起到引导、劝说、敦促消费者采取行动的作用。例如：

① 原文：Just do it.
　　译文：想做就做。（耐克）

② 原文：Begin your own tradition.
　　译文：代代相传，由你开始。（百达翡丽）

3. 多用疑问句

疑问句能够缩短广告与消费者的距离，增加渲染力度，加强语势，启发思考，吸引注意力。所以，商务广告也经常使用疑问句。例如：

① 原文：Have you ever drunk mineral water?
　　译文：你喝过山泉水吗？（农夫山泉）

② 原文：Are you going gray too early?
　　译文：您的头发是不是白得为时过早？（乌发乳）

4. 多用主动语态

主动语态更能表达一种主观感觉或感受，所以英语广告语多使用主动语态，以让人感觉真实，贴近自己。例如：

① 原文：What we do, we do well.
　　译文：我有我的品质。

② 原文：Look again, and you will never look back.
　　译文：再看一看，你将不再追忆过去。

5. 多用现在时

除叙事式广告使用过去时外，英文广告为了营造身临其境的气氛，多用现在时或现在完成时。例如：

① 原文：Golden Monkey takes me everywhere.
　　译文：穿金猴皮鞋，走金光大道。（金猴皮鞋）

② 原文：It happens at the Hilton!
　　译文：希尔顿酒店有求必应！（希尔顿酒店）

（三）商务广告的修辞手法

1. 比喻

比喻是一种常见的修辞手法，包括明喻和暗喻。广告语中使用明喻，能使广告商品的特征一目了然，形象生动；使用暗喻则可以使人发挥丰富的想象力，更巧妙地增强语言的美感。例如：

① 原文：Light as a breeze, soft as a cloud.
　　译文：轻如微风，柔似彩云。（明喻）

② 原文：Ebel, the architects of time.
译文：玉宝手表，时间设计师。（暗喻）

2. 拟人

拟人手法是把所宣传的事物人格化，赋予其人的品格和言行。广告语中使用拟人手法会使所宣传的商品更生动形象，富有人情味，使消费者产生亲切感，从而激发消费者的购买欲望。例如：

① 原文：Strong tractor, strong farmer.
译文：勇猛的拖拉机，勇猛的耕田夫。（把拖拉机比拟为钢铁巨人，以农民的好帮手的形象打动消费者）

② 原文：Flowers by Interflora speak from the heart.
译文：Interflora 鲜花，用心表达。（speak 一词突显了鲜花的灵动）

3. 双关

中英文广告都会使用双关的修辞手法，使广告语耐人寻味，读起来朗朗上口。双关主要是利用谐音双关和语义双关。例如：

① 原文：百衣百顺。（蒸汽熨斗广告）
译文：All clothes are always well pressed.

② 原文：口服心服。（矿泉水广告）
译文：Drinking is believing.

这两句广告语分别使用了"百依百顺"的谐音双关和"心服口服"的语义双关，既体现出产品的特征和属性，又简单明了、朗朗上口。

4. 反复

为了表达的需要，重复使用同一词语或句子的修辞手法叫作反复。广告语中使用反复，在语言形式上有承上启下的作用，在语气上能渲染气氛，营造一种特殊的情调，从而增加消费者对所宣传产品的印象。例如：

① 原文：Everything is extraordinary; everything tempts.
译文：件件超凡脱俗，样样新颖诱人。（卡地亚）

② 原文：如意如意，尽如人意。（如意保温瓶）
译文：All as you wish.

5. 押韵

押韵是诗歌中常用的手法，而广告中使用押韵可以使其富有节奏感，使消费者从广告语中获得美的享受，记住产品的效果，加深对广告产品的印象。押韵分为头韵、尾韵和内部押韵。例如：

① 原文：Don't just dream it. Drive it.
译文：心动不如行动。（头韵：dream 和 drive）

② 原文：A Mars a day keeps you work, rest and play.
译文：每日一块玛氏巧克力，工作满意，舒适惬意。（句内押韵：day 和 play）

③ 原文：Go well, use Shell.
译文：行万里路，用壳牌油。（尾韵：well 和 Shell）

6. 夸张

广告语中使用夸张的手法是为了生动地揭示产品的本质并加强语言的感染力，给消费者以深刻的印象，激发其丰富的想象力，形成一种艺术渲染。例如：

原文：We have hidden a garden full of vegetables where you'd never expect. In a pie.

译文：在您意想不到的地方，我们珍藏了满园的蔬菜——就在那小小的馅饼里。

（四）商务广告的翻译技巧

1. 直译法

直译法是指在不违背译入语语言规范及不引起曲解原文含义的情况下，译文中保留原文表达方式的一种翻译方法，这是广告翻译中最常用的方法。这种方法主要用来处理一些原文意思较明确、语句结构较完整简单、按字面意思翻译能同时表达句子的表层意思和深层意思的广告语。例如：

原文：Winning the hearts of the world.

译文：赢取天下心。

2. 意译法

意译是一个相对于"直译"的概念，这种翻译方法在形式上较为自由、灵活，基本保留原文的意思，但可在原文的基础上进行适当发挥。对于采用了修辞手法的广告语，有时无法在译入语中再现其修辞特征，只能传译其意义，这时要用到意译法。例如：

原文：FedEx: We live to deliver.

译文：联邦快递，诚信为本。

3. 创译法

创译法是指创造性翻译，但绝不是指脱离原文的纯粹的创造。译文尽管在表层意义上与原文少有相似之处，却能与原广告神似。该译法比一般的简单翻译意境更高、感染力更强。例如：

原文：Bridging the distance.

译文：沟通无限。

4. 增补法

增补是在原文的基础上进行适当的添加，从而取得更好的广告效果。一般说来，英译汉更容易采用增补的手法，因为汉语的广告语可以更长一些，而且更多时候是为了前后对仗。例如：

原文：Good to the last drop!

译文：滴滴香浓，意犹未尽！（麦斯威尔咖啡）

5. 仿译法

仿译法是指使用译入语文化背景中常用的名言名句等，通过套用的方式，跨越不同的文化背景，再现原文的含义。例如：

原文：Where there is a South, there is a way.

译文：有南方，事竟成。

解析：原文套用"Where there is a will, there is a way."的句式。译文采用仿译法，套用中国人熟知的"有志者，事竟成"，将原文翻译成"有南方，事竟成"，准确地传达出原文的信息。

二、经典广告语和商标翻译

(一) 经典广告语翻译

① A diamond lasts forever.
钻石恒久远,一颗永流传。(戴·比尔斯)
② Things go better with Coca-Cola.
饮可口可乐,万事如意。(可口可乐)
③ M&M's melt in your mouth, not in your hand.
只溶在口,不溶在手。(M&M's 巧克力)
④ No business too small, no problem too big.
没有不做的小生意,没有解决不了的大问题。(IBM)
⑤ Intelligence everywhere.
智慧演绎,无处不在。(摩托罗拉手机)
⑥ To me, the past black and white, but the future is always colorful.
对我而言,过去平淡无奇;而未来,却是绚烂缤纷。(轩尼诗酒)
⑦ Time is what you make of it.
天长地久。(斯沃琪手表)
⑧ Start ahead.
成功之路,从头开始。(飘柔)
⑨ Where there is a way, there is a Toyota.
有路就有丰田车。(丰田汽车)
⑩ Apple thinks different.
苹果电脑,不同凡"想"。(苹果电脑)

(二) 经典商标翻译

Siemens	西门子
Facebook	脸书
Starbucks	星巴克
Unilever	联合利华
Carrefour	家乐福
Longines	浪琴
IKEA	宜家
Hazeline	夏士莲
Revlon	露华浓
Citibank	花旗银行
Dabao	大宝
Lego	乐高

Konka	康佳
Kelon	科龙
Septwolves	七匹狼
Lenovo	联想
Peak	匹克
Canon	佳能
Colgate	高露洁
Flyco	飞科

Section 4　巩 固 练 习

一、翻译以下英文广告。

1. Intel inside. (Intel Pentium)

2. Every time a good time. (McDonald's)

3. You are at 35,000 feet. Your head is in New York. Your heart is in Paris. Your Rolex can be in both places at once. (Rolex)

4. She's the nimblest girl around. Nimble is the way she goes. Nimble is the bread she eats. Light, delicious, nimble. (Nimble)

5. The relentless pursuit of perfection. (Lexus)

6. A journey is not a trip. It's not a vacation. It's a process, a discovery; it is a process of self-discovery. A journey brings us face to face with ourselves. A journey shows us not only the world, but how we fit in it. Does the person create the journey, or does the journey create the person? The journey is life itself. Where will life take you? Louis Vuitton. (Louis Vuitton)

7. Introducing the new Toshiba 2230 Turbo, the first turbocharged copier in history. Beneath its sleek exterior is a copying system. So remarkable it's actually patented. With it, you can produce 22 copier a minute, or hit the turbo button and turn out 30 copier a minute. So now you have the power to work 40% more efficiently, while using 33% less toner. And what's even more revolutionary, we've managed to do it without turbo charging the price. To arrange for a free demonstration, just call 1-800-Go-TOSHIBA. (Toshiba)

二、翻译以下中文广告。

1. 健康笑容来自佳洁士。（佳洁士）

2. 提神醒脑，喝七喜。（七喜）

3. 《读者文摘》给世人带来欢乐。（读者文摘）

4. 要想皮肤好，早晚用大宝。（大宝）

5. 一包好牛奶，是感情与理智巧妙平衡的结晶。这富含天然优质乳蛋白的牛奶，滴滴融入乳牛的幸福。从奶源基地到进入包装，更是对于理性的考验，堪称全球楷模的样板工厂，领先世界的先进工艺,确保牛奶闻更香、饮更浓。如此无与伦比的醇香感受,只在特仑苏。高贵的人生,来自精神和物质的双重给养。用心工作,用心享受生活,以金牌的标准要求自己,亦只感受金牌品质的人生。而此刻,就像我们只喝特仑苏。我只纵情这无可比拟的绿色,于天地间放飞自由心灵,这就是特仑苏人生。(特仑苏)

6. 别具匠心的苏州园林驰名中外。亭台楼阁,池石林泉,疏密适度,相映生辉;廊榭曲折,沟壑幽深,移步换景,引人入胜;布局结构,各显特色。(苏州园林)

Chapter 2

产品说明书

Section 1 概 述

一、产品说明书的定义

产品说明书在英语中通常有三种说法,即使用指导(instruction)、用法说明(direction)、说明书(description)。

产品说明书是一种常见的说明文,是生产者向消费者全面、明确地介绍产品名称、用途、性质、性能、原理、构造、规格、使用方法、保养维护、注意事项等内容而写的准确、简明的文字材料。产品说明书是产品标识的重要组成部分,是在产品或包装上用于识别产品或其特性、特征的各种表达和指示的统称。

二、产品说明书的功能

产品说明书作为展现企业产品的最直接的手段,必须具备一定的功能和特性,以达到生产产品和消费产品的目的。具体来说,一个合格的产品说明书应具备以下三种功能。

(一)宣传产品

宣传产品可以激发消费者的购买欲望,从而实现购买,促进商品流通。宣传产品是产品说明书的基本属性。

(二)扩大消息

产品说明书在信息传播、复制、交流、利用、反馈等方面,作用十分重要,因为它在社会生产过程中,实现了生产、交换、分配、消费四个环节中交换和消费两个环节的必然连接。

(三)传播知识

产品说明书的内容涉及科学文化知识等的普及、宣传和利用,凝聚着知识的结晶。生产者实现销售,是从制作产品说明书开始;消费者认识产品,往往也是从阅读产品说明书开始。

三、产品说明书的类型

产品说明书应用广泛，类型多种多样，按不同的分类标准可分类如下。

（1）按对象、行业的不同分类，可分为工业产品说明书、农业产品说明书、金融产品说明书、保险产品说明书等。

（2）按形式的不同分类，可分为条款（条文）式产品说明书、图表式产品说明书、条款（条文）和图表结合式说明书、网上购物产品说明书、音像型产品说明书、口述产品说明书等。

（3）按内容的不同分类，可分为详细产品说明书、简要产品说明书等。

（4）按语种的不同分类，可分为中文产品说明书、外文产品说明书、中外文对照产品说明书等。

（5）按说明书性质的不同分类，可分为特殊产品说明书、一般产品说明书等。

四、产品说明书的结构

产品说明书的结构通常由标题、正文和落款三个部分构成。

（一）标题（title）

产品说明书的标题通常由产品名称或说明对象加上文种构成，一般放在说明书的第一行，要注重视觉效果，可以有不同的样式设计。

（二）正文（body）

正文是产品说明书的主体部分，是介绍产品的特征、性能、使用方法、保养维护、注意事项等内容的核心所在。常见的主体包括以下内容：

（1）概述（general description）。
（2）指标（index）。
（3）结构（structure）。
（4）特点（features）。
（5）使用方法（methods/usage）。
（6）注意事项（notes）。
（7）保养（maintenance）。
（8）责任（responsibilities）。

（三）落款（signature）

即写明生产者和经销者的名称、地址、电话、邮政编码、邮箱等内容，为消费者进行必要的联系提供方便。

Section 2　译 例 分 析

Passage One

Product Introduction

[Features[1] of product]

Luxury wide door series, European optimized man-machine design. No door handle, open it by pulling of the door edge. High energy saving.[2] Phasing in high energy-saving compressor, three cycling system and thick insulation get the appliance having high cooling efficiency and better energy saving.

[Safety information]

Make sure[3] to use a separate earthed socket. Pull out the mains plug when you repair or clean the machine. Do not store inflammable or explosive materials in appliances to avoid explosion or fire.

[Transportation and placement]

Do not move the appliance by holding a door or door handle. You should lift it from the bottom. You can not lie down or reverse the appliance to move.[4]

[Connecting the appliance]

The rated voltage of the appliance is 220V alternating current[5] and the rated frequency is 50Hz. It can vary from 180V to 220V.

[Operations]

Take away all the packing components, including the bottom foam pad, other pads and adhesive tape for fixing as accessories in appliance.

[Cleaning and maintenance]

Defrosting

Cleaning

...

[Technical parameters and packing list]

Technical parameters

Packing list

...

[Customer service]

Warranty instructions
...

Key Words

optimized man-machine design	最优化人机工程设计
door handle	门把手
compressor	压缩机
energy saving	节能
earthed socket	接地插座
inflammable or explosive materials	易燃、易爆物品
lie down	横抬
rated voltage	额定电压
alternating current	交流电
adhesive tape	胶带
accessories	附件
packing components	包装组件
technical parameters	技术参数
packing list	装箱单

Notes

1. 在电器类说明书中，表示产品的性能、特点、特征时，一般用 features 来表达，或者可用 characteristics、traits 等词语来表达，而在其他说明书，如药品类说明书中，一般使用 properties 来表达。对于不同种类说明书的同一名词应熟练掌握不同译法。

2. 此句中，一连串描述电器类产品特点的短语可以译为中文的四字短语，表达清楚明了，也体现了中文句式的对称性和简洁性。在翻译电器类说明书时应留意这种中英文的译文表达方式。

3. 电器类说明书的主要作用是告诉使用者应如何操作和使用，其主体并不是必须指明的，所以祈使句是此类说明书最常见的句型，如 Make sure...、Pull out...、Do not...等。相应地，译成汉语时也可以采用祈使句进行处理。

4. 虽然该句中有主语 you，但译文可以不用完全照译，而是省略主语，将具体的搬运方法翻译出来。

5. 电器类说明书经常会出现额定电压、额定频率的表达，该句译为"额定电压为交流 220 V"。要注意积累"额定电压"的表达方式及"交流电"的翻译方法。

 参考译文

产品说明书

【产品特点】

豪华宽门系列,欧洲最优化人机工程设计,无门把手,随处开门;高效节能,采用高效节能压缩机、三循环制冷系统及加厚保温层,制冷效率更高、更节能。

【安全注意事项】

务必使用单独的、带接地线的三芯电源插座。维修或清洁冰箱时,必须拔下电源插头。禁止将易燃、易爆物品放在冰箱中,以防爆炸和火灾。

【搬运和放置】

不可抓着门或门把手来搬运冰箱,应从底部抬起冰箱。不宜将冰箱横抬或倒置。

【电器连接】

冰箱的额定电压为交流220 V,额定频率为50 Hz,允许电压波动范围为180 V到220 V。

【使用】

拆除所有包装组件,包括冰箱底部的泡沫垫及箱内固定附件用的泡沫垫和胶带。

【清洁与维护】

除霜

清洁

....

【技术参数与装箱单】

技术参数

装箱单

....

【客户服务】

保修说明

....

Passage Two

盐酸曲美他嗪片说明书[1]

(请仔细阅读说明书并在医师指导下使用)

【药品名称】

通用名称:盐酸曲美他嗪片

商品名称:万爽力®[2]

【成分】

本品主要成分:盐酸曲美他嗪

化学名称：1-(2,3,4-三甲氧基苄基)哌嗪二盐酸盐

分子式：$C_{14}H_{22}N_2O_3 \cdot 2HCl$

分子量：339.26

【性状】

本品为红色薄膜衣片，去除薄膜衣后呈白色。

【适应症】

心绞痛发作的预防性治疗。眩晕和耳鸣的辅助性对症治疗。[3]

【用法用量】

口服，每 24 小时 60 mg，每日 3 次，每次 1 片，三餐时服用。[4]

【不良反应】

罕见胃肠道不适（恶心，呕吐）。

【注意事项】

此药不作为心绞痛发作时的对症治疗用药，也不适用于对不稳定心绞痛或心肌梗死的初始治疗。此药不应用于入院前或入院后最初几天的治疗。心绞痛发作时，对冠状动脉病况应重新评估，并考虑治疗的调整（药物治疗和可能的血运重建）。

【孕妇及哺乳期妇女用药】

妊娠：动物实验没有提示致畸作用，但是由于缺乏临床资料，致畸的危险不能排除。因此，从安全的角度考虑，最好避免在妊娠期间服用该药物。

哺乳：由于缺乏通过乳汁分泌的资料，建议治疗期间不要哺乳。

【药物相互作用】

为避免不同药物之间可能的相互作用，您必须将您接受的其他治疗告知您的医生或药剂师。

【贮藏】遮光，密封保存。

【包装】药品包装用铝箔/聚氯乙烯固体药用硬片包装，30 片/盒，48 片/盒[5]。

【有效期】24 个月。

【执行标准】YBH00572010

【批准文号】国药准字 H20083596

Key Words

通用名称	generic name
分子式	molecular formula
薄膜衣片	film-coated tablet
预防性治疗	prophylactic treatment
注意事项	precautions
哺乳期妇女	lactation
致畸	teratogenicity
临床资料	clinical data

Notes

1. 药品说明书的英文表达有 instructions、directions、description 等，现在多用 package insert。或简称 insert。insert 原意为"插入物，插页"，药品说明书即为附在每种药品包装盒中的一份用药说明。

2. 药品说明书中的商品名称右上角有一个®标记，如"万爽力®"。R 是 Register（注册）的缩写，表示该产品已经由本国的有关部门批准，取得了专用的注册商标（registered trademark）。

3. 此句译为英文时，可以只列出两个名词性短语（Prophylactic treatment of episodes of angina pectoris 和 Adjuvant symptomatic treatment of vertigo and tinnitus）。句式虽简单，却短小精悍，点明要义。

4. "用法用量"是药品说明书中不可缺少的内容，但详略不一，在翻译时常使用祈使句和省略句，句中谓语动词多用被动语态。此外，还应特别注意本项中关于给药方式、剂量、剂量单位、给药时间等用词的准确性，尤其是剂量单位，稍不小心，则差之千里，可能会造成不可估计的人身伤害。

5. "包装"内容的结构特点是内容简单，多为不完整句，在翻译时仅仅列出包装工具、剂型、装量等即可。

 参考译文

Insert of Trimetazidine Dihydrochloride Tablets

(Carefully read insert and conform to the physician's prescription)

[Drug names]
Generic name: Trimetazidine dihydrochloride tablets
Trade name: VASOREL®
[Ingredients]
Main ingredients: Trimetazidine dihydrochloride
Chemical name: 1-(2, 3, 4-trimethoxybenzyl) piperazine dihydrochloride
Molecular formula: $C_{14}H_{22}N_2O_3 \cdot 2HCl$
Molecular weight: 339.26
[Description]
Red film-coated tablet with white core.
[Indications]
Prophylactic treatment of episodes of angina pectoris. Adjuvant symptomatic treatment of vertigo and tinnitus.
[Dosage and Administration]

60 mg per 24 hours: 1 tablet to be taken 3 times a day at meal times.

[Adverse reactions]

Rare cases of gastrointestinal disorders (nausea and vomiting).

[Precautions]

This drug is not a curative treatment for angina attacks, nor is it indicated as initial treatment for unstable angina, or myocardial infarction. It should not be used in the pre-hospital phase nor during the first days of hospitalization; in the event of an angina attack, the coronary artery should be reevaluated and an adaptation of the treatment considered (drug treatment and possibly revascularisation).

[Pregnancy and lactation]

Pregnancy: Studies in animals have not demonstrated a teratogenic effect; however, in the absence of clinical data, the risk of teratogenicity cannot be excluded. Therefore, for safety reasons, it is preferable to avoid prescription during pregnancy.

Breastfeeding: In the absence of data on excretion in breast milk, breastfeeding is not recommended during treatment.

[Interactions of drugs]

In order to avoid possible interactions between various medicines, you must always tell your doctor or pharmacist about any other treatment you are receiving.

[Storage] Stored in sealed and cool condition.

[Package] Aluminium foil or medicinal PVC film; 30, 48 tablets/box.

[Shelf life] 24 months.

[Specification No.] YBH00572010

[Approval No.] SFDA Approval No. H20083596

Section 3 实 践 总 结

一、翻译技巧

（一）产品说明书的翻译原则

产品说明书是企业与消费者沟通的桥梁和纽带。企业若想在激烈的国际竞争中将产品成功打入国际市场，其产品说明书的译文必须准确、真实。倘若译文失真或错误百出，不仅会给消费者留下极坏的印象，而且会影响到产品的形象与销售。更严重的是，那些劣质的译文还可能影响到正常的生产秩序，甚至危及消费者的生命与财产安全。产品说明书的翻译需遵循以下原则。

1. 忠实和准确原则

要做到译文"忠实""准确"，就要在遣词造句方面加以注意。说明书的语言大都简洁浅显,译者在处理其中的词语时并无多大困难。不过,倘若不小心,译者还是很容易掉入某些"陷阱"的。语法错误是说明书翻译中的一个问题,译者应当注意。例如:

原文:【产品特点】富含多种人体必需的维生素、矿物质及各种氨基酸,有动植物蛋白互补作用,促进成人营养的合理平衡。

译文:[Property] Be rich in various vitamin, mineral and acid. The animal and plant protein are mutually complementary, so it will promote nutrition absorption reasonable and balanced.

解析:该译文存在的错误有五处。第一,property 应为复数 properties,因为该产品特点不止一个。第二,be 应该省去不用。在这里使用系动词,不仅违背说明书翻译中的简洁原则,而且不符合英文行文规范。第三,说明书重在陈述客观事实,因此谓语动词一般用现在时,尽量不使用将来时等时态。第四,因产品含多种维生素、矿物质和氨基酸,故应将 vitamin、mineral、acid 改为复数形式。第五,"植物蛋白"和"动物蛋白"并非同一类型蛋白质,所以 protein 也应为复数。

2. 可读性原则

说明书翻译的主要目的是实现彼得·纽马克所说的祈使功能。要做到这点,译者就必须考虑如何使译文既能有效地传递信息内容,又能在语言上符合译入语的表达习惯和读者的审美情趣。从语言角度来看,美感的制造可以采用不同的方法,如词语的选择、语序的排列、句子的搭配组合,等等。所以,译者应该从多个层面对译文进行反复推敲。例如:

原文:本品是传统医药验方,选用纯正中药材及蜂蜜,用最新科学方法炼制而成的纯中药滋补药膏。

译文:This product is prepared from the selected Chinese medical materials and refined with modern scientific methods on the basis of the active principle of traditional Chinese medicine.

解析:将译文与原文进行比较,我们发现,译者为了迎合读者的审美标准和阅读习惯,较大幅度地调整了原文,涉及语序、词性和句法结构。此外,译文中增加了 the active 一词,暗示传统药方并未过时。而为了使译文简洁,语义清楚,"纯正""蜂蜜""纯中药滋补膏剂"等次要信息更是被译者省略未译,译者只需考虑汉、英行文方面的差异,依据译入语规范对原文进行适度调整,以保证译文更加流畅地道,具有较强的可读性。

因此,译者在翻译时必须处理好译文"准确性"与"可读性"之间的关系,才能最大限度地避免译文产生负面效果。

(二)产品说明书的句法特点

1. 主语+be(情态动词)+形容词(或过去分词)+目的状语

产品说明书中句子的主语通常是产品名称,主要是突出产品具体的特性(功能),直观简洁地描述产品,以使读者更加了解产品的相关信息。例如:

原文:本装置仅限于由接受过导管插入诊断及治疗培训的医生使用。

译文:The device should be used only by physicians trained in diagnostic and therapeutic catheter procedures.

2. 现在分词(介词)+名词(非谓语动词形式)

产品的维护或操作程序可以通过非谓语动词的结构来表达,这是产品说明书的另一个较为明显的句法特点。例如:

原文：使用本产品时须注意遵守消毒规定。
译文：Observe sterile technique when using this product.

3. 使用祈使句

产品说明书的指示说明部分经常使用祈使句，尤其是在表达命令或警告时。例如：

原文：早晚刷牙后含漱 2~5 分钟。
译文：Gargle with the product 2-5 minutes after brushing in the morning and evening.

4. 使用被动语态

产品说明书的重点在于产品的性能和使用方法，比起产品的主体，使用者更想了解的是使用方法，因此翻译使用方法时可巧妙地将主动语态转换为被动语态。例如：

原文：该产品用于温度在 225 ℃ 以下的热水管或蒸汽管道上。
译文：The product can be used in hot water or steam line with the temperature limited to 225℃.

5. 使用不完整句或省略句

产品说明书的语言特点是简洁明了，短而精确，因此译文也应该简洁精练。例如：

原文：Contains the antioxidants of Vitamin C&E. Helps delay aging and maintain healthy lips.
译文：富含维生素 C 和 E 抗氧化成分，延缓双唇衰老，保持双唇健康。

（三）产品说明书的翻译技巧

产品说明书是一种较为特殊的文体，翻译时不仅要做到上述的"忠实""准确"，也有一些技巧可以借鉴，主要可归纳为顺译、音译、多用三字结构和四字结构、增减词语、语序调整、词类转换等。具体示例如下。

1. 顺译

产品说明书属于科技类文体，较少运用文学类表达方式，因此，在翻译时，译者可以基本保留原文的意思，按照原文语序进行翻译。例如：

原文：Whether or not upper and lower limit values are printed is designated.
译文：无论上限和下限值是否打印，均需要指定。

2. 音译

对产品品名和商标的翻译，经常使用音译法，以达到谐音又谐义的目的，增强感染力。例如：

Canon	佳能（相机）
Pampers	帮宝适（纸尿裤）
Lacovo	乐口福（饮料）

3. 多用三字结构和四字结构

说明书具有简洁精练、醒目有力的特点。为体现其语言风格，说明书中的祈使句、省略句或 to be 短语，一般译成四字结构；对于单个形容词，多译为三字结构。例如：

Keep away from moisture	切勿受潮
Not to be laid flat	不可平放
With care	小心谨慎
Inflammable	易燃品

4. 增减词语

为了使译文更符合目的语的特点，翻译说明书时还可以在不改变原文意思的基础上，增加或者删减一些成分。例如：

① 原文：If there is smoke, smelliness, noise and so on, please stop at once, or it may cause a fire or electric shock.

译文：若出现冒烟、怪味、噪音等情形，请立即停止使用，以免导致火灾或触电等危险。（增译）

② 原文：As soon as you start charging the empty shaver, the green pilot light will go on.

译文：电剃刀充电时，绿色指示灯马上亮起。（减译）

5. 语序调整

汉英两种语言有不同的表达习惯，如表示时间或地点时，汉语习惯先大后小，英语则习惯先小后大。例如：

原文：中国深圳市福田区振华路 52 号 402 栋中联大厦 308 室

译文：Room 308, Building 402, #52 Zhenhua Road, Futian District, Shenzhen, China

6. 词类转换

在英译汉时，原文的某些词类应根据汉语的表达习惯作适当转换才能使译文更自然、地道。英语中的动词、名词、形容词、副词等在汉译时都能转换成其他词类。

（1）英语名词译为汉语动词，例如：

原文：We find it a necessity to change the country's economic developing pattern.

译文：我们发现必须要改变国家的经济发展模式。（necessity 在此译作"必须要"）

（2）英语名词译为汉语形容词，例如：

原文：Independence of thinking is an absolute necessity in study.

译文：独立思考对于学习是绝对必要的。（necessity 在此译作"必要的"）

（3）英语副词译为汉语动词，例如：

原文：After careful investigation they found the design behind.

译文：经过仔细研究后，他们发现这个设计落后了。（behind 在此译作"落后"）

（4）英语介词短语译为汉语动词，例如：

原文：The plane crushed out of control.

译文：这架飞机失控坠毁了。（out of control 在此译为"失控"）

二、常用术语和表达

（一）常用术语

shake well before use	使用前请摇匀
moisturize the skin	润肤
unblock the pores	改善毛孔堵塞
increase the brightness and transparency of the skin	提升肌肤亮度和透明质感
keep the skin tender and smooth	令肌肤水润柔滑
indication	适应证
contraindication	禁忌证

side effects	副作用
expiry	失效期
manufacturing date	生产日期
solubility	溶解度
ingredients	成分
molecular weight	分子量
pharmacological property	药理特性
be used for (in) the treatment of	用于治疗
be prepared from	由……制备
be contraindicated in (for)	对……禁忌
maximum output power	最大输出功率
charging time	充电时间
output impedance	输出阻抗
operating temperature	工作温度

（二）常用表达

① 本产品性能可靠、经济划算、特色众多，在许多国家和地区享有盛誉。

The product has gained an excellent reputation in many countries and regions by virtue of its reliability, cost-effectiveness and a wealth of features.

② 本产品广泛应用于……，它能满足……的需求/需要。

The product is greatly used in..., it meets/satisfies the demands/needs of...

③ 本产品经久耐用，外形美观。

The product features high durability and good appearance.

④ 本产品耐高温、抗热。

It is resistant to high temperature and heat.

⑤ 本产品便于操作，易于维修。结构简单，安装方便，使用安全可靠。

The product is convenient in operation and maintenance. It is simple in structure, easy to install, and safe and reliable in operation.

⑥ 勿在近火源处存放或使用，宜放在阴凉、儿童不宜碰到的地方。

Do not use or store near fire. It should be kept in cool place and kept away from the children.

Section 4　巩固练习

一、翻译以下短语。

1. 净重　　　　　　　6. distilled water
2. 维修，维护　　　　7. medicinal herb

3. 耐磨的
4. 能源消耗
5. 开袋即食
8. seasoning
9. whitening essence
10. manufacturer

二、翻译以下句子。

1. Designed to restructure and protect the hair fiber. The hair regains strength, shine and is revitalized. Neofibrine, a unique combination of bio-mimetic ceramide, shine perfecting agent and a UV filter for hair.

2. An anesthetic effect on the oral mucous membranes may occur occasionally, but may be avoided by swallowing the drug quickly with water without crashing the tablet.

3. Should you encounter some problems during the installation or use of this computer, please refer to this trouble-shooting guide prior to calling the helpdesk. Look up the problem in the left column and then check the suggestions in the right column.

4. No side-effects are to be expected, but some patients may develop the well-known "nitrate headache" which in itself is harmless. In such instances, it is recommended that the dosage be reduced. Because this nitrate effect is subject to tachyphylaxis, the medicine need not be interrupted. Security for angina pectoris patients for 8-10 hours. In case of extreme severity, immediate relief can be obtained by chewing this tablet.

5. Keebler Snack Crackers are baked to a secret recipe of specially selected wholesome ingredients. The light and crispy crackers bring you and all your family that uncommonly good taste and freshness as only Keebler knows how. As an established world leader, we are committed to baking biscuits of the highest quality. Our products are sold in over 90 countries around the world.

6. 洁面后将面膜贴从胶袋中取出，敷于面部10～20分钟后揭下，轻轻按摩至吸收，2～3次每周，每天使用一次效果更好。

7. 在开机状态下连接USB，拉下通知栏，选择USB连接，之后选择"打开USB存储设备"，此时您就可以操作电脑进行手机与电脑之间的数据传输了；同时，与电脑USB连接后还可以为手机充电。

8. 该产品具有使用安全、耐候、耐磨、机械强度高、线路耗损小等特点，广泛应用于城市和林区电网改造，能大大提高电网的安全可靠性。

9. 该空调广泛应用于各种场合，如宾馆、饭店、医院、托儿所、住宅等，为您创造舒适的生活环境。

10. 如在使用本品的过程中，有强烈刺痛、皮疹或灼痛现象发生，请立即用温水冲洗干净。

Chapter 3

企业宣传资料

Section 1 概　　述

一、企业宣传资料的定义和作用

企业宣传资料是企业为树立自身形象，通过文字、图画、宣传片等形式使受众了解和相信自己，以达到拓展业务、提升经营层次的一种书面材料。

企业宣传作为企业的一项常规性工作，具有对内和对外的双重作用。对内，它作为企业文化的一部分，可以促进对内沟通，鼓舞团队士气，增强团队凝聚力；对外，它是外界了解企业的一个重要窗口，担负着提高企业知名度，树立企业良好形象，促进企业蓬勃发展的重任。

在全球化的经济浪潮中，不断有中国的企业走出国门，迈入国际市场，拓展全球业务。与此同时，也有一大批的外资企业入驻中国，在华投资。不管是中国企业还是外国企业，要想在异国赢得声誉，获得成功，必须要做好企业宣传且保证企业相关信息得以全面且准确的传递，因此企业宣传资料的翻译就扮演着举足轻重的角色。鉴于中外企业宣传资料在语言习惯、行文风格等方面的差异，译者在译前必须充分了解两种语言的特点，根据不同的风格选择不同的翻译策略，以便能准确、清楚、明了、完整地传递信息。

二、企业宣传资料的功能

企业宣传资料按其语篇功能来看，属于信息和呼唤类语篇，具有呼唤功能和宣传功能。

企业宣传资料具有呼唤功能。根据英国翻译理论学家彼得·纽马克的文本类型理论，企业宣传资料属于呼唤型（vocative）文体。呼唤型文体的功能在于号召读者采取行动、进行思考或感受，其实质就是号召读者按照文体意图作出"反应"。企业宣传最重要的目的在于树立公司良好形象，吸引国内外投资商、厂家、消费者等群体，使得这些群体对其销售的产品和提供的服务产生兴趣。

企业宣传资料具有宣传功能。企业宣传资料向宣传对象提供了一些有关公司的实质信息，其目的是让受众对公司有一个真正的了解。一般来说，企业宣传资料包括公司背景、公司经营范围、产品及服务内容、公司结构、公司发展历史等信息。

三、企业宣传资料的内容

企业宣传资料的内容主要包括以下六个部分。

（一）成立时间、行业定位与综合性概括

该部分尤为重要，介绍的内容包括公司的成立时间、行业定位与综合性概括等，主要是为了获得读者对企业的认同和信任感。例如：

Wrigley Company is headquartered in the Wrigley Building in Near North Side, Chicago, Illinois. The company was founded on April 1, 1891, originally selling products such as soap and baking powder. In 1892, William Wrigley, Jr., the company's founder, began packaging chewing gum with each can of baking powder.（箭牌公司）

（二）证明企业实力的相关资料

企业为证明其实力，建立顾客信心，通常会列举一系列数据来吸引顾客的注意力，包括经权威机构认证的公司排名、销售业绩、员工和客户数量等。例如：

Apple has about 35,000 employees worldwide and had worldwide annual sales of US$32.48 billion in its fiscal year ending September 29, 2008. In 2014, *Fortune* magazine named Apple the most admired company in the United States.（苹果公司）

（三）品牌信息

企业在宣传资料中会向顾客介绍企业的主打产品，这有利于客户加深对企业的了解，从而达到推介产品的目的。例如：

Samsung Electronics is a multinational electronics and information technology company headquartered in Suwon and the flagship company of the Samsung Group. Its products include air conditioners, computers, digital televisions, liquid crystal displays, mobile phones, monitors, printers, refrigerators, semiconductors and telecommunications networking equipment.（三星公司）

（四）研发与创新信息

该部分主要介绍的是企业产品研发和创新的相关信息，目的在于向消费者展示企业所拥有的强大发展潜力和发展实力，并塑造一种不断开拓进取、具有生机活力的企业形象。例如：

In China, Motorola has invested US$600 million in R&D, building 17 R&D centers and labs in Beijing, Tianjin, Shanghai, Nanjing, Chengdu and Hangzhou. The number of R&D staff is about 3,000 now.（摩托罗拉公司）

（五）社会公益活动记录

该部分介绍的是企业以支持社会公益而开展的公关活动，通过相关公益活动的介绍，在公众心里树立企业重视社会责任、不忘回报社会的形象，从而提高企业的美誉度和知名度。这是提升企业品牌形象和品牌价值的重要途径。例如：

P&G is providing everyday essentials that help create the experience of home for families who can't afford them or who have been displaced. We leverage the strength of partner organizations to deliver programs which help address both short-term and long-term housing-related issues, including those associated with sanitation and water. Our employees team up as volunteers to build, clean and repair homes in virtually every region where P&G conducts business.（宝洁公司）

（六）企业标语或口号

企业标语是企业理念的概括，是对企业形象和企业产品形象的重要补充。例如：
Ideas for life.（松下电子）
Communication unlimited.（摩托罗拉公司）

Section 2 译例分析

Passage One

Boeing Overview[1]

Boeing is the world's largest aerospace company and leading manufacturer of commercial jetliners, defense, space and security systems, and service provider of aftermarket support. As America's biggest manufacturing exporter, the company supports airlines and U.S. and allied government customers in more than 150 countries. Boeing products and tailored services include commercial and military aircraft, satellites, weapons, electronic and defense systems, launch systems, advanced information and communication systems, and performance-based logistics and training.

Boeing has a long tradition of aerospace leadership and innovation.[2] The company continues to expand its product line and services to meet emerging customer needs.[3] Its broad range of capabilities includes creating new, more efficient members of its commercial airplane family; designing, building and integrating military platforms and defense systems; creating advanced technology solutions; and arranging innovative financing and service options for customers.

With corporate offices in Chicago, Boeing employs about 145,000 people across the United States and in more than 65 countries. This represents one of the most diverse, talented and innovative workforces anywhere.[4] Our enterprise also leverages the talents of hundreds of thousands more skilled people working for Boeing suppliers worldwide.

Boeing is organized into three business units: Commercial Airplanes; Defense, Space & Security; and Boeing Global Services, which began operations on July 1, 2017. Supporting these units is Boeing Capital Corporation, a global provider of financing solutions.

In addition, functional organizations working across the company focus on engineering and program management; technology and development-program execution; advanced design and manufacturing systems; safety, finance, quality and productivity improvement and information technology.

Commercial Airplanes

Boeing has been the premier manufacturer of commercial jetliners for decades. Today, the company manufactures the 737, 747, 767, 777 and 787 families of airplanes and the Boeing Business Jet range. New product development efforts include the Boeing 787-10 Dreamliner, the 737 MAX, and the 777X. More than 10,000 Boeing-built commercial jetliners are in service worldwide, which is almost half the world fleet. The company also offers the most complete family of freighters, and about 90 percent of the world's cargo is carried onboard Boeing planes.

Defense, Space & Security

Defense, Space & Security (BDS) is a diversified, global organization providing leading solutions for the design, production, modification and support of commercial derivatives, military rotorcraft, satellites, human space exploration and autonomous systems. It helps customers address a host of requirements through a broad portfolio and is seeking ways to better leverage information technologies and continues to invest in the research and development of enhanced capabilities and platforms.

Boeing Global Services

As the leading manufacturer for commercial and defense platforms, Boeing is positioned to provide unparalleled aftermarket support for mixed fleets worldwide. Boeing Global Services delivers innovative, comprehensive and cost-competitive service solutions for commercial, defense and space customers, regardless of the equipment's original manufacturer. With engineering, digital analytics, supply chain and training support spanning across both the government and commercial service offerings, Boeing Global Services' unsurpassed, around-the-clock support keeps our customers' commercial aircraft operating at high efficiency, and provides mission assurance for nations around the world.

Boeing Capital Corporation

Boeing Capital Corporation (BCC) is a global provider of financing solutions for Boeing customers. Working closely with Commercial Airplanes and Defense, Space & Security, BCC ensures customers have the financing needed to buy and take delivery of their Boeing products. With a year-end 2016 portfolio value at approximately $4.1 billion, BCC combines Boeing's financial strength and global reach, detailed knowledge of Boeing customers and equipment and the expertise of a seasoned group of financial professionals.

Key Words

tailored services	定制服务
Commercial Airplanes	民用飞机集团
jetliner	喷气客机
Boeing Business Jet	波音公务机
freighter	货机
Defense, Space & Security	防务、空间与安全集团
military rotorcraft	军用旋翼机
broad portfolio	完善的产品布局
leverage	利用
digital analytics	数字化分析
supply chain	供应链
seasoned	经验丰富的，老练的

Notes

1. 波音公司（Boeing）是全球航空航天业的领袖公司，也是世界上最大的民用和军用飞机制造商之一。它设计并制造旋翼飞机、电子和防御系统、导弹、卫星、发射装置，以及先进的信息和通信系统。此外，波音公司还是美国国家航空航天局的主要服务提供商。此例详细介绍了波音公司的地位、业务范围、服务对象、公司规模和特色等各种信息。文中有许多航空航天专业术语，译者在译前需要收集相关的资料，避免错译或漏译。此外，译者还需要在准确传达原意的基础上把握中英文表达的特点，遣词造句力求符合中文习惯。

2. 译者在处理这一句时要注意不能完全直译原文，将 has a long traditional of aerospace leadership 机械地译为"有着航空航天业领头羊的传统"，而应翻译成"一直是航空航天业的领袖公司"。与此类似的还有在第八段出现的 be positioned to 这个词组的汉译。be positioned to 原意为"定位于"，译者可以巧妙地将其译为"波音公司能够为……"，既未曲解原意，又符合中文的表达，让中国读者更容易理解。

3. 该句和后面一句是两个单独的句子，但前后两句在意思上有重叠，因此译者可以将两句合并成一句翻译，使得译文语义更加连贯，避免赘述。

4. 译者在处理该句的几个形容词时，要充分考虑到汉语在这类文体中多使用辞藻华丽、描述性很强的词汇，因此可以将这一句翻译为"这是一支非常多元化、人才济济且极富创新精神的队伍"，译文中的程度副词和四字成语的使用提升了原文的表达效果，更符合中文的表达习惯。

 参考译文

波 音 简 介

波音公司是全球最大的航空航天业公司,也是世界领先的民用飞机和防务、空间与安全系统制造商,以及售后支持服务提供商。作为美国最大的制造出口商,波音公司为分布在全球 150 多个国家和地区的航空公司和政府客户提供支持。波音的产品及定制的服务包括:民用和军用飞机、卫星、武器、电子和防御系统、发射系统、先进的信息和通信系统,以及基于性能的物流和培训等。

波音公司一直是航空航天业的领袖公司,也素来有着创新的传统。波音公司不断扩大产品线和服务,满足客户的最新需求,包括开发更新、更高效的民用飞机家族成员;设计、构筑、整合军事平台及防御系统;研发先进的技术解决方案;为客户安排创新的融资和服务方案等。

波音公司的总部位于芝加哥,在美国境内及全球 65 个国家和地区共有员工约 14.5 万人。这是一支非常多元化、人才济济且极富创新精神的队伍。波音公司还非常重视发挥成千上万分布在全球供应商中的人才。

波音公司下设三个业务部门:民用飞机集团,防务、空间与安全集团,以及于 2017 年 7 月 1 日投入运营的波音全球服务集团。作为金融解决方案的全球提供者,波音金融公司负责支持这些业务集团。

此外,还有一些在整个公司层面工作的职能组织,负责关注工程和项目管理、技术和研发项目执行、先进的设计和制造系统、安全、财务、质量和生产力改进,以及信息技术。

民用飞机集团

波音公司一直是领先的民用飞机制造商。目前,波音公司制造了 737、747、767、777 和 787 家族及波音公务机。正在研发中的新机型包括:787-10 梦想飞机、737 MAX 和 777X。在世界各地运营的波音民用飞机超过 10 000 架,占全球机队的近一半。此外,波音公司提供最完善的货机家族,全球 90% 的航空货物是由波音货机运输的。

防务、空间与安全集团

防务、空间与安全集团是集多元化与全球化于一身的组织机构,提供设计、制造、改装及支持民用飞机改型、军用旋翼机、卫星、载人航天探测和自主系统的领先解决方案。该集团通过完善的产品布局满足客户的各种需求,并寻求更好的方法,以利用信息技术,持续增加能够提升能力和平台的研发投入。

波音全球服务集团

作为民用和军用平台的领先制造商,波音公司能够为全球混合机队提供无与伦比的售后支持。无论设备的原始制造商是谁,波音全球服务集团可以向民用、防务和航天客户交付创新、全面且具有成本效率的服务解决方案。凭借覆盖政府和民用领域服务方案的工程、数字化分析、供应链和培训支持能力,波音全球服务集团拥有的无可比拟、全天候的支持可以让客户的民用飞机高效运营,并给世界各国提供任务保障。

波音金融公司

波音金融公司是一家为波音客户提供融资方案的全球性公司。波音金融公司通过同波音民用飞机集团及波音防务、空间与安全集团的紧密合作，确保客户在购买及接收波音产品时的融资需求。截至2016年年底，波音金融公司的产品服务资产约为41亿美元，拥有融资实力、全球客户、翔实的客户经验及专业且经验丰富的金融团队。

Passage Two

西门子简介 [1]

西门子股份公司是全球领先的技术企业，创立于1847年，业务遍及全球200多个国家，专注于电气化、自动化和数字化领域。[2] 作为世界最大的高效能源和资源节约型技术供应商之一，西门子在高效发电和输电解决方案、基础设施解决方案、工业自动化、驱动和软件解决方案，以及医疗成像设备和实验室诊断等领域占据领先地位。

西门子最早在中国开展经营活动可以追溯到1872年，当时西门子向中国出口了第一台指针式电报机，并在19世纪末交付了中国第一台蒸汽发电机及第一辆有轨电车。1985年，西门子与中国政府签署了合作备忘录 [3]，标志着西门子与中国进行深入合作。145年来，西门子以创新的技术、卓越的解决方案和产品坚持不懈地为中国的发展提供全面支持，并以出众的品质和令人信赖的可靠性、领先的技术成就、不懈的创新追求，在业界独树一帜。[4]

西门子见证了中国改革开放带来的巨大变化，同时也顺应时代潮流，不断积极进行自身的改革与发展。2016财年（2015年10月1日至2016年9月30日），西门子在中国的总营收达到64.4亿欧元。西门子在中国拥有约31 000名员工，是中国最大的外商投资企业之一。

西门子已经发展成为中国社会和经济不可分割的一部分，以其环保业务组合与创新解决方案全面投入到与中国的合作中，共同致力于实现可持续发展。[5] 2016年，西门子发布全新品牌宣言"博大精深，同心致远"。为实现"2020公司愿景"，公司专注于电气化、自动化、数字化领域，逐一实现为客户、员工和社会创造可持续的价值。

Key Words

电气化	electrification
自动化	automation
数字化	digitalization
指针式电报机	pointer telegraph
蒸汽式发电机	steam generator
有轨电车	tram line
财年	fiscal year

| 环保业务组合 | a wide array of environmental portfolio |

Notes

1. 该例是全球电子电气工程领域的领先企业德国西门子公司的公司简介。原文语言简洁精练，内容详尽，介绍了西门子公司的行业地位、发展历史、业务范围等信息。译者要注意对一些带有渲染色彩词汇的翻译，并且要注意句子语序和句与句之间是否要拆分或合并的问题。

2. 这句信息量较大，介绍了西门子公司的公司地位、创立时间和业务范围等相关信息。在做句子处理时，可将最重要的部分作为主句，通过使用非谓语、独立结构、定语从句等将其余信息依次添加。此外，为符合英语表达习惯，译者也可多使用插入语结构。因此，这句可译为："Siemens AG, founded in 1847, is a global technology powerhouse active in more than 200 countries, focusing on the areas of electrification, automation and digitalization."。

3. "合作备忘录"只是一个概括性的说法，并没有详细列出备忘录的名称。在翻译时，译者应当阐释清楚，将其完整名称译出，帮助外国读者理解，力求译文的准确。

4. 这一句有许多修饰性词语，如"卓越的""领先的""不懈的"等，在翻译时我们要遵循英语的表达原则，把一些不必要的表达删掉。因此，这句可译为："For 145 years, Siemens has pioneered cooperation with the country with its solutions, technologies and products, and has been known in the country for its quality and reliability, technological excellence and innovation."。

5. 在这一句中，句子的前一部分和后一部分联系并不是那么紧密，在译成英文时将其放在一个句子中并不妥当，因此译者可以将句子拆分成两个句子分别进行翻译。

 参考译文

Siemens Overview

Siemens AG, founded in 1847, is a global technology powerhouse active in more than 200 countries, focusing on the areas of electrification, automation and digitalization. As one of the world's largest producers of energy-efficient and resource-saving technologies, Siemens has leading positions in efficient power generation and power transmission solutions, infrastructure solutions, automation, drive and software solutions, as well as medical imaging equipment and laboratory diagnostics.

The history of Siemens in China dates back to 1872, when the company delivered the first pointer telegraph to China. The company manufactured the first steam generator and built the country's first tram line by the end of the 19th century. In 1985, *Memorandum of Comprehensive Cooperation between Machinery, the Electric and Electronics Industries of the People's Republic of China and Siemens AG* marked a comprehensive cooperation between Siemens and China. For 145 years, Siemens has pioneered cooperation with the country with its solutions, technologies and products, and has been known in the country for its quality and reliability, technological excellence and innovation.

Siemens has witnessed the tremendous changes that have taken place since China opened up and embarked on its reform drive. In fiscal year 2016 (October 1, 2015 – September 30, 2016), Siemens generated revenue of €6.44 billion in China. With about 31,000 employees, Siemens is one of the largest foreign-invested companies in the country.

Siemens has become an integral part of the Chinese economy and society. Offering a wide array of environmental portfolio and innovative solutions in cooperation with local partners, Siemens is committed to the sustainable development of China. In 2016, Siemens launched the new brand declaration "Ingenuity for Life". On the way to "Vision 2020", the company will focus on electrification, automation and digitalization, and make real what matters to create sustainable values for the customers, employees and the society.

Section 3 实 践 总 结

一、翻译技巧

（一）企业宣传资料的翻译原则

企业宣传资料具有客观准确、条理清晰、流畅简洁的语言特征，在翻译时要力求准确、完整。译者在翻译此类文本时要遵循以下几个原则。

1. 忠实性原则

忠实性原则是翻译企业宣传资料的首要原则。译者在翻译时必须做到忠实原文，译文要准确传达原文信息，不能漏译、错译。

2. 语用等效原则

语用等效可分为语言语用等效和社交语用等效。语言语用等效要求译文不拘泥于原文的形式，只求保存原文的内容，以求等效。社交语用等效要求译者在充分考虑目的语读者的文化观念和价值标准的前提下，按目的语的语言文化习惯表达出其语用含义。在企业宣传资料的翻译中要达到社交语用等效，译者就要从社会、文化交际的角度去考察语言的使用。

3. 信息性原则

企业宣传资料具有信息功能，翻译时要遵循传达原文主要信息的原则。译者要以保留主要内容为宗旨，排除与翻译目的关系不大的其他信息，如文体信息和语言信息等，采用变通的方法进行翻译。

4. 术语译名统一性原则

在翻译企业宣传资料中涉及的行业术语时，译者切不可闭门造车，自编自造。即使有些术语暂时没有一致认可的译名，译者也要参照权威的文献进行翻译。此外，译者还要尽量避免概念术语在同一译作中出现前后不统一的现象。

（二）企业宣传资料的翻译技巧

企业宣传资料具有呼唤功能和信息功能，其目的是让消费者通过阅读宣传资料，了解认识企业，并进一步激起消费者购买该企业产品的欲望。在翻译企业对外宣传资料时，由于中英文表达上的诸多不同，例如英语语言朴实、中文重渲染，英文重形合、中文重意合等，译者除了要保证基本的翻译原则之外，常常需要根据不同目的语的语言特点，选择不同的表达形式。企业宣传资料有着不同的翻译技巧，具体如下。

1. 不拘泥原文形式，学会拆分合并

英文宣传资料重形合，注重以"形"驱"神"，在行文结构上具有高度的形式化和严密的逻辑性，多用复合句和长句。反之，中文宣传资料重意合，注重以"神"驭"形"，在行文结构上少用显性连接手段，句子各成分之间的逻辑关系靠上下文和事理顺序来间接显示，常用短句和分句。根据两者之间的差异，译者在将中文译成英文并表达多重信息时，要注意句子合并，通过调整各部分顺序，使用连接词、不定式、独立主格、非谓语动词、从句等方法串联起整个句子的逻辑。译者在将英文译成中文时，先要厘清英文句子的逻辑结构，做到分清主次，按时间先后顺序依次阐述，在造句时要学会将冗长的句子结构拆分成一个个分句。例如：

① 原文：康菲石油是由美国康纳和石油公司和菲利普斯石油公司于2002年合并而成立。合并后的新公司承袭了原来两家公司在能源行业共200多年的丰富经验和在石油领域的优越技术，使之成为当今世界杰出的公司之一。康菲石油如今业务遍及近40个国家和地区，全球雇员约3万人。

译文：When Conoco Inc. and Phillips Petroleum Company merged in 2002, one of the world's leading integrated energy companies was born. Bringing together more than 200 years of experience, including a rich history of discoveries and world firsts, ConocoPhillips now operates in nearly 40 countries and employs about 30,000 people across the globe.

② 原文：Combining safety, performance and efficiency, Model S has reset the world's expectations for the car of the 21st century with the longest range of any electric vehicle, over-the-air software updates that make it better over time, and a record 0-60 mph acceleration time of 2.28 seconds as measured by *Motor Trend*.

译文：Model S集安全、性能和高效于一身，其行驶里程完全超越其他电动车并且可以通过OTA空中升级助力车辆不断完善。经美国《汽车族》杂志的测试，Model S的0～60英里每小时加速仅需2.28秒，彻底颠覆了人们对于21世纪汽车的期待。

在例①中，中文原文共三句，但英文译文则仅有两句，这是因为译者在翻译时并未完全按照中文材料原有格式进行翻译，而是在理解原文的基础上对句子结构进行重新整合。"使之成为当今世界杰出的公司之一"本来是第二句的成分，但是译者将其同中文的第一句放在一起翻译，意思上并没有什么改变，但是逻辑上却显得更紧密顺畅。通过例②，我们也会发现，译者对句子结构做出了调整，把原有的长句变换成几个短句。此外，中文常常把表达结果的成分放在后面，例②的译文也正好体现了这一点。

2. 迎合读者阅读习惯，既能增亦能减

中文的企业宣传资料惯用辞藻华丽的形容词和修饰语，多用四字、五字、六字等结构，

注重句子的工整对仗。英文的企业宣传资料以通俗易懂、富于表现力的日常用语为基础，注重充分表述事实，传输真实信息，用事实说话。因此，英文宣传资料倾向于使用朴实、简洁、抽象的词语。在翻译时，对于英文中一些简单的表达，我们要做出一些必要发挥，对语言和文字进行加工；对于中文中一些不必要的表达，我们要学会取舍，迎合外国受众的阅读习惯。例如：

① 原文：诞生于上世纪末的虎豹集团，信守孜孜以求、永不言退的发展理念，在市场经济的大潮中，任凭浊浪排空，惊涛拍岸，独有胜似闲庭信步的自信，处变不惊，运筹帷幄。尽握无限商机于掌间，渐显王者之气于天地。虎豹人以其特有的灵气，极目一流，精益求精，集世界顶尖服装生产技术装备之大成。裁天上彩虹，绣人间缤纷，开设计之先河，臻质量之高峰，领导服装潮流，尽显领袖风采。

译文：Founded in the late l980s, the Hubao Group has its philosophy to seize the business chances and achieves its brilliance in the ever-changing and competitive market based on the ever-aggressive concept. Hard work rewards. The Hubao Group, equipped with the world's most advanced technology and their efforts, has been taking a leading role in designing newest fashions and producing fine-quality products for years, appearing a king-like manner in the garment world.

② 原文：We will offer systematic and all-around service tailored for the customers. We have a team of honest, experienced, responsible and excellent staff, who hold it as our work principle to offer our customers quick and satisfying services.

译文：我们将根据客户的需求，为客户精心设计、量身定制并提供系统的、全方位的服务。公司汇聚了一支以诚信为本、从业经验丰富、具有高度敬业精神和责任感的高素质员工队伍。公司的每一名员工都以为客户提供到位、满意、快捷的服务为基本工作原则。

通过对两个例子进行观察和分析可知，中英文在用词上的差异显而易见。例①的原文中充斥着华丽的修辞手法和繁杂的意象，初学翻译的人会感觉无从下手。但实际上，译者在处理此种风格的文本时要做到精简翻译，抓住重点，用简单短小的英文单词或词组表达同样的中文意思。例①的译文很好地体现了英文宣传资料以朴实见长的文体风格。中文重语言的堆砌，例②在翻译几个英语形容词时就做了很好的转换，符合中国人的思维模式。

相似的处理手法还体现在对一些带有文化信息的词句的翻译上。中国企业为凸显企业形象常常引经据典，这在中国读者中可以引起良好的效应。英译时，考虑到文化差异，译者只需译出其精神即可，强行对译只会让外国读者一头雾水。例如：

③ 原文：华夏之子，鸿鹄之志。华鸿控股集团诞生于浙江义乌这片神奇的沃土。

译文：The company was founded in Yiwu City, Zhejiang Province, and we have great ambitions to improve it.

3. 以信息传达为纲，不可望文生义

企业宣传资料对于传达企业现状、历史、构成、业务范围、业务特色等基础信息有着重要作用。译者在翻译时要确保关键信息准确、全面、有效地传达给读者。因此，译者必须以信息传达为纲，对一些自己拿不准的地方不能想当然地进行翻译，尤其是在一些专业词汇的翻译上，译者一定要做好事前准备，切勿望文生义。例如：

① 原文：Pros love iMac. So when they asked us to build them a killer iMac, we went all in. And then we went way, way beyond, creating an iMac packed with the most staggeringly powerful collection of workstation-class graphics, processors, storage, memory, and I/O of any Mac ever.

译文：专业人士对 iMac 情有独钟。因此，当他们要我们打造一款性能顶尖的 iMac 时，我们自然全力以赴。在设计上，我们不断突破极限，为这款 iMac 集成了 Mac 自诞生以来最强大的工作站级图形处理器、中央处理器、存储设备、内存和 I/O 端口。

② 原文：For 90 years, Caterpillar Inc. has been making sustainable progress possible and driving positive change on every continent. Customers turn to Caterpillar to help them develop infrastructure, energy and natural resource assets. With 2015 sales and revenues of $47.011 billion, Caterpillar is the world's leading manufacturer of construction and mining equipment, diesel and natural gas engines, industrial gas turbines and diesel-electric locomotives. The company principally operates through its three product segments — construction industries, resource industries and energy & transportation — and also provides financing and related services through its financial products segment.

译文：90 年来，卡特彼勒不懈努力，促使可持续进步成为可能，并在全球各大洲积极推动变革。卡特彼勒协助客户进行基础设施建设、能源和自然资源的开发。2015 年，卡特彼勒全球销售及收入总额为 470.11 亿美元，是建筑工程机械、矿用设备、柴油和天然气发动机、工业燃气轮机及电传动内燃机车领域的全球领先企业。公司主要运营三大业务板块：建筑行业、资源行业、能源和交通行业，并通过金融产品部门提供融资及相关服务。

以上两例中，一个是苹果公司的产品介绍，一个是重工业巨头卡特彼勒的公司介绍。与普通公司介绍不同，这两个例子中有很多专业性术语需要翻译，译者在翻译时一定要保证相关信息的准确传达。

二、常用术语和表达

（一）常用术语

全资子公司	a wholly-owned subsidiary
跨国公司	transnational corporation
财富全球 500 强企业之一	a Fortune Global 500 company
畅销全球	sell well all over the world
长期盈利能力	long-term financial viability
方便群众	make things convenient for the people/suit the people's convenience
兑现承诺	deliver on commitments
各式俱全	wide selection/large assortment
顾客第一	customers first
开拓进取	blaze new trails and forge ahead
规格齐全	a complete range of specifications
花样繁多	a wide selection of colors and designs
高瞻远瞩的决策	a visionary/far-sighted decision
款式新颖	fashionable (in) style/novel (in) design/up-to-date styling
深受国内外客户的信赖和称誉	win a high admiration and be widely trusted at home and abroad

减员增效	downsize to improve efficiency
供不应求	in short supply/demand exceeding supply
货源充足	ample supply and prompt delivery
价格公道	reasonable price/street price/moderate price
结构坚固	sturdy construction
居同类产品之首	rank first among similar products
科学精制	by scientific process
品质优良	excellent (in) quality
审时度势	size up the trends of event
拳头产品	knockout product
使用寿命长	long performance life
性能可靠	reliable performance
选材精良	superior materials
沿用传统的生产方式	with traditional methods
业务责任	line responsibility
做工讲究	exquisite (in) workmanship
遵守、践行最高道德标准	practice and uphold the highest ethical standards
制定工作重点	prioritize issues
世界闻名	internationally renowned

（二）常用表达

① Founded in…, … Co., Ltd, with the old company name …, specializes in manufacturing…
……有限公司成立于……，原名……，专业生产……

② Located in…, … company was founded and put into operation in… with an investment of…, and now has employment of more than… people.
……公司坐落于……，于……成立并投入运营，初始投入资本为……，现有员工……余名。

③ As a Fortune Global 500 company with more than… employees, … has established more than… branches in… countries by the end of….
……公司名列财富全球 500 强企业名录，截止到……年底，全球拥有员工……名，在……个国家中设立了超过……个分公司。

④ Adopting advanced equipment with solid techniques, our products are strictly tested before being put into the market.
我公司采用先进的生产设备，拥有雄厚的技术力量，产品在投放市场前均经过严格的测试。

⑤ Our strong brand names and new product development capabilities enjoy worldwide recognition.
我公司的品牌知名度、新产品研发能力在全球范围内享有极高的声誉。

⑥ The capital assets of our company is… while the output is… per year.

我公司固定资产为……，年产量达……

⑦ Our company will consistent our tenet: all work for customers' standard, and try to produce more high quality products in order to requite stable and new customers.

我公司将始终如一地坚持以迎合客户为标准的信条，努力生产更多高质量的产品，以此来回馈新老客户。

⑧ People in all walks of life are welcomed to come for an inquiry!

欢迎各界垂询！

Section 4　巩　固　练　习

一、翻译以下短语。

1. 经营范围
2. 企业理念
3. 享有良好声誉
4. 注册资本
5. 招商引资
6. pragmatic
7. flagship store
8. spare no efforts
9. service supremacy
10. equality and mutual benefit

二、翻译以下句子。

1. Today, six Johnson & Johnson affiliations are operating in China, employing more than 3,000 people and producing a wide range of consumer, pharmaceutical and medical products in our mission to promote the healthcare of Chinese people.

2. Standard Chartered employs more than 40,000 people in 56 countries with widely varying business cultures. The bank has added about 10,000 staff in the last year, including more than 5,000 in Korea, where we bought Korea First Bank (now SC First Bank) last year.

3. We cultivate creativity and development ability, learn new information, new knowledge and new concepts, establish advanced concepts and systems, break through the limitation of regulations, develop the best technologies and techniques, and achieve first-class performance and pattern.

4. DuPont puts science to work by creating sustainable solutions essential to a better, safer, healthier life for people everywhere. Operating in more than 70 countries, DuPont offers a wide range of innovative products and services for markets, including agriculture, nutrition, electronics, communications, safety and protection, home and construction, transportation and apparel.

5. ConocoPhillips' longstanding commitment to the communities in which it operates reflects our belief that no individual or corporation can be a good citizen without getting actively involved—exercising imagination, donating time and skills and providing financial support. Both as a corporation and through individual employees, COP is taking positive action in our community by improving education, protecting the environment, ensuring employee safety and conducting technology transfers. It's a commitment that has not gone unnoticed, ensuring that our efforts and

performance are recognized by the general public.

6. 公司已着手在亚洲、欧洲、美洲地区组建三个独立的跨国集团公司，实行自主经营，独立核算，自负盈亏。

7. 萃华楼烹制的菜肴选料精细，操作严谨，刀法娴熟，讲究火候。成品具有"清、鲜、脆、嫩"的特色，而且"色、香、味、形、养"五质具备。

8. 本公司是一家大型国有房地产上市公司、国家一级房地产开发资质企业，连续五年荣膺中国房地产行业领导品牌。2006年7月，公司股票在上海证券交易所上市，截止到2015年年底，公司总资产突破3 600亿元，实现签约金额1 366.76亿元。

9. 作为推动中国社会经济发展的值得信赖的合作伙伴，西门子一直致力于开展企业社会责任活动，通过技术推广、教育推广和社会发展项目，为社会做出积极而持续的贡献。成立于2012年的西门子员工志愿者协会已在全国15个城市开展志愿服务，惠及数万民众。

10. 百年苏宁，人才为本。人才资源是苏宁电器的核心竞争力，苏宁电器将人力资源视为企业长久发展的战略资本，建立了系统化的招聘选拔、培训培养、考核激励与发展规划体系。秉承人品优先、能力适度、敬业为本、团队第一的用人理念，坚持自主培养、内部提拔的人才培养方针，苏宁电器先后实施了"1200工程""总经理梯队""采购经理梯队""店长梯队""督导梯队""销售突击队""监领工程"等10多项人才梯队计划，倡导员工与企业共同成长，长远发展。

Chapter 4

商 务 报 告

Section 1 概 述

一、商务报告的定义及功能

商务报告是日常商务活动中常见的一种公文文体。商务报告是指针对某种特殊的、有意义的商务目的,就某一重大事件或重大问题向一个人或多个人提供的公正、客观和系统的事实陈述。报告中所陈述的事实必须与事件、条件、质量、进展、结果、问题或提议的解决方案有关,以帮助当事人了解复杂的商业情况和计划进程,解决问题,提供建议,使上级领导就一系列事件做出决策。

商务报告应用极其广泛,在财务、金融、投资、管理、营销、生产、外贸等方面更为常用,如营销人员需要对产品情况、销售对象、广告方式、销售手段、销售状况、竞争对手等进行分析和调查,从而制定策略以提升销售量。从商务报告的定义可以看出,商务报告提供的信息包括调研过程、结果和建议等,提交决策者,帮助决策者制定决策。商务报告还可以就某事进行解释、说服或鼓动管理人员做出某项决策,商务报告也可以就某事提供启发性的建议或者意见,供领导参考。因此,商务报告具有如下功能:信息功能(informative function)、解释功能(explanatory function)、说服功能(persuasive function)、鼓动功能(inciting function)及启发功能(suggestive function)。

商务报告是商务文书的重要组成部分,在商务交往中起着重要的桥梁作用,尤其是作为对外交流沟通使用的商务报告,在现代企业中使用得更为频繁。在当今经济全球化的背景下,熟练掌握商务报告的翻译技巧,已是从事商务活动的人员,特别是职业经理人必备的文书处理技能之一。

二、商务报告的分类

商务报告的使用范围很广，种类众多，根据不同的分类标准有不同的分类方法。

（1）根据报告的语体，可分为正式报告（formal report）和非正式报告（informal report）。

（2）根据报告频率，可分为周报（weekly report）、月报（monthly report）、季报（quarterly report）、年报（annual report）、例行报告（routine report）和定期报告（periodical report）。

（3）根据报告的内容，可分为事件调查报告（investigation report）、意见调查报告（survey report）、工作进展报告（progress report）、市场调查报告（market research report）、商务旅行报告（business trip report）、可行性报告（feasibility report）、促销报告（promotion report）和效益报告（business results report）。

（4）根据报告的写作手法，可分为信息式报告（informational reports）和分析式报告（analytical reports）。

不同种类的商务报告既具有报告的基本特点，又各有自身特点，但因其复杂性，分类互有重叠，不能穷尽。本章讲述的商务报告的翻译主要是指正式的商务报告的翻译。

三、商务报告的构成

商务报告包括呈送对象、标题、正文和结尾等部分。通常情况下，一份完整、正式的商务报告包括题目（title）、呈送对象（transmittal）、目录（table of contents）、摘要/提要（abstract）、前言/引言/导言/序言（introduction）、正文（body）、结论（conclusion）、建议（recommendation）、参考文献/参考资料（bibliography/reference）、附录/附件（appendix）等。其中，题目、前言、正文和结论是商务报告中必不可少的重要组成部分。

Section 2   译 例 分 析

>> *Passage One*

This report was commissioned to examine why[1] the sales volume of Super Chocolate has dropped over the past four years since its peak[2] in 2001 and to recommend ways of increasing the volume.

The research draws attention to[3] the fact that in 2005 Super Chocolate's share had actually increased by 1% to 39%. However, the sales volume had decreased because the market size of chocolate dropped. Further investigations reveal that there are a growing number of people who tend to regard the milk and sugar ingredients in chocolate as bad for health.[4] Moreover, an increasing number of rival "healthy candies" had appeared on the market.[5]

The report concludes that the primary reason for the decline in sales is brought about by a reduction in the market size of chocolate due to an increased health consciousness of consumers.[6] There is also the mounting challenge of rival "healthy candies".

It is recommended that immediate measures be taken to launch and promote new products alongside its existing product range.[7]

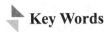 Key Words

was commissioned to	受托
sales volume	销售额
decline in sales	销售下降
a reduction in the market size	市场萎缩
alongside its existing product range	在已有产品的基础上

Notes

1. 英语中由 why、what 等引导的定语从句一般有两种翻译方法：第一种是直译，翻译成句子，如 I don't know why he was late（我不知道他为什么迟到）；第二种是意译，翻译成名词，如上面这句话可以翻译成"我不知道他迟到的原因"。译者要根据上下文，灵活选择。

2. peak 如直接翻译成"顶峰"，则太抽象，可以采取增译法，翻译成"销售顶峰"，更具体。

3. draw attention to 翻译成"指出"，相当于 reveal 或者 show。

4. 这个句子比较长，宾语从句里含有一个定语从句，因此应该采取分译法。但是 there are 在上下文中没有什么实际意义，所以只需把定语从句的意思表达出来即可。

5. 此句中，rival 表示"竞争的"，如果将该句直译成"越来越多的（参与）竞争的'健康糖果'出现在市场上"则比较拗口，所以翻译时拆分为"越来越多的'健康糖果'出现在市场上，参与竞争"，更符合汉语的表达习惯。

6. 此句中，is brought about 意义很虚，可以省译。另外，due to 翻译成汉语时，可以单独成句。

7. 该句中 alongside 本意为"一起"，在这里可以引申为"在已有产品的基础上"。launch 表示"推出（新产品）"，promote 表示"促销"。在商务报告中，被动语态使用较多，如 it is concluded that..., it is suggested that..., it is recommended that... 等，在翻译时，需要将被动语态译为主动语态。

 参考译文

本报告受托调查了 Super 牌巧克力自 2001 年销售顶峰后，销售量连续四年下滑的原因，并对增加销售额提出了建议。

研究指出，2005 年 Super 的市场份额增长了 1%，达到 39%，但销售量却下降了，因为整个巧克力市场的规模缩小了。进一步的调查发现，越来越多的消费者倾向于认为巧克力中的牛奶和糖分有损健康。而且越来越多的"健康糖果"出现在市场上，参与竞争。

报告得出结论，销售下降的最主要原因是市场萎缩，因为消费者的健康意识在不断加强。其次，"健康糖果"的挑战也与日俱增。

建议立即采取措施，在已有产品的基础上，推出新产品进行促销。

Passage Two

在道路建设方面[1]，吉尔吉斯斯坦伊塞克湖环湖公路连接线修复、塔吉克斯坦艾尼—彭基肯特高速公路项目竣工，两国总统出席通车仪式并对项目高度评价[2]；乌兹别克斯坦安格连—帕普铁路隧道、塔吉克斯坦瓦赫达特—亚湾铁路隧道工程进展顺利，质量和进度多次受到领导人肯定。

在跨境物流运输合作方面，连云港已成为中亚国家对日韩及东南亚转口的重要货物中转基地，预计到2015年年底转运货物总量25万标准集装箱[3]；中哈霍尔果斯国际边境合作中心改善了跨境基础设施条件；中俄同江铁路桥[4]中方一侧已完成工程总进度的65%，计划2016年年中开工建设黑河—布拉戈维申斯克公路桥及跨黑龙江索道。截至10月底，中欧班列共开行1 070列，其中回程207列，比上年增长15倍。[5]

Key Words

高度评价	speak highly
竣工	completion
跨境物流运输	cross-border logistics transportation
货物中转基地	cargo transshipment base
增长15倍	increase by 15 times

Notes

1. "在道路建设方面""在跨境物流运输合作方面"中的"在……方面"英译时，采用了两种形式的短语：in terms of 和 in the aspect of。这一处理方式使译文表达更为多样，不拘泥于固定形式。

2. 在翻译此句时，应将原文的顺序进行调整，突出汉语重心在后的特点，英语往往是判断或结论在前，事实或描写在后，"两国总统出席通车仪式并对项目高度评价"是结论，前面所述的两个项目的进行情况是事实，因此，将汉语的语序调整后再翻译是可取的。这一方法也同样适用于后一句的翻译。

3. 该句译为"its total volume of transshipment cargo is expected to reach 250 thousand standard containers by the end of 2015."。"总量"在商务报告中通常被译为 total volume；"预计达到"的表达为 be expected to reach，此类的表达在商务报告翻译中经常用到，要多积累。

4. "塔吉克斯坦艾尼—彭基肯特高速公路项目""乌兹别克斯坦安格连—帕普铁路隧道""塔吉克斯坦瓦赫达特—亚湾铁路隧道工程""中俄同江铁路桥"这些涉及国家的专业工程项

目名称在翻译前一定要查找专业资料或询问专业人士,确保翻译的准确性。

5. 该句应译为"By the end of October, China-Eurasia railways have totally opened 1,070 including 207 for return trip, which have increased by 15 times more than last year."汉语多短句,英语多长句。在将汉语译成英语时,要将个别短句整合成一句。此外,"比上年增长15倍"这样的表达在商务报告中也经常见到,关于数字的翻译必须谨慎,相关的表达也要多积累。

 参考译文

In terms of road construction, two presidents from Kyrgyzstan and Tajikistan were present at the road opening ceremony, and spoke highly of such projects as the connecting line's repairing of road around the Issyk Kul in Kyrgyzstan and the completion of freeway from Ayni to Panjakent in Tajikistan; the quality and progress of tunnel projects, namely, Angren-Pape railway tunnel in Uzbekistan and Vahdat-Yovon railway tunnel in Tajikistan, which went well, have been recognized by leads for more than once.

In the aspect of cross-border logistics transportation cooperation, Lianyungang has become an important cargo transshipment base for Central Asian countries re-exporting goods to Japan, South Korea and Southeast Asia, and its total volume of transshipment cargo is expected to reach 250 thousand standard containers by the end of 2015; the China-Kazakstan Horgos Frontier International Cooperation Center has improved cross-border infrastructure conditions; in the China-Russia Tongjiang-Nizhneleninskoye railway bridge project, China has finished 65% of total progress, and plans to start the construction of Heihe-Blagoveshchensk highway bridge and cross-Heilongjiang river ropeway in the middle of 2016. By the end of October, China-Eurasia railways have totally opened 1,070 including 207 for return trip, which have increased by 15 times more than last year.

Section 3 实 践 总 结

一、翻译技巧

(一)商务报告的语言特点

1. 准确性(accurate)

商务报告必须用词准确、数据无误,不允许有任何含糊不清或数据矛盾的地方,如China's total import and export from Jan. to Dec. in 2009 amounted to US$ 2.207 27 trillion, down by 13.9% on a year-on-year basis. 商务报告的数据必须有真凭实据或来自官方的统计数据,尽量避免使用about、approximately等比较模糊的词语。

2. 简洁性（brief）

商务报告的最大特点在于其简洁性，比其他文体更加注重表达效果的准确性、时效性，客观描述性语句较多，不主张使用修饰或夸张性语言。商务报告如果语言累赘、啰唆，只会耽误时间，延误决策的制定，甚至影响公司的业绩。因此，商务报告必须简洁明了，言简意赅，如 Of which export was US$ 130.72 billion, up by 17.7%, and import was US$112.29 billion, up by 55.9%. 这里用 up 一词表示增幅，而没有用 with an increase of 或者 representing an increase of。此外，该句使用的都是客观描述性词汇，没有使用夸张或修饰性或表达感情色彩的词汇。

3. 清晰性（clear）

商务报告的每个部分必须结构合理、条理清晰、逻辑清楚。例如：In general, the demand for home appliances has shown the biggest increase for many reasons. Especially there has been a sharp increase in our sales in rural areas in the west regions. 该例先综述需求增长，然后指出特别之处，符合人们认识事物的逻辑规律，清晰易懂。

4. 客观性（objective）

商务报告必须客观公正，不掺杂任何个人感情。商务报告中尽量少用 I think、We think 之类的语言，即使有关建议可能具有一定的主观性，但这是基于调查研究的客观基础之上提出的合理建议，本身就具有客观性，如 Through comparison and analysis, it is recommended that the price of our products should be lowered by 3-5 percent. 从表面看，该句数据不是十分精确，但这确实是经过调查比较得出的客观结果。

5. 逻辑性（logical）

商务报告，尤其是可行性报告和调查报告多用长句、复合句、并列复合句等句式，并通过使用介词短语、插入语、同位语、倒装句、被动语态等特殊句型，使语句结构更严密，细节更突出，句子的逻辑性更强，如 The reason why I choose this plan over the other optional ones is that I find this plan has several advantages which might be easily ignored. 该句看似有些啰唆，其实不然，这种句式上的复杂性是实现严密逻辑表达效果的保障。

6. 专业性（professional）

商务报告中往往包括各行各业的专门术语或者缩略语，如 external and fiscal balances、year on year（YOY）等。因此，商务报告的语言具有一定的专业性。

（二）商务报告的翻译原则

要进行切实有效的商务报告翻译，必须要有相应的原则来规范。有了原则，才会有商务报告翻译工作的规章，也才会有处理商务报告翻译问题的理论框架。商务报告翻译应遵循"忠实""准确""统一"的原则，具体如下。

1. 忠实

商务报告翻译中的"忠实"原则是指正确地将原文语言的信息用译文语言表达出来。这个原则不苛求语法与句子结构的一致，却要达到信息内涵上的对等，即信息等值。

商务报告属于表达型文本，针对这类文本的翻译，纽马克建议使用"语义翻译法"，即尽可能使用贴近原文的句法和语义结构将原文语境意义准确地表达出来。在进行这类文本的翻译时，译者进行发挥的自由度是十分小的。译者需要忠实地反映原作的基本思想和观点，不能将自己的主观态度和情绪强加于译文之中。

例如,"现场捣毁两条正在非法生产 VCD 的生产线"译为...destroyed on the spot two production lines that were illegally manufacturing VCDs。原文想要说明的是所生产出来的 VCD 不是经过正规途径生产而得的,属于非法;而译文则偏离了原意,illegally 这个副词修饰的是 manufacture 这个动词,这样的修饰关系意思是生产 VCD 这个行为是违法的。生产 VCD 本身并没有违法与不违法之说,只有生产出来的 VCD 本身是否合法。所以,译文应改为...manufacturing illegal VCDs。该例体现了"忠实"原则,译者要将原文的意思准确地理解,然后跳出语言的框架,将汉语转换成相应的英语。虽然两种语言的语法与句子结构并不完全一致,但是其句子想要表达的信息和内涵却得到了充分的体现。这样才是意义等值,才符合"忠实"的原则。

2. 准确

商务报告翻译中的"准确"原则是指译者在将原文语言内容转换到译文语言内容的过程中做到选词准确,概念表达确切,物与名所指正确,数码与单位精确。

例如,"工作组"这一名词译为 working group。动词的 ing 形式,大多表示一个正在进行的动作,在这里有失恰当;而要表示其本身的性质,则应该用动词原形,因而"工作组"应译为 work group。"突出重点领域"的"突出"可使用动词 highlight,意为"强调,突出,使显著,加亮"。因此,为使商务报告的内容翻译准确,译者应谨慎选用词语。

3. 统一

商务报告翻译中的"统一"原则是指在翻译过程中译名、概念、术语等应始终保持统一,不允许随意变换译名。

例如,中华人民共和国公安部、国家广播电视总局、国家知识产权局、最高人民法院、最高人民检察院,其相应的译文分别是:the Ministry of Public Security of the People's Republic of China、National Radio and Television Administration、State Intellectual Property Office、the Supreme People's Court of the People's Republic of China、the Supreme People's Procuratorate of the People's Republic of China。商务报告翻译经常涉及各种各样的组织机构名称,这些名称的英语译名大多已经固定下来,没有变通的余地。这就要求译者必须用统一的、通用的、既定的译名来传递信息。任何译者自造的与所涉机构沿用已久的译名不一致的情况,在商务报告的翻译中都是不可接受的。

(三) 商务报告的翻译技巧

商务报告的翻译主要采用直译法,视具体情况而言,需要特别关注视角转换法的使用,包括词类转换法、语态转换法、肯定与否定转换法等;商务报告中往往有一些句式结构复杂的长句,可以根据实际情况采用顺译法或者拆译法,以符合目的语的语言表达习惯。

1. 省译法

原文:Finally, the ownership model of the farms as well as financial subsidies, investors and funding sources would give an idea of linkages within the production and consumption network.

译文:最后,农场的所有制模式、财政补贴、投资者、资金来源会告诉我们生产和消费网络内部之间的关系。

解析:这句采用了省译法。英语连词众多,属于形合语言;汉语属于意合语言,翻译时省略了 as well as、and 这些连接词。

2. 结构调整法

原文：Adherence with government regulations is a basic benchmark for evaluating farmers as often the regulation in practice is below what should be enforced and implemented.

译文：评估农民的基本标准是执行政府规定，这些规定在实践中往往没有很好地贯彻落实。

解析：译文采用了结构调整法和视角转换法。如果按原文结构翻译成"执行政府规定是评估农民的基本标准，这些规定在实践中往往没有很好地贯彻落实"，显得前后不够连贯，把"政府规定"后移，可以使译文更连贯。另外，below 表示"低于"的意思，此处无法直译，必须转换角度，"低于"不是"没有执行"，而是"没有很好地执行或没有完全执行"，所以，这里翻译成"没有很好地贯彻落实政府规定"。

3. 增词法

原文：In all developing regions, except Latin America, the Caribbean and Southeast Asia, girls are less likely than boys to remain in school. The gap between girls and boys is greatest in the 22 countries where fewer than 60 percent of children complete their primary education.

译文：所有的发展中地区，除拉美、加勒比海和东南亚地区外，女孩比男孩失学的可能性更大。在完成小学教育人数不到60%的22个国家中，女孩和男孩的入学情况差距最大。

解析：译文采用了增词法和视角转换法。原文 girls are less likely than boys to remain in school 如果译成"女孩不大可能跟男孩一样上学"就显得不清楚，译者需要转换视角，把"男孩"和"女孩"对调，把"上学"改为"失学"，译成"女孩比男孩失学的可能性更大"。此外，the gap between girls and boys 如果只是翻译成"男孩和女孩的差距"就显得语义不是很清楚，加上"入学情况"就非常清楚了。

4. 顺译法

原文：In dishwashers, where Matsushita has led the market since it produced Japan's first model 46 years ago, the company's aggregate production reached 5 million units in May 2006.

译文：在洗碗机方面，自从46年前制造出第一台洗碗机以来，三菱一直领先市场。2006年5月，三菱公司总产量达500万台。

解析：鉴于原文是带有非限制性定语从句的长句，译文采用了顺译法。

5. 拆译法

原文：Extreme poverty remains a daily reality for more than 1 billion people who subsist on less than $1 a day.

译文：超过10亿人口每天都处于极度贫困状态，他们每天的生活费用不到1美元。

解析：译文采用了拆译法。原文是定语从句，如果直译，显得不够清晰，因此，译文把定语从句拆译成两个分句，意思清楚明了。

（四）商务报告中的数字翻译

商务活动中，任何时候都离不开数字，数字可以准确地表达事物的状况，可以翔实记录事物的发展状态，也可以科学地证明某些观点。在商务报告中，数字的应用比比皆是。因此，数字的翻译及与数字紧密相关的准确表达显得尤为重要。

1. 表示数量增加

英语中，表示数量增加的词语包括 increase、rise、grow、up、reach，增长了多少可以用 up、by 表示，增长到多少可以用 increase to、arrive at 表示。另外，表示迅速增长或者急剧上升可以用 rocket、skyrocket、jump、leap、soar、shoot up、increase dramatically、increase sharply 等表示。例如：

① 原文：China's actual foreign direct investment (FDI) rose by 24% to $4.58 billion in the first two months of this year while contracted FDI shot up by 37.8% in the same period.

译文：中国今年头两个月实际外商直接投资增长了 24%，达到 45.8 亿美元，而同期合同外商直接投资猛增 37.8%。

② 原文：Through optimizing the economic structure and improving economic returns while reducing consumption of resources and protecting the environment, China will have quadrupled its GDP per capita of the year 2000 by 2020.

译文：通过优化结构、提高效益、降低消耗、保护环境，2020 年中国将实现人均国内生产总值比 2000 年翻两番。

2. 表示数量减少

英语中，可以用 decrease、fall、reduce、down、drop、slide、slip、shrink、dip、diminish、lessen、descend、come down 等表示减少、下降或下降百分之多少，用 plunge、plummet、fall dramatically 可以表示迅速降低、大幅下跌、暴跌，也可以通过比较级如 less than 来表示减少。例如：

① 原文：It is expected that the cost of superconducting cable might plummet soon with the rapid advancement of technology in the near future.

译文：可以预见，随着技术的快速发展，超导电缆的成本不久就会大幅下降。

② 原文：Through rounds of WTO negotiations, the average tariff rate has been reduced dramatically from nearly 40% right after the Second World War to about 4% of the developed nations and 13% of the developing countries in recent years.

译文：经过几轮 WTO 谈判，近年来平均关税已从二战后的 40% 大幅下调到发达国家的 4% 和发展中国家的 13%。

3. 表示数量保持不变

英语中，stand at、remain at 可以表示保持在某种特定的水平或程度上；而 hover around、fluctuate 则表示保持在某种水平或程度上下。例如：

① 原文：China's GDP growth rate in the first half of this year was 7% — among the highest in the world — and is forecast to remain at 7% for the whole year.

译文：中国上半年 GDP 增长率为 7%，是世界上增长最快的国家之一，据预测，今年全年增长率将保持在 7%。

② 原文：Due to the changeable weather, the prices of vegetables fluctuate between 6 yuan and 12 yuan per kilo.

译文：由于天气变幻无常，蔬菜价格波动很大，每公斤价格在 6~12 元。

4. 表示约数

商务报告中可以用一些约数作为谈判技巧，翻译时也需要准确翻译原文约数的"不确定性",英语往往用 about、around、nearly、some、approximately、roughly、more or less、or so 表示约数。例如:

原文:This year's floods, which affect 250 million people or so and 2.25 million hectares of farmlands, have caused more than 200 billion yuan of direct losses.

译文:今年的洪灾受灾人口大约为 2.5 亿,农田受灾面积为 225 万公顷,造成的直接经济损失超过 2 000 亿元人民币。

5. 表示增幅

英语是形合语言,往往只能有一个动词。需要特别注意的是,在汉译英时,需要把增幅译成非谓语动词,如 up、increasing by、representing an increase of 等。例如:

原文:今年 1—8 月,广东与加拿大进出口贸易总值达 25 亿美元,增长 20.9%。其中,广东对加拿大出口 17.38 亿美元,增长 38.2%。

译文:From January to August this year, total import and export trade volume between Guangdong Province and Canada reached US$2.5 billion, representing an increase of (increasing by) 20.9%. Export from Guangdong Province to Canada amounted to US$ 1.738 billion, an increase of 38.2%.

二、常用术语和表达

(一)常用术语

analyze...	分析……
describe some features of...	描述……的一些特征
deal with the problem of...	处理……问题
explore two aspects of...	探讨……的两个方面
get feedback from...	从……中得到反馈
look at...	考虑/审视……
assess/estimate	评估
evaluate	评价
focus on...	重点关注……
investigate	调查
recommend	推荐
set out to...	旨在……
launch new products	推出新产品
senior management	高级管理层
upon request of...	应……的要求
enclosed is...	附上……
it was decided/agreed/felt that...	决定/同意/认为……
with a view to doing sth.	有做某事的打算和希望
technical support	技术支持
sluggish market	市场疲软

（二）常用表达

① I am submitting the following report about...
提交的报告是关于……
② The major findings of the present investigation can be summarized as follows.
本调查的主要发现可以归结为如下几个方面。
③ According to the finding above, it can be concluded that...
根据上述发现，可作出如下结论……
④ It is strongly recommended that the marketing strategy be improved.
强烈建议改进营销策略。

Section 4　巩　固　练　习

一、翻译以下短语。

1. 目前市场走向　　　　6. preliminary part
2. 优先权，居先　　　　7. feasibility report
3. 利润损失　　　　　　8. after-sales service
4. 问卷调查　　　　　　9. by and large
5. 公开招标　　　　　　10. regular meeting

二、翻译以下句子。

1. This report ranks 50 appliance manufacturers selected according to their volume of sales.

2. Despite the gigantic population, Chinese consumption of juice beverages is quite low. The annual juice beverage consumption per capita was below 10 litres in 2009.

3. According to China's clothing industry, the following eight trends will dominate the domestic garment market for some time to come.

4. Our findings suggest that although, for the most part, there are considerable similarities between the terms and conditions of the two companies, there are a number of slight differences between the ways that local and expatriate managerial-grade staff are treated at transpacific shipping and international airfreight.

5. The total turnover of the analyzed companies is worth around EUR 587 billion, including EUR 125 billion of the major appliances considered in this report: refrigerators and freezers, washers and driers, dishwashers, cooking appliances, microwave ovens, air conditioners, vacuum cleaners.

6. 77 国集团中有 35 名外长将出席这次为期两天的会议，而其余的国家则将派出非部长级别的高级代表团到会。

7. 数字运输网络系统是一个安全、中立而且低成本的共享基础设施，可为区内和全球众多的贸易和物流业参与者提供渠道，使彼此之间的信息流通更便捷，从而大大改善货物和信息的流通。

8. 对各界新老朋友莅会参展表示热烈欢迎，并真诚预祝买卖双方合作愉快，生意兴隆。

9. 第 20 届中国地毯交易会的规模为历届之最，来自全国各地的专业外贸公司和有地毯出口经营权的各类外贸公司及 108 家地毯厂踊跃参展；来自 30 多个国家和地区的 200 多家公司和商社欣然应邀。

10. 随着加入世界贸易组织，中国开始了历史性的市场开放改革，这场改革带来的变化将影响所有的地区及社会各个阶层。

Chapter 5

商 务 谈 判

Section 1　概　　述

一、商务谈判的概念

商务谈判是买卖双方为了促成交易而进行的活动,也是为了解决买卖双方的争端,并取得各自的经济利益的一种方法和手段。商务谈判是在商品经济条件下产生和发展起来的,它已经成为现代社会经济生活必不可少的组成部分。可以说,没有商务谈判,经济活动便无法进行,小到生活中的讨价还价,大到企业法人之间的合作、国家与国家之间的经济技术交流,都离不开商务谈判。

二、商务谈判的基本类型

商务谈判可以根据不同的标准划分为若干类型。根据谈判的规模可分为一对一谈判、小组谈判、大型谈判;根据谈判的地域可分为国内谈判与国际谈判。此外,根据谈判的内容,商务谈判可分为以下几种。

(一)商品谈判

商品谈判实际上就是货物买卖谈判,主要涉及两种形式:现货贸易谈判和期货贸易谈判。这是商务谈判的基本类型。商品谈判的内容一般包括商品的具体名称、数量、质量、价格、日期、验收、责任等条款。

(二)投资谈判

投资谈判是以获取(或借出)资金为目的,围绕资金展开谈判内容的谈判类型,如联合投资谈判、联合开发谈判、引进外资谈判、借贷款谈判等。投资谈判比较复杂,包括内容较多,因此谈判时要对有关法律法规熟悉和了解。

（三）技术谈判

技术谈判包括技术引进、技术转让、技术咨询服务等多方面内容。技术谈判中对转让形式、价格条件、支付方式、商业秘密、使用期限等都要进行磋商。

（四）服务贸易谈判

服务贸易谈判是目前商务活动中发展最快的一种，服务贸易包括运输、咨询、项目管理、旅游等方面。它涉及的常常不是货物，也不是有形企业或工程，而是提供某一方面的服务。随着第三产业的发展和国际交流的频繁，服务贸易发展越来越多样化，在谈判中所占的比重也越来越大。

三、商务谈判的原则

（1）双赢原则。
（2）平等原则。
（3）合法原则。
（4）时效性原则。
（5）最低目标原则。

四、商务谈判"八字真言"

谈判力在每种谈判中都起到重要的作用，无论是商务谈判、外交谈判，还是劳务谈判，在谈判中，双方谈判力的强弱决定了谈判结果的差别。对于谈判中的每一方来说，谈判力均来源于八个方面，即用八个英文字母代替——NO TRICKS。

（1）NO TRICKS 中的 N 代表需求（need）。对于买卖双方来说，如果买方的需求较多，卖方就拥有相对较强的谈判力。

（2）NO TRICKS 中的 O 代表选择（options）。如果买方认为卖方的产品或服务是唯一的或者没有太多选择的余地，卖方就拥有较强的谈判资本。

（3）NO TRICKS 中的 T 代表时间（time）。谈判中可能会出现有时间限制的紧急事件，如果买方受制于时间的压力，卖方的谈判力自然会增强。

（4）NO TRICKS 中的 R 代表关系（relationships）。如果卖方与顾客之间建立良好的关系，在同潜在顾客谈判时就会拥有关系力。但是，也许有的顾客觉得卖方只是为了推销，因而不愿建立深入的关系，这样，卖方在谈判过程中将会比较吃力。

（5）NO TRICKS 中的 I 代表投资（investment）。投资是指在谈判过程中投入了多少时间和精力。对达成协议承诺较多的一方往往拥有较少的谈判力。

（6）NO TRICKS 中的 C 代表可信性（credibility）。可信性也是谈判力的一种。如果卖方的产品具有价格和质量等方面的优势，无疑会增强卖方的可信性，但这一点并不能决定最后是否能成交。

（7）NO TRICKS 中的 K 代表知识（knowledge）。知识就是力量。如果卖方充分了解顾客的问题和需求，并知道如何满足顾客的需求，也会增强对顾客的谈判力。反之，如果顾客对产品拥有更多的知识和经验，顾客就有较强的谈判力。

(8) NO TRICKS 中的 S 代表技能（skill）。这可能是增强谈判力最重要的内容了，不过，谈判技巧是综合的学问，需要广博的知识、雄辩的口才、灵敏的思维等。

总之，在商务谈判中，谈判者应该善于利用 NO TRICKS 中的每一种能力。

Section 2　译 例 分 析

Passage One

A: Our price is $50 per square meter. Isn't this about right[1]?

B: May I present my frank opinion[2]?

A: Yes, please go ahead.

B: I think that will price us out of the market[3]?

A: Why? Please explain.

B: That will make Stoneplat twice as expensive as our competitors' products.

A: We have no competitors as such.

B: I admit Stoneplat has admirable attributes. If, however, one can bear a little less luster and lower impact strength, Duraface can be accepted in most of the markets we are targeting.

A: That is your opinion.[4] We believe, however, that the two are totally different.

B: Never underestimate your opponent. No product is without competitors.

A: All right. I am prepared to[5] go to $40, but no further.

B: That is better. Let's shake on[6] $40, and see how it goes.

A: Shall we discuss delivery[7] terms?

B: Yes, let's talk about delivery dates. Say[8] I gave you an order today, when could I expect to get the products?

A: Today is the 2nd of May. If the order were for standard colors and sizes, we would be to shop it out by the end of June.

B: What does that mean in real terms[9]? My question is when I can "receive" the products.

A: It normally takes 45 days to ship by sea from China to the US.

B: In other words, it takes about three months even for standard items.

A: For your better understanding, I would like to explain the details of our production schedule. Please remember that our production plan for the next month is fixed on the 20th of each month. If your order is placed today, it will be scheduled on the 20th of May for the production in June.

B: In the age of instant global communications, this is unbelievably slow. You have to improve the production system. Otherwise, we will lose all our customers. Can't you devise

something better, like stockpiling some standard items here in the US?
A: We have no plans to do so at present. But that may have to be an alternative at a later date.

Key Words

admirable attributes	令人称赞的特质
impact strength	冲击强度
shake on	以……成交
stockpile	储存

Notes

1. about right 表示价格合适，通常用于不是积极地肯定时。
2. frank opinion 表示直白的观点，通常预示会出现反对意见。
3. price us out of the market 指由于价格过高，势必遭到市场的淘汰。
4. That is your opinion 表示"你的意见不代表一切"，比较缓和的说法还有 So you say（那只是你的意见）。
5. be prepared to (do) 表示"打算……"或是"准备……"。
6. shake on 表示"以……成交"或是"双方达成协议"。
7. delivery 是 deliver 的名词形式，表示"交货"，是指对方收到货物。而 ship 和 dispatch 则表示"出货"。但是，要注意 receive 与 accept 的区别，receive 单纯表示收到货物，而 accept 则包含货物检查完毕。
8. Say 有"假设"的意思，通常译为"比如说"。
9. in real terms 并非抽象的用语，而是带有"具体"的意思。

参考译文

A：我们的价格是每平方米 50 美元。这可还合理吗？
B：我可以坦白地表示我的见解吗？
A：请说。
B：我认为那将使我们因价格而遭市场淘汰。
A：为什么？请说明原因。
B：因为 Stoneplat 的价格将会是我们的竞争对手产品的两倍。
A：我们没有这样的对手。
B：我承认 Stoneplat 确实有令人称赞的特质。但是如果有人愿意忍受少一点的光泽和低一点的冲击强度，Duraface 就能够取代我们而占有我们预估的目标市场。
A：那是您的意见。我们认为这两种商品完全不同。
B：绝对不要看轻你们的对手。没有商品是可以避免竞争的。
A：好吧，这样的话我可以降到 40 美元，这已经是最低价了。

B：这样会好一点。让我们暂定在 40 美元，再评估看看。
A：接下来让我们讨论交货事宜吧？
B：好，让我们讨论交货日期。假设我今天下订单，什么时候可以拿到产品呢？
A：今天是 5 月 2 日。如果是标准颜色和尺寸的订单，我们会在 6 月底前出货。
B：这是什么意思？我的问题是我什么时候能够"收到"产品。
A：通常从中国装船后运送到美国需要 45 天。
B：换句话说，依照标准程序来做的话仍然需要大约 3 个月的时间。
A：为了使您更好地理解，我想说明一下我们生产计划表的细节。请记住我们在每个月 20 日确定我们下个月的生产计划。如果您今天下订单，我们会在 5 月 20 日的生产计划表里安排在 6 月生产。
B：在全球快速流通的时代，这种速度慢得令人无法置信。你们必须改进生产系统，否则我们将会失去所有的顾客。你们不能设法改善吗？例如在美国储存一些标准规格的产品。
A：目前我们并没有这样的计划。但是日后也许会这么处理。

▶▶ *Passage Two*

A：进一步想[1]，如果[2]Stoneplat 在市场上销售良好，我们可以考虑在此地直接生产。
B：我个人认为我们双方都应该牢记这一点。如果这样的计划得以实现，Novel 应该是你们的合作伙伴。
A：我正期待你这么说。但是中国华润集团必须对任何这样的合资企业[3]拥有控股权益[4]。
B：因为这在我们国家是新的尝试，Novel 必须至少与你们有同等的地位，尤其是合资企业的市场营销活动，必须利用到我们销售部门的良好商誉。
A：在这个阶段，对于股权比例，我们是有弹性的，并且不排除[5]50/50 的合资形式。
B：对合资形式我有一个建议[6]。在美国有所谓的合伙制[7]，提供了合伙公司的某些优势。例如，如果合伙公司前几年出现损失，可以用来抵消母公司的利润。我建议可以考虑这个形式。
A：我们对合伙制非常熟悉，但是我们并不考虑。因为如果我们参与合伙制，我们必须受到美国法院的管辖。请仔细考虑以上的提议。
B：你们可以考虑在美国设立一个子公司，以其名义参与合伙制。
A：我们无法接受为此目的来投资成立子公司。
B：合资公司至少有一个常驻的总裁，而目前我们已有一些考虑人选。
A：我希望总裁在管理公司的同时必须身兼公关人员。因此他必须熟悉这个国家的文化和习惯。我建议他最好是美国公民。
B：谢谢，我会记下您的宝贵建议。然而，我们认为，各国国情不同，总裁人选不仅是在技术方面，而且在市场需求方面都必须很熟悉。因此，他可能会一个日本人，因为一开始并没有适当的当地人选。然而，情况并不一定永远这样，我们希望将来会有最好的人选来担任总裁一职。

Key Words

合资企业	joint venture (JV)
中国华润集团	China Resources Group
合伙制	partnership
子公司	subsidiary
常驻总裁	resident President

Notes

1. "进一步想"译为 think ahead，还有几种相似的说法，如"长期来看"译为 take a long term view；"拟定基本计划"译为 construct a grand design。
2. "如果……"译为 assuming that...。
3. "合资企业"译为 joint venture，简称 JV。
4. "拥有控股权益"译为 have a controlling interest。如果是股份有限公司，则表示持有超过半数以上的股数。50/50 的持股比例并不具有控股的能力。
5. "排除"译为 rule out。
6. 该句可译为 I would like to offer a suggestion。这是提出建议时比较客气的说法。
7. "合伙制"译为 partnership，这是比较类似日本的企业形态，与正式的企业形态不同，合伙制企业的特征为损益直接归属于出资者。

参考译文

A: Thinking ahead, assuming that Stoneplat sells well in this market, we may consider the possibility of producing it here.

B: I personally think it is something we both should bear in mind. If such a scheme materializes, Novel should be your partner.

A: I was hoping you would say that. But China Resources Group must have a controlling interest in any such joint venture.

B: Since it would be a venture in our country, Novel must have at least an equal footing with you. Especially, the marketing and sales activities of the JV would have to utilize the goodwill generated by our sales organization.

A: At this stage, we are flexible about the ownership ratio, and do not rule out a 50/50 JV.

B: I would like to offer a suggestion on the form of the JV. In the US, there is an entity called partnership. It offers certain advantages to the parent companies. Namely, if the JV shows any losses in the initial years, they may be used to offset the profits of the parent. I suggest we consider this form for the JV.

A: We are quite familiar with the partnership system. But we prefer not to consider it. The reason is that we may be subject to jurisdiction of a US court if we participate in partnership. Please consider this matter closed.

B: You may consider establishing a subsidiary in the US and have the subsidiary participate in a partnership.

A: We cannot tolerate spending money to established subsidiary only for that purpose.

B: We plan to have at least one resident President for the JV. We have a few candidates in mind.

A: I just want to note that the President must act as a king of public relations person, as well as running the company. So, the President must be familiar with the culture and customs of this country. We suggest that the President be a US citizen.

B: Thank you. I will take due note of your valuable advice. However, while we recognize that each country is different, I believe the President must be someone who is familiar not only with the technology, but also with the demands of the market. The logical conclusion is that it probably will be a Japanese because no local has such qualification in the beginning. However, I do not mean that this situation will continue indefinitely, and the person who has the best qualification should be the President in the future.

Section 3 实 践 总 结

一、翻译技巧

（一）商务谈判英语的特点

作为英语的一个功能性变体，商务谈判英语在语言使用方面有其显著特色，主要表现在以下几个方面。

1. 具有极强的专业性

商务谈判英语的语言形式、词汇及内容等方面与专业密切相关。商务谈判英语所承载的是商务理论和商务实践等方面的信息，没有承载商务理论和商务实践等方面的信息的英语不能称为商务谈判英语。所以，进行商务谈判翻译的译者们除了要掌握专业的英语翻译知识以外，同时还要具备比较完整的商务知识。

2. 用词准确

商务谈判英语的用词明白易懂、简短达意。在用词明白易懂方面，尽量多用较为常用的词语，如多用 approval 而不用 approbation，以保证所有词语具有通用性，能为普通大众所理解。但与此同时，商务谈判英语所使用的语言又不能过于非正式。例如，在介词和连词使用方面，由于现代英语中的介词和连词非常简短，将这些介词和连词置于商务英语谈判中，会与谈判中所使用的比较正式和规范的名词、动词等不协调，故在谈判中往往采用介词短语来替代简单的介词和连词。例如，可以用 in the nature of 替代 like，用 for the purpose of 替代 for，用 in the case of 替代 if，用 in the event that/of 替代 if，用 on the grounds that 替代 because 等。

3. 遵守陈述原则

商务谈判英语翻译在陈述事物时要具体、明确，不能含糊其辞、不着边际。例如，商务谈判中不说 we wish to confirm our telex dispatched yesterday，而要说成 we wish to confirm our telex of July 2nd, 2018。因为前者含糊笼统，后者清晰明了。

4. 遵守礼貌原则

在商务谈判中，礼貌是非常重要的语言特点。良好的素养和谈吐能在对方的心里树立起一种正直、热情、有良好职业道德的形象，从而使对方愿意合作，达成谈判目的。

（二）商务谈判英语的翻译方法与技巧

要做好商务谈判的翻译工作，译者必须在翻译的过程中，在充分理解原话的基础上把握好以下 3 点。

1. 商务谈判英语的模糊翻译

这里的模糊翻译与意译有一些不同。意译是无法找到对应的译出语时所采取的迂回的翻译方法；而模糊翻译则是一种属性，是指翻译过程中不可避免的模糊性。商务语言具有一定的模糊性，为了实现等效的目的，译文也应具有一定的模糊性。在商务谈判中，对于模糊信息的理解必须忠实地反映谈判双方模糊用词的意图。在商务语言的模糊翻译中，对等法是最常用的方法。例如：

① 原文：合资企业的注册资本一般以人民币表示，也可以用合营各方约定的外币表示。

译文：The registered capital shall generally be represented in Renminbi, or may be in a foreign currency agreed upon by the parties to the joint venture.

② 原文：How does one register the joint venture?

译文：怎样注册合资企业呢？

③ 原文：We'll prepare all the necessary documentation and present it to the responsible authority. We'll do it well in three months.

译文：我们要准备所有必要的文件，提交给负责该事务的机构，三个月之内会办好的。

2. 商务谈判英语的缩略语翻译

英语缩略语用简单的几个字母表达复杂的含义，具有言简意明的特点，广泛应用于国际贸易、国际金融、国际经济技术合作等领域，在商务谈判这一语境的交际中起着十分重要的作用。商务英语缩略语和普通英语词语一样，具有同等的句法功能。例如：

① CIF is the basis we are to offer.

到岸价是我们的报价基础。（CIF 在句中做主语）

② When can I have your CIF firm offer?

我们何时能得到贵方到岸价的实盘？（CIF 在句中做定语）

③ What do the abbreviations CIF and FOB mean?

缩写语 CIF 和 FOB 指的是什么？（CIF and FOB 在句中做同位语）

④ Send YR L/C.

请惠寄你方信用证。（YR L/C =your letter of credit，在句中做宾语）

3. 正确使用礼貌用语

正确使用礼貌用语对于谈判的效果有很大的促进作用，并能加速谈判目的的实现。现介绍一些如下：

1）将命令式改为请求式

将祈使句改为以 will、would 开头的疑问句。例如：

① Would you please make your lowest quotation CIF Shanghai?

请报上海最低到岸价。

② Would you please tell us the quantity you require so as to enable us to work out the offer?

请告知贵方所需货物的数量，以便我方算出报价。

2）虚拟语气使用过去式

过去式形式的虚拟语气如 would ask、should be、might make、could effect 等，可以用来表达委婉的语气和礼貌的情感以改进谈判的效果。例如：

① We would ask you to make a prompt shipment.

务请贵方即期装运。

② We wish you could effect insurance on the goods with PICC.

希望贵方能向中国人民财产保险公司投保该货物。

3）使用缓和法

在谈判翻译中，为了避免翻译时过分强调自己，应当使用缓和句式，如 We are afraid…; We would say…; We might (may) say…; We would think…; It seems (would seem)…等。例如：

① I'm afraid that we cannot deliver the goods all at one time.

我方恐怕不能一次性交货。

② We would say that it was unwise of you not to accept this favorable offer.

我们会说，贵方放弃这一优惠报盘是不明智的。

③ We might say that our goods are the very goods on the current market.

可以说，我们的货物是目前市场上最好的。

④ It seems (would seem) to us that you ought to have accepted the offer.

我们认为，贵方应该接受该报盘。

二、常用术语和表达

（一）价格条件

运费	freight
单价	unit price
码头费	dock charges
卸货费	landing charges
关税	customs duty
净价	net price
印花税	stamp duty
含佣价	price including commission

折扣	discount
批发价	wholesale price
零售价	retail price
现货价格	spot price
现行价格（时价）	current price/prevailing price
国际市场价格	world (international) market price

（二）交货条件

交货	delivery
轮船	steamship（S.S.）
装运、装船	shipment
租船	charter a ship
定程租船	voyage charter
定期租船	time charter
班轮	regular shipping liner
驳船	lighter
舱位	shipping space
油轮	tanker
提货	take delivery of goods
选择港（任意港）	optional port
选港费由买方负担	optional charges to be borne by the buyers/optional charges for the buyers' account
一月份装船	shipment during January/January shipment
一月底装船	shipment not later than January 31/shipment on or before January 31
在……（时间）分两批装船	shipment during...in two lots
在……（时间）平均分两批装船	shipment during....in two equal lots

（三）交易磋商、合同签订

指示性价格	price indication
速复	reply immediately
参考价格	reference price
习惯做法	usual practice
交易磋商	business negotiation
不承担义务	without engagement
限……复	subject to reply…
有效期限	time of validity
购货合同	purchase contract
购货确认书	purchase confirmation

销售确认书　　　　　　　　　sales confirmation
一般交易条件　　　　　　　　general terms and conditions
以未售出为准　　　　　　　　subject to prior sale

Section 4　巩 固 练 习

一、翻译以下短语。

1. 卖出汇率　　　　　　　6. time of validity
2. 来料加工　　　　　　　7. port dues
3. 招标　　　　　　　　　8. clearance of goods
4. 溢短装条款　　　　　　9. return commission
5. 指示性价格　　　　　　10. prompt shipment

二、翻译以下句子。

1. 如果你们不太为难，我希望你们在两年内还清贷款。
2. 我方希望你方提供装配零件所使用的必要技术。
3. 你能否告诉我加工装配的费率和支付方式？
4. 发货后，我们根据项目安装的进度，分4次付清其余款项。
5. 投标者提供的设备，其技术指标应符合标书中每个品目中的技术指标要求。
6. We require that the equipment and technology to be provided by you should be up to advanced world standards reasonable in price and suitable to our condition of production.
7. For the purpose of mastering all the techniques of operating your equipment, we request you give technical training to the personnel for operating and servicing the equipment.
8. What concerns us is when the opening bank will be able to make this payment.
9. We hope you will let us have an outline of your proposal so that we can make a preliminary evaluation of the economic feasibility of your proposal.
10. All the materials are provided by you, while our company is only responsible for processing, for which we would charge a processing fee.

Chapter 6

代 理 合 同

Section 1 概　述

随着我国加入世贸组织,以及近年来提出"一带一路"的倡议,我国对外开放水平不断提高。在国际贸易中,各类合同显然成了经贸交流的重要媒介,代理合同在中外商务合作中的需求也越来越大。

一、代理的定义和分类

根据《中华人民共和国民法通则》第 63 条规定,代理人在代理权限内,以被代理人的名义实施民事法律行为。被代理人对代理人的代理行为,承担民事责任。此外,《中华人民共和国民法通则》第 64 条规定,代理包括委托代理、法定代理和指定代理。委托代理人按照被代理人的委托行使代理权,法定代理人依照法律的规定行使代理权,指定代理人按照人民法院或者指定单位的指定行使代理权。国际贸易中所采用的代理方式一般为委托代理。按委托授权的大小,委托代理可分为以下几种。

1. 独家代理（exclusive/sole agency）

独家代理是指在特定地区、特定时期内享有代销指定商品的专营权,同时不得再代销其他来源的同类商品。凡是在规定地区和规定期限内做成该项商品的交易,除双方另有约定外,无论是由代理做成,还是由委托人直接同其他商人做成,代理商都有享受佣金的权利。

2. 一般代理（agency）

一般代理又称佣金代理,是指在同一地区,同一时期内,委托人可以选定多个客户作为代理商,根据推销商品的实际金额支付佣金,或者根据协议规定的办法和百分率支付佣金。我国的出口业务中,运用此类代理商的较多。

3. 总代理（general agency）

总代理是指在特定地区和一定时间内委托人的全权代表,除有权代表委托人签订买卖合同、处理货物等商务活动外,也可以进行一些非商业性的活动,而且还有权指派分代理,并可享受分代理的佣金。

4. 特约代理（special sales agency）

有些国家的厂商和跨国集团公司，常在国外指派特约代理，为其推销技术性的工业产品或为其提供技术和维修服务。例如，三菱、丰田等日产汽车公司在其特约代理网点，既有维修和零部件供应服务，又有技术咨询服务，从而为买方解除了维修服务的后顾之忧。

二、代理合同的定义和分类

代理合同是商务合同的一种，它是用以明确委托人和代理人之间权利与义务的法律条文。但代理合同又不同于其他的商务合同，主要表现在以下两点：第一，代理合同的内容更侧重于代理服务，即规定委托人和代理人各自的权利与义务，而其他的商务合同大多侧重于商业活动中的各个交易环节及交易的具体细节；第二，相比较于其他的商务合同而言，代理合同中不会有那么多的数据。

代理协议也是代理合同。合同是法律用语，源自法语 contractus，也就是"契约"的意思。《中华人民共和国合同法》第 2 条规定：合同是平等主体的自然人、法人、其他组织之间设立、变更、终止民事权利义务关系的协议。而商务合同是合同中最常见的一种，是商业法人之间为实现一定的经济目的、明确相互权利和义务的一种文体。根据格式的繁简程度不同，国际商务合同可以采取正式合同（contract）、协议书（agreement）、确认书（confirmation）、备忘录（memorandum）、订单（order）等书面形式。在合同签订和履行过程中，当事人之间的往来信函、电子邮件、传真等也是合同的组成部分。所以说代理协议也是代理合同。

依据不同的代理内容，代理合同可以分为：销售代理合同、注册代理合同、广告代理合同、法律事务代理合同、缴款代理合同、发行代理合同等；依据不同的代理类型，代理合同又可以分为：独家代理合同、一般代理合同、总代理合同、特约代理合同等。

三、代理合同的功能

代理合同作为商务合同的一种，主要有两种功能：一是提供合同信息，即明确当事人的权利和义务；二是祈使功能，即要求当事人履行义务。

四、代理合同的内容与结构

代理合同的主要内容包括：① 协议双方姓名和地址；② 代理商名称、数量和代理区域；③ 代理人、委托人各自的权利与义务；④ 佣金的支付；⑤ 有效期。除上述基本内容外，关于不可抗力和仲裁等条款的规定，与经销协议和一般买卖合同的做法大致相同。

尽管代理合同有不同的种类，但是就其结构而言，大体上同其他商务合同相似。其构成部分通常包括以下 3 个部分（当事人根据实际情况可做适当调整）。

（1）标题（title）：标题主要为了标明合同性质和合同号（contract number），如独家代理协议（exclusive agency agreement）。

（2）前文（preamble）：前文一般包括订约日期和地点（signing date/place）、合同当事人及其国籍、主要营业场所或住所（signing parties and their nationalities, principal place of business or residence address）；当事人合法的权威依据（each party's authority）；说明条款（WHEREAS clause）。

（3）正文（body）：包括定义条款（definition clause）、基本条款（basic clause）、一般条

款（general terms and conditions）和结尾条款（WITNESS clause）。

Section 2 译例分析

Passage One

SALES AGENCY AGREEMENT[1]

No.:
Date:

This Agreement is entered into between the parties concerned on the basis of equality and mutual benefit to develop business on terms and conditions mutually agreed upon as follows:

1. Contracting Parties

Supplier:　　　　(hereinafter called "Party A")

Agent:　　　　　(hereinafter called "Party B")

Party A hereby[2] appoints Party B to act as his selling agent to sell the commodity mentioned below.

2. Commodity

***

3. Quantity or Amount

It is mutually agreed that Party B shall undertake to sell not less than ＿＿＿ of the aforesaid commodity in the duration of this Agreement.

4. Territory

In＿＿＿ only.

5. Confirmation of Orders

The quantities, prices and shipment of the commodities stated in this Agreement shall be confirmed for each transaction, the particulars of which are to be specified in the Sales Confirmation signed by the two parties hereto.

6. Payment

After confirmation of the order, Party B shall arrange to open a confirmed, irrevocable L/C[3] available by draft at sight in favour of Party A within the time stipulated in the relevant S/C. Party B shall also notify Party A immediately after L/C is opened, so that Party A can get prepared for delivery.

7. Commission

Upon the expiration of the Agreement and Party B's fulfilment of the total turnover mentioned in Article 3, Party A shall pay to Party B _____% commission on the basis of the aggregate amount of the invoice value already paid by Party B of the shipments effected.

8. Reports on Market Conditions

Party B shall forward once every three months to Party A detailed reports on current market conditions and of consumers comments. Meanwhile, Party B shall, from time to time, send to Party A samples of similar commodities offered by other suppliers, together with their prices, sales information and advertising materials.

9. Advertising & Publicity Expenses

Party B shall bear all expenses for advertising and publicity within the aforementioned territory in the duration of this Agreement and submit to Party A all patterns and/or drawings and description for prior approval.

10. Validity of Agreement

This Agreement, after its being signed by the parties concerned shall remain in force for _____ year(s) as from _____ to _____. If either party wish to extend this Agreement, he shall notice, in writing, the other party one month prior to its expiration. The matter shall be decided by consent of the parties hereto.

Should either party fail to implement the terms and conditions herein, the other party is entitled to terminate the Agreement.

11. Arbitration

All disputes arising from the execution of this Agreement shall be settled through friendly consultations. In case[4] no settlement can be reached, the case in dispute shall then be submitted to the Foreign Trade Arbitration Commission of China Council for the Promotion of International Trade[5] for arbitration in accordance with its provisional rules of procedure. The decision made by this Commission shall be regarded as final and binding upon both parties. Arbitration fees shall be borne by the losing party, unless otherwise awarded.

12. Other Terms & Conditions

(1) Party A shall not supply the contracted commodity to any other buyers in the above mentioned territory. Direct enquiries, if any, will be referred to Party B. However, should any other buyers wish to deal with Party A directly, Party A may do so, but Party A shall send to Party B a copy of Sales Confirmation and give Party B _____% commission(s) concluded.

(2) Should Party B fail to pass on his orders to Party A in a period of _____ months for a minimum of _____, Party A shall not bind himself to this Agreement.

(3) For any business transacted between governments of both Parties, Party A may handle such direct dealings as authorized by Party A's government without binding himself to this Agreement. Party B shall not interfere in such direct dealings, nor shall Party B bring forward any demand for compensation therefrom.

(4) This Agreement shall be subject to the terms and conditions in the Sales Confirmation signed by both parties hereto.

This Agreement is signed[6] on ___/___/_____ at _____ and is in two originals; each party holds one.

Party A: Party B:
Signature: Signature:

Key Words

hereinafter	下文
territory	经销地区
supplier	供货人
confirmation	确认书
irrevocable	不可撤销的
compensation	补偿,赔偿
delivery	交货
expiration	期满
breach	违反,不履行
arbitration	仲裁
dispute	纠纷,争端
divergence	分歧,歧异
in accordance with	依据,按照
provision	规定
award	裁决,授予,判给
arbitral award	仲裁裁决
valid	有效的
null	无效的
void	无效的
letter of credit (L/C)	信用证
commission	佣金
contracting parties	订约人,合同当事人
shipment	装船
validity	有效性
provisional rules of procedure	暂行议事规则
sales agent	销售代理人

Notes

1. 销售代理协议是指,代理人为委托人销售某种特定产品或全部产品并对价格、条款及其他交易条件可全权处理的与委托人签订的协议。从法律上来讲,销售代理人与委托人之间的关系属于委托代理关系。销售代理人在代理权限内替委托人销售商品,但其所有权不属于代理人,因此销售收入归委托人所有,而代理人只领取佣金。

2. hereinafter、hereby、hereunder 在法律文本中经常出现,可分别译为"在下文中""特此"和"如下的"。例如:"This Contract shall come into force from the date of execution hereof by the Buyer and the Builder."(本合同自买方和建造方签署之日生效)。

3. L/C，letter of credit，译为信用证。信用证结算是当今国际贸易中的主要货款支付方式。

4. in case 引导状语从句时，相当于 should，汉译时一般翻译成"若……（发生）"。

5. China Council for the Promotion of International Trade，中国国际贸易促进委员会（简称 CCPIT）。

6. 在法律文本中，表示协议的"订立"可用以下 4 个动词：sign、make、conclude、enter into。根据同义词连用的写作特点，也可用上述 4 个动词中的两个来表示"订立"。

 参考译文

销售代理协议

编号：
日期：

本协议双方为了发展贸易，在平等互利的基础上，按下列条件签订本协议。

1. 订约人

供货人：　　　　　　　　（以下简称"甲方"）

销售代理人：　　　　　　（以下简称"乙方"）

甲方委托乙方为销售代理人，推销下列商品。

2. 代理商品

***

3. 数量或金额

双方约定，乙方在协议有效期内，承销不少于＿＿＿＿的上述商品。

4. 经销地区

只限在＿＿＿＿销售。

5. 订单的确认

关于协议所规定的上述商品的每笔交易，其数量、价格及装运条件等须经甲方确认，并签订销售确认书，对交易做具体规定。

6. 付款

订单确认后，乙方须按照有关确认书所规定的时间开立以甲方为受益人的保兑的、不可撤销的即期信用证。乙方开出信用证后，应立即通知甲方，以便甲方准备交货。

7. 佣金

在本协议期满，乙方完成了第 3 条所规定的数额时，甲方应按装运货物所收到的全部发票金额付给乙方＿＿＿＿%的佣金。

8. 市场情况报告

乙方每三个月向甲方提供一次有关当时市场情况和用户意见的详细报告。同时，乙方应随时向甲方提供其他供应商所给的类似商品的样品及其价格、销售情况和广告资料。

9. 广告及宣传费用

在本协议有效期内，乙方在上述经销地区所做广告宣传的一切费用，由乙方自理。乙方须事先向甲方提供广告宣传的图案及文字说明，由甲方审阅同意。

10. 协议有效期

本协议由双方签字后生效，有效期＿＿＿年，自＿＿＿至＿＿＿。若一方希望延长本协议，则须在本协议期满前一个月书面通知另一方，经双方协商决定。

若协议一方未履行协议条款，另一方有权终止协议。

11. 仲裁

在履行协议过程中，如产生争议，双方应友好协商解决。若通过友好协商未能达成协议，则提交中国国际贸易促进委员会对外贸易仲裁委员会，根据该会仲裁程序暂行议事规定进行仲裁。该委员会的决定是终局的，对双方均有约束力。仲裁费用，除另有规定外，由败诉一方负担。

12. 其他条款

（1）甲方不得向经销地区其他买主供应本协议所规定的商品，如有询价，当转给乙方洽办。若有买主希望从甲方直接订购，甲方可以供货，但甲方须将有关销售确认书副本寄给乙方，并按所达成交易的发票金额付给乙方＿＿＿％的佣金。

（2）若乙方在＿＿＿月内未能向甲方提供至少＿＿＿的订货，甲方不承担本协议的义务。

（3）对双方政府间的贸易，甲方有权按其政府的授权进行有关的直接贸易，而不受本协议的约束。乙方不得干涉此种直接贸易，也无权向甲方提出任何补偿或佣金要求。

（4）本协议受签约双方所签订的销售确认书条款的制约。

本协议于＿＿＿年＿＿月＿＿日在＿＿＿签订，正本两份，甲乙双方各执一份。

甲方： 乙方：
签字： 签字：

Passage Two

独家代理协议 [1]

本协议于 2017 年 5 月 20 日在中国青岛由有关双方在平等互利的基础上达成，按双方同意的下列条件发展业务关系 [2]：

1. 协议双方

甲方：青岛×××有限公司　　　　　　乙方：新加坡×××有限公司
地址：中国山东省青岛市瞿塘峡路 25 号　地址：新加坡滑铁卢街 126 号
电话：****832　　　　　　　　　　　　电话：****436
传真：****415　　　　　　　　　　　　传真：****862

2. 委任

甲方指定乙方为其独家代理,为第 3 条所列商品从第 4 条所列区域的顾客中招揽订单,乙方接受上述委任[3]。

3. 代理商品

"金鱼"牌洗衣机。

4. 代理区域

仅限于新加坡。

5. 最低业务量

乙方同意,在本协议有效期内从上述代理区域内的顾客中招揽的上述商品的订单价值不低于 10 万美元。

6. 价格与支付

每一笔交易的货物价格应由乙方与买主通过谈判确定,并须经甲方最后确认[4]。付款使用保兑的、不可撤销的信用证,由买方开出,以甲方为受益人。信用证须在装运日期前 15 天到达甲方。

7. 独家代理权

基于本协议授予的独家代理权,甲方不得直接或间接地通过乙方以外的渠道向新加坡销售或出口第 3 条所列商品,乙方不得在新加坡经销、分销或促销与上述商品相竞争或类似的产品,也不得招揽或接受以到新加坡以外地区销售为目的的订单。在本协议有效期内,甲方应将其收到的来自新加坡其他商家的有关代理产品[5]的询价或订单转交给乙方。

8. 商情报告

为使甲方充分了解现行市场情况,乙方须至少每季度一次或在必要时随时向甲方提供市场报告,内容包括与本协议代理商品的进口与销售有关的地方规章的变动、当地市场发展趋势及买方对甲方按协议供应的货物的品质、包装、价格等方面的意见。乙方还须向甲方提供其他供应商类似商品的报价和广告资料。

9. 广告及费用

乙方负担本协议有效期内在新加坡销售代理商品所做广告宣传的一切费用,并向甲方提交所用于广告的音像资料,供甲方事先核准。

10. 佣金[6]

对乙方直接获取并经甲方确认接受的订单,甲方按净发票售价向乙方支付 5%的佣金。佣金在甲方收到每笔订单的全部货款后支付。

11. 政府部门间的交易

在甲、乙双方政府部门之间达成的交易不受本协议条款的限制,此类交易的金额也不应计入第 5 条规定的最低业务量。

12. 工业产权

在本协议有效期内,为销售有关洗衣机,乙方可以使用甲方拥有的商标,并承认使用于或包含于洗衣机中的任何专利商标、版权或其他工业产权为甲方独家拥有。一旦发现侵权,乙方应立即通知甲方并协助甲方采取措施保护甲方权益。

13. 协议有效期

本协议经有关双方如期签署后生效,有效期为 1 年,从 2017 年 7 月 1 日至 2018 年 6 月 30 日。除非作出相反通知,本协议期满后将延长 12 个月。

14. 协议的终止

在本协议有效期内,如果一方违反协议条款,另一方有权终止协议[7]。

15. 不可抗力

由于水灾、火灾、地震、干旱、战争或协议一方无法预见、控制、避免和克服的其他事件导致不能或暂时不能全部或部分履行本协议,该方不负责任。但是,受不可抗力事件影响的一方须尽快将发生的事件通知另一方,并在不可抗力事件发生15天内将有关机构出具的不可抗力事件的证明寄交对方。

16. 仲裁

因履行本协议所发生的一切争议应通过友好协商解决。如协商不能解决争议,则应将争议提交中国国际经济贸易仲裁委员会(北京),依据其仲裁规则进行仲裁。仲裁裁决是终局的,对双方都有约束力。

甲方:青岛×××有限公司　　　乙方:新加坡×××有限公司
(签字)　　　　　　　　　　　(签字)

Key Words

平等互利	equality and mutual benefit
订单	order
委任	appointment
以……为受益人	in favor of...
经销、分销或促销	sell, distribution or promote
询价	inquiry
商情报告	market report
最低业务量	minimal turnover
音像资料	audio and video materials
独家代理	exclusive agency
净发票售价	net invoiced selling price
佣金	commission
如期签署	be duly signed
违反条款	violate the stipulations
终止协议	terminate the agreement
出具证明	send a certificate
友好协商	friendly negotiation
有约束力的	binding
保兑的	confirmed
不可撤销的	irrevocable

Notes

1. 独家代理是指委托人根据独家代理协议，在一定期间、一定地区内委托代理商代销某种商品，并按销售额的比例付给代理商佣金。

2. 此句英译时要结合合同的句式特点来进行。英文合同的开头通常是一个比较复杂的被动语态长句，通过各种插入成分把签约双方、签约地点、签约时间、签约原则等融在一句话中。该句两个主谓结构的主语都和"本协议"有关，因此可以把"协议"作为主语，"达成"作为谓语，其余成分全部转为状语。另外，要注意合同文件中常使用后置定语，如常用 the parties concerned，而不用 the concerned parties。

3. "委任"可翻译为 appoint，名词形式是 appointment。其相关句式有：① appoint sb. (to be) +职位（注意职位前不用冠词）；② appoint sb. as...。该句翻译时应注意词性的选用和搭配的选择。

4. 此处的"经甲方最后确认"应采用被动句式译出。英文合同大量使用被动句，以求客观严谨，因此很多中文的主动句式也可以考虑用被动句式译出。再如第 13 条中的"除非作出相反通知，本协议期满后将延长 12 个月"，可将"协议"作为主语，采用被动句式译出，体现条款的客观公正性。

5. "有关代理产品"可译为 commodity in question。

6. "佣金"可译为 commission，指的是代理人为委托人提供服务所获得的报酬。

7. 此句为条件句，翻译时应谨慎对待主、从句时态的选择。

参考译文

EXCLUSIVE AGENCY AGREEMENT

This agreement is made and entered into by and between the parties concerned on May 20, 2017 in Qingdao, China on the basis of equality and mutual benefit to develop business on terms and conditions mutually agreed upon as follows:

1. The Parties Concerned

Party A: Qingdao ××× Co., Ltd.

Add: 25 Qutangxia Road, Qingdao, Shangdong, China

Tel: ****832

Fax: ****415

Party B: Singapore ××× Co., Ltd.

Add: 126 Waterloo Street, Singapore

Tel: ****436

Fax: ****862

2. Appointment

Party A hereby appoints Party B as its exclusive agent to solicit orders for the commodity stipulated in Article 3 from customers in the territory stipulated in Article 4, and Party B accepts and assumes such appointment.

3. Commodity

"Golden Fish" Brand Washing Machines.

4. Territory

In Singapore only.

5. Minimum Turnover

Party B shall undertake to solicit orders for the above commodity from customers in the above territory during the effective period of this agreement for not less than USD 100,000.

6. Price and Payment

The price for each individual transaction shall be fixed through negotiations between Party B and the buyer, and subject to Party A's final confirmation. Payment shall be made by confirmed, irrevocable L/C opened by the buyer in favor of Party A, which shall reach Party A 15 days before the date of shipment.

7. Exclusive Right

In consideration of the exclusive rights granted herein, Party A shall not, directly or indirectly, sell or export the commodity stipulated in Article 4 to customers in Singapore through channels other than Party B; Party B shall not sell, distribute or promote the sales of any products competitive with or similar to the above commodity in Singapore and shall not solicit or accept orders for the purpose of selling them outside Singapore. Party A shall refer to Party B any enquiries or orders for the commodity in question received by Party A from other firms in Singapore during the validity of this agreement.

8. Market Report

In order to keep Party A well informed of the prevailing market conditions, Party B should undertake to supply Party A, at least once a quarter or at any time when necessary, with market reports concerning changes of the local regulations in connection with the import and sales of the commodity covered by this agreement, local market tendency and the buyer's comments on quality, packing, price, etc. of the goods supplied by Party A under this agreement. Party B shall also supply Party A with quotations and advertising materials on similar products of other suppliers.

9. Advertising and Expenses

Party A shall bear all expenses for advertising and publicity in connection with the commodity in question in Singapore within the validity of this agreement, and shall submit to Party A all audio and video materials intended for advertising for prior approval.

10. Commission

Party A shall pay to Party B a commission of 5% on the net invoiced selling price on all orders directly obtained by Party B and accepted by Party A. No commission shall be paid until Party A receives the full payment for each order.

11. Transactions between Governmental Bodies

Transactions concluded between governmental bodies of Party A and Party B shall not be restricted by the terms and conditions of this agreement, nor shall the amount of such transactions be counted as part of the turnover stipulated in Article 5.

12. Industrial Property Rights

Party B may use the trade-marks owned by Party A for the sale of the washing machines covered herein within the validity of this agreement, and shall acknowledge that all patents, trademarks, copy rights or any other industrial property rights used or embodied in the washing machines shall remain to be the sole properties of Party A. Should any infringement be found, Party B shall promptly notify and assist Party A to take steps to protect the latter's rights.

13. Validity of Agreement

This agreement, when duly signed by both parties concerned, shall remain in force for 12 months from July 1, 2017 to June 30, 2018, and it shall be extended for another 12 months upon expiration unless notice in writing is given to the contrary.

14. Termination

During the validity of this agreement, should either of the two parties be found to have violated the stipulations herein, the other party has the right to terminate this agreement.

15. Force Majeure

Either party shall not be held responsible for failure or delay to perform all or any part of this agreement due to flood, fire, earthquake, draught, war or any other events which could not be predicted, controlled, avoided or overcome by the relative party. However, the party affected by the event of Force Majeure shall inform the other party of its occurrence in writing as soon as possible and thereafter send a certificate of the event issued by the relevant authorities to the other party within 15 days after its occurrence.

16. Arbitration

All disputes arising from the performance of this agreement shall be settled through friendly negotiation. Should no settlement be reached through negotiation, the case shall then be submitted for arbitration to the China International Economic and Trade Arbitration Commission (Beijing) and the rules of this Commission shall be applied. The award of the arbitration shall be final and binding upon both parties.

Party A: Qingdao ×××Co., Ltd.　　　　　Party B: Singapore ××× Co., Ltd.
(Signature)　　　　　　　　　　　　　　(Signature)

Section 3　实 践 总 结

一、翻译技巧

（一）英文代理合同的文体特点与翻译

1. 词汇特点与翻译

1）使用古词语

古词语在法律文件中广泛使用，体现了法律契约性行文正式、严肃与古板的文体特征。

英文代理合同的一个显著特点是古词语的使用，这增加了文体的严肃性和规范性，保持了合同的威严性和正式性，同时也保持了内容的准确性，避免造成合同双方的误解。这些古词语均为副词，一般是由 here、there 或 where 与 after、by、from、in、on、to、under、of、upon、with 等介词结合而构成的复合词。例如：

hereafter	此后，今后
hereby	特此，兹
herein	此中，于此，本合同中
hereinafter	以下，此后，在下文中
herefrom	由此，从此
hereto	对此
hereunder	在下面，在下文中
hereof	关于，由此，其中
hereunder	在其下，据此，依据
whereas	鉴于

2）使用专业术语和缩略语

合同是一种庄重的文体，用词要选择意义明确、不含歧义的词语，以免引起不必要的误解和纠纷。由于专业术语和缩略语具有国际通用性，意义准确，因此代理合同中常使用许多专业术语以描述代理的各个细节。例如：

commission	佣金
contracting parties	订约人，合同当事人
sales agent	销售代理人
supplier	供货人
letter of credit (L/C)	信用证

3）使用情态动词

代理合同中权利和义务的约定部分构成了合同的主体，对当事人双方都具有约束力。代理合同中经常使用 shall、must、may (not) 等情态动词，虽然这些词很常见，但是在合同中却具有特殊的含义，翻译时要谨慎。

（1）shall：在合同中该词出现的频率最高，是一个极为严谨的法律文件专用词。shall 不仅表示单纯的"将"的意思，还常常表示法律上可以强制执行的义务，或者当事人应该承担的义务，有"应该""必须"之意，翻译时要根据合同条款的具体内容采用灵活的译法，有时可以不译。

（2）must：用于强制性义务，表示必须做什么。

（3）may：在合同中对权利、权限或特权作选择性约定时使用。

（4）may not (shall not)：用于禁止性义务，表示不得做什么。

4）使用并列同义词

代理合同中同义词（近义词）并列现象十分普遍，这体现了商务合同用词的严谨性、准确性与完整性的特点。并列词语各成分之间通常意义交叉，可以在内容上互相补充，从而使词义更具有唯一性，而不产生语义歧义。例如：

any and all	全部
customs and usages	惯例
null and void	无效
made and entered into	签订
benefit and interest	利益
duty and obligation	责任
costs and expenses	各种费用
free and clear of	无，没有
terms and conditions	条款
by and between	由（甲方和乙方）
fulfill and perform	履行

5）使用多个介词或介词短语

代理合同中常用较为复杂的介词或介词短语来代替常见的简单介词和连词，以突出合同的正式与严谨。例如：

prior to	在……之前
in accordance with	根据，按照
with regard to	就……，关于……

6）使用外来词

外来词常见的有拉丁语和法语。例如：

agent ad litem	（拉丁语）诉讼代理人
force majeure	（法语）不可抗力
as per	（拉丁语）按照

2. 句法特点与翻译

1）多用长句

代理合同中长句很多，句法结构复杂，往往是从句套从句，环环相扣；句型变化多端，以复合句居多。在翻译英语长句时，如果完全按照原句的顺序硬译，译出的句子就会生硬啰唆，甚至不知所云。应该按照由先到后、由具体到一般、由因到果、由现象到本质、由条件到事实、由事实到结论的顺序翻译，先找出原文的主干，分析整个句子的逻辑关系，再分析从句和短句的功能，看句子中是否有固定搭配、插入语等其他成分，透彻理解原文的意思，然后再按照汉语句子的结构顺序将原文的意思重新组织起来。在翻译实践中常见的长句译法一般包括以下4种。

（1）顺译法：指按照原文的顺序进行翻译。如果英语句子的内容安排与汉语的表达习惯基本一致，翻译时就不需要做大的调整。

（2）逆译法：指颠倒原句的顺序，按照与原句相反的顺序翻译。英语句子表达的方式一般是开门见山，先交代主要内容。而汉语句子多是把重要的内容放在句子的最后。因此，有些英语长句在翻译的过程中要颠倒原句的顺序，先译后半部分，再译前半部分。

（3）拆译法：指将原文按照意群拆分成多个独立的句子，即把长句的从句或短语拆分成独立的句子分开来叙述。有时为了使语意连贯，还需要适当增加词语。

（4）综合法：指翻译一个英语长句时，并不只是单纯地使用一种翻译方法，而是综合使用各种方法。尤其在某些情况下，一些英语长句单纯采用上述任何一种方法都不方便，这就需要译者仔细分析，或按照时间的先后顺序，或按照逻辑顺序，顺逆结合、主次分明地对全句进行综合处理，以便把英语原文翻译成通顺忠实的汉语句子。例如：

① 原文：WHEREAS the principal and the general agent have agreed that the general agent shall be appointed as the principal's sole exclusive agent to negotiate, on behalf of the principal, with the seller the price and other terms and conditions for, and all other matters connected with, the acquisition of the technology by the principal, subject to the terms and upon the conditions hereinafter set forth.

译文：鉴于委托人和总代理人双方同意，由委托人指定的总代理人系独家全权代表，委托人授权其代表可根据本协议所列的条款和条件，与卖方洽谈引进技术的价格及其他有关事项。双方兹同意下列条款。（顺译法）

② 原文：Either party shall not be held responsible for failure or delay to perform all or any part of this agreement due to flood, fire, earthquake, draught, war or any other events which could not be predicted, controlled, avoided or overcome by the relative party.

译文：由于水灾、火灾、地震、干旱、战争或协议一方无法预见、控制、避免和克服的其他事件导致不能或暂时不能全部或部分履行本协议，该方不负责任。（逆译法）

2）多用条件句

代理合同通常是约定当事人的权利、义务和责任，具有一定的法律效力，因此，合同条款中必须考虑到各种可能发生的情况，附有各种条件。只有符合这些条件，双方才能履行各自的权利和义务。条件句多由一些连词引导，如 if、should、in case (of)、in the event of/that、provided (that)、except、with the exception of、in the absence of、unless、whereas、in consideration of、subject to 等。

3）多用被动语态

代理合同强调客观事实，因此，合同中的一些条款多以被动语态的形式出现，旨在突出动作的承受者，尽量减少个人情感的影响。

（二）中文代理合同的文体特点与翻译

中文代理合同在词汇与句法结构的严谨性与准确性上与英文代理合理有些相似之处，但还是有一定的差异。

1. 词汇特点与翻译

1）常用文言词汇

中文代理合同中的语言正式、客观、逻辑性强，除了使用专业术语外，还常用文言词汇以体现合同的正式与规范，在合同中常用"兹""特""本""以""之""即"等词汇。例如：

原文：兹证明：双方授权各自代表，于上述规定的日期签订本合同。本协议一式两份。

译文：IN WITNESS WHEREOF, the parties hereto have caused this contract to be executed in duplicate by their duly authorized officers or representatives at the date written above.

2）用词严密

中文代理合同通常用词严密、具体而准确，以防在履约过程中发生争议，从而避免不必要的麻烦。

2. 句法特点与翻译

1）常用主动语态

中文代理合同常用主动语态，即使有时表达被动含义，也使用形式上的主动句，这是汉语的表达习惯，相对应的英文通常采用被动语态。

2）常用"的"字结构

"的"字结构在中文代理合同中也频繁出现，即省略真正的名词。这实际上也是一种客观、公正的表现，在翻译时要体现出合同的严肃性。例如：

原文：有下列情形之一<u>的</u>……

译文：<u>Where</u> one of the following happens...

（三）中英文代理合同的翻译原则

1. 用词严谨准确，合乎规范

由于涉外合同具有专业性和兼容性，所以要求译者在翻译合同时，把"严谨"放在首位。尤其是合同中的法律术语和关键词语的翻译，例如，accept 在一般情况下译为"接受""认可"就可以了，但在涉外合同中，这个词可能要译成"承兑"，相应地，acceptor 和 acceptee 就要分别译成"承兑人"和"接受承兑人"。由此可见，正确翻译合同中的术语是合同翻译最基础的工作。

2. 行文规范通顺，条理清楚

代理合同是契约性文件，属于庄严性文体；合同条款较多，句子结构比较复杂，均以完整句子为主，陈述句居多。另外，中文代理合同中主动语态较多，英文中被动语态较多。翻译时要按照合同文体的特点，弄清各层次的脉络，根据逻辑关系组织成文。同时，词语运用也要规范，符合约定俗成的含义。

通顺是对任何一种译文的基本要求，通顺的合同译文应着重体现在"条理清楚"这一方面。涉外合同的条款往往比较繁复，翻译时应首先弄清全文的条理，对各条款的制约关系仔细琢磨，吃透其实质含义，尽量使译文明确清楚、通顺易懂。

二、常用术语和表达

sales agent	销售代理人
arbitration	仲裁
as from	自……日起
as per/in accordance with	按照，根据
be obliged to	有义务
be entitled to	有权，有……的资格
binding force	约束力
both parties to the contract	合同双方
breach the contract	违约
breaching party	违约方
cause annulment to	使作废

come into effect/force	生效
commence	开始
commission	佣金
comply with	遵照
confirmed	保兑的
constraint	约束，强制
contracting parties	订约人，合同当事人
dispute adjudication board	争端裁决委员会
dispute	纠纷，争端
disrupt	中断
divergence	分歧，歧异
enforceable	可强制执行的
entitlement	权利
equality, mutual benefit, and friendly consultation	平等互利，友好协商
exclusive agency	独家代理
expiry	期满
force and effect	效力
force majeure	不可抗力
general terms	总条款
give approval of	许可，批准
grant consent to	赞同，同意
hereinafter to be referred as	以下简称为……
hereinafter	下文
in favor of...	以……为受益人
in duplicate	一式两份
inconsistent with	与……不符
infringement	侵权
invoice	发票
irrevocable	不可撤销的
letter of credit (L/C)	信用证
market report	市况报告
minimal turnover	最低业务量
net invoiced selling price	净发票售价
obligation/liability	责任，义务
observant party/non-breaching party	守约方
pertaining to/in respect to	关于……
prevailing market conditions	现行的市场状况
rectify	纠正，改正
said	上述的
settlement of disputes	争议的解决

sign the contract/agreement	签订合同
supplement	增加,补充
supplier	供货人
terminate the contract	终止合同
terms and conditions	条款
territory	经销地区
turnover	业务量
unduly	不适当地,不合理地
unforeseeable	不可预见的
unfulfilled obligations	未能履行的义务
validity	有效性
variation/alteration/modification	改变,变更
whereas	鉴于
whilst	当……的时候
witness	见证方

Section 4 巩固练习

一、翻译以下英文代理合同。

EXCLUSIVE AGENCY AGREEMENT

This Agreement is made and entered into this_____day of_____, by and between ABC Co., Ltd., a corporation duly organized and existing under the laws of the People's Republic of China, with its principal place of business at ___ (hereinafter called Seller) and XYZ Co., Ltd., a corporation duly organized and existing under the laws of _____, with its principal place of business at ___ (hereinafter called Agent). Whereby it is mutually agreed as follows:

Article 1   Appointment

During the effective period of this Agreement, Seller hereby appoints Agent as its exclusive agent to solicit orders for products stipulated in Article 4 from customers in the territory stipulated in Article 3 and Agent accepts and assumes such appointment.

Article 2   Agent's duty

Agent shall strictly conform with any and all instructions given by Seller from time to time and shall not make any representation, warranty, promise, contract, agreement or do any other act binding Seller. Seller shall not be held responsible for any acts or failures to act by Agent in excess of or contrary to such instructions.

Article 3 Territory

The territory covered under this Agreement shall be expressly confined to____(hereinafter called Territory).

Article 4 Products

The products covered under this Agreement shall be expressly confined to____(hereinafter called Products).

Article 5 Exclusive right

In consideration of the exclusive right herein granted, Seller shall not, directly or indirectly, sell or export Products to Territory through channels other than Agent and Agent shall not sell, distribute or promote the sale of any products competitive with or similar to Products in Territory and shall not solicit or accept orders for the purpose of selling Products outside Territory. Seller shall refer to Agent any inquiries or orders for Products Seller may receive from other customers in Territory during the effective period of this Agreement.

Article 6 Minimum transaction and price

In the event that during one year (12 months) during the effective period of this Agreement, aggregate payment received by Seller from customers on orders obtained by Agent under this Agreement amounts to less than_____, Seller shall have the right to terminate this Agreement by giving thirty (30) days written notice to Agent.

Seller shall from time to time furnish Agent with a statement of the minimum prices and the terms and conditions of sales at which the goods are respectively to be sold.

Article 7 Orders

In soliciting orders, Agent shall adequately advise customers of the general terms and conditions of Seller's sales note or contract note and of any contract being subject to the confirmation of acceptance by Seller. Agent shall immediately dispatch any order received to Seller for its acceptance or rejection.

Seller shall have the right to refuse or accept any such orders or any part thereof and Agent shall not be entitled to any commission in respect of any such rejected order or part thereof refused.

Article 8 Expenses

All expenses and disbursements such as cabling, traveling and other expenses incurred in connection with the sale of Products shall be for the account of Agent, unless especially arranged. Further, Agent shall, at its own expenses, maintain office(s), salesmen and others sufficient for the performance of the obligation of Agent in conformity with any and all instructions given by Seller.

Article 9 Commission

Seller shall pay to Agent commission in____currency at the rate of ____% on the net invoiced selling price on all orders directly obtained by Agent and accepted by Seller. Such commission shall be payable every six months only after Seller receives the full amount of all payments due to Seller. Payments of such commission shall be made to Agent by way of remittance.

Article 10 Information and report

Both Seller and Agent shall quarterly and/or on the request of either party furnish information and market report each other to promote the sale of Products as much as possible.

Article 11　Sales promotion

Agent shall diligently and adequately advertise and promote the sale of Products throughout Territory. Seller shall furnish with or without charge to Agent reasonable quantity of advertising literatures, catalogues, leaflets, and the like as Agent may reasonably require.

Article 12　Industrial property rights

Agent may use the trade-mark(s) of Seller during the effective period of this Agreement only in connection with the sale of Products, provided that even after the termination of this Agreement, Agent may use the trade-mark(s) in connection with the sale of Products held by it in stock. Agent shall also acknowledge that any and all patents, trade-marks, copyrights and other industrial property rights used or embodied in Products shall remain to be sole properties of Seller and shall not dispute them in any way. If any infringement being found, Agent shall promptly notify Seller and assist Seller to take steps to protect its right.

Article 13　Duration

This Agreement shall enter into force on the signing of both parties. At least three (3) months before the expiration, both Seller and Agent shall consult each other for renewal of this Agreement. If the renewal of this Agreement is agreed upon by both parties, this Agreement shall be renewed for another _____ year(s) under the terms and conditions herein set forth, with amendments, if agreed upon by both parties. Otherwise, this Agreement shall expire on_____.

Article 14　Termination

In case there is any nonperformance and/or violation of the terms and conditions including Article 5, 6, 11 under this Agreement by either party during the effective period of this agreement, the parties hereto shall do their best to settle the matter in question as prompt and amicable as possible to mutual satisfaction. Should settlement not be reached within thirty (30) days after notification in writing of the other party, the other party shall have the right to cancel this Agreement and the loss and damages sustained thereby shall be indemnified by the party responsible for the nonperformance and/or violation. Further, in case of bankruptcy or insolvency or liquidation or death and/or reorganization by the third party of the other party, either party may forth with terminate this Agreement without any notice to the other party.

Article 15　Force majeure

Either party shall not be held responsible for failure or delay to perform all or any part of this Agreement due to acts of God, government orders or restrictions or any other events which could not be predicted at the time of the conclusion of the Agreement and could not be controlled, avoided or overcome by the parties. However, the party affected by the event of force majeure shall inform the other party of its occurrence in writing and a certificate of the event as soon as possible.

Article 16　Trade terms and governing law

The trade terms under this Agreement shall be governed and interpreted under the provisions of INCOTERMS 1990 and this Agreement shall be governed as to all matters including validity, construction, and performance under the laws of the People's Republic of China.

Article 17　Arbitration

All disputes arising from the performance of the Agreement should be settled through friendly negotiations.

Should no settlement be reached through negotiation, the case shall then be submitted for arbitration to the China International Economic and Trade Arbitration Commission (Beijing) and the rules of this Commission shall be applied. The award of the arbitration shall be final and binding upon both parties. The arbitration fee shall be borne by the losing party unless otherwise awarded by the arbitration organization.

WITNESS THEREOF: This Agreement shall come into effect immediately after it is signed by both parties in two original copies; each party holds one copy.

ABC Corp.　　　　　　　　XYZ Corp.
BY　　　　　　　　　　　　BY

二、翻译以下中文代理合同。

独家销售代理协议

制造商：
代理商：

本着平等自愿、协商一致的原则，签订此协议。双方均应严格遵守。

第一条　独家销售代理

制造商同意将其生产的下列产品在中国的独家销售代理权授予代理商：

产品名：＿＿＿＿＿＿＿

第二条　代理商的职责

代理商利用自身的销售网络在中华人民共和国积极拓展用户。代理商向制造商转送接收到的询价和订单。代理商无权代表制造商签订任何具有约束力的合约。代理商应把制造商规定的技术参数和商业条款对用户解释。采取措施配合制造商获得订单。

相关代理商只能介绍自己是这些产品的"销售服务代理商"，不得以制造商授权自居去从事给制造商带来不良印象的活动。所有报价和订单须包括这样一个条款："需经 M/s Veejay Lakshmi Engineering Works Limited 批准"。制造商有权保留收到的订单和商品的销售发票。

未经制造商书面授权，代理商不得做出对产品的承诺、担保或保证、陈述。

除非制造商提供或批准，代理商不得使用任何与此产品相关的广告、促销和销售材料。

代理商须获得规定的商品和服务的代理许可权，还应该告知制造商进口税率、优惠条件及适用于中国的加工方法的法律法规、商品标记等，一旦意识到制造商的产品触犯了中国的法律法规，代理商应及时告知制造商。

第三条　培训

为使代理商能了解所推销产品的技术性能，制造商同意派人来中国对代理商的销售团队进行系统培训。培训人数及地点由双方协商确定。

为了在保修期内向顾客提供售后服务（如安装、试车和服务热线），制造商委托代理商进行必要的售后服务，制造商为代理商培训两名技师（机械和电器技师各一名）。如果两名技师需要在印度培训，制造商应当承担他们在印度的食宿费和当地的交通费用。代理商承担他们往返机票费用。同样，如果制造商派工程师来中国培训，往返机票费用应自理，代理商负责制造商工程师在中国的食宿及交通费用。保修期内的售后服务费用由制造商负担，假如超出保修期范围，代理商向客户收取售后服务费，此费用应当另行商定。

第四条　广告和展览会

双方应就各种促销活动的费用展开讨论，诸如在报纸上刊登广告、路演、研讨会、参展等活动。费用由双方共同承担。分担模式由双方共同讨论后确定。制造商须出资提供印刷有当地语言的产品目录。代理商负责提供翻译和印刷的帮助。

第五条　代理商的财务责任

代理商有义务按时收回信用证支付条件下的货款和订单条款下的兑现。在赊账付款条件下，代理商应采取适当方式了解当地订货人的信誉和支付能力。假如出现对货款回收的诉讼，代理商应全力提供帮助。通常的索款及协助收回应付货款的开支应由制造商负担。

未经同意，代理商无权利也无义务以制造商的名义接受付款。

第六条　用户意见

代理商有权留心并接受用户对产品的意见和申诉，及时通知制造商并关注制造商的切身利益。

第七条　提供信息

代理商应尽力向制造商提供当前商品的市场行情和市场竞争等方面的信息，每季度需向制造商寄送工作报告。为了促进销售，代理商需定期走访代理区域的所有客户及潜在的客户，还要保留一份客户及潜在客户的更新清单。假如制造商要求，还应提供一份给制造商。代理商还应把潜在客户对产品的询价及报价告知给制造商。

第八条　公平竞争

代理商应遵从以下要求：

不能与制造商或帮助他人与制造商竞争；

不能制造代理产品或类似于代理的产品；

不能从与制造商竞争的任何企业中获利；

不能代理或销售与代理产品相同或类似的任何产品。

此合约一经生效，代理商应将与其他企业签订的有约束性的协议告知制造商。不论是作为代理的或经销的，此后再签订的任何协议均应告之制造商，代理商在进行其他活动时，决不能忽视此条约中对制造商承担的义务。

第九条　保密

代理商不得泄露制造商的商业机密，也不得将该机密超越协议范围使用。

所有产品设计和说明均属制造商所有，代理商应在协议终止时归还给制造商。

第十条　分包代理

代理商事先经制造商同意后可聘用分包代理商，代理商应对该分包代理商的活动负全部责任。

第十一条　工业产权的保护

如发现第三方侵犯制造商的工业产权或有损于制造商利益的任何非法行为，代理商应据实向制造商报告。在和制造商磋商后，代理商应尽最大努力并按制造商的指示，帮助制造商使其不受这类行为的侵害，制造商将承担正常代理活动以外的费用。一切依照制造商先前书面承诺的相关费用分担。

第十二条　独家销售权的范围

这是一份该地区独家代理协议。在协议执行期间，制造商不得同意其他任何人、团体或公司作为该地区促销、销售或服务的代理商。然而，制造商可以利用代理商书面批准的第三方为其提供服务。在制造商和代理商讨论并同意的情况下，制造商可以有权使用那些长期合作过的第三方提供的服务。当第三方参与进来时，关于佣金的分配，由三方共同商量决定。

第十三条　技术帮助

制造商应帮助代理商培训雇员，使其获得代理产品的技术知识。

第十四条　佣金数额

制造商支付给代理商货物 FOB 价格的 5%作为佣金。超出正常销售价格，另行商谈确定。只有在货物开出发票且制造商得到全部货款时，代理商才能得到佣金。若是由于产品质量问题用户没有付清全部货款，代理商可以根据制造商实收货款提取佣金。

第十五条　平分佣金

不同地区的两个代理商为争取一份订单都作出极大努力，当订单来自于某一代理商所在地，而供货的制造厂位于另一代理商所在地时，则佣金由两个代理商平均分配。

第十六条　商业失败、合约终止

如制造商不接受订单，则代理商无佣金。代理商所介绍的订单合约已中止，代理商无权索取佣金，若该合约的中止是由于制造商的责任，则不在此限。

第十七条　佣金计算方法

佣金以净实现价值计算，净实现价值是开发票货物的 FOB 价格减去第三方费用（如果有）。

第十八条　支付佣金的时间

制造商在收到货款后，应在 30 天内支付佣金。对于信用证或延期付款方式进行的销售，如果有信用证或银行担保保证买方信用，在交货后三十天内支付佣金。如果佣金支付货币转移到国外需要印度政府的许可，佣金会在收到许可后支付。

支付佣金时，制造商还应提供一份保值单据，上面列有支付佣金方式的详细资料和关于总发票金额、FOB 离岸价和佣金总数的详单。除此之外，制造商还应每一季度寄送给代理商报表，上面涉及该区域的销售详情，以及每个季度信用证和货款详单。这个报表在每一季度的最后一月寄出。

第十九条　支付佣金的货币

佣金按照开给顾客发票的货币种类来计算和支付。

第二十条　协议期限

本协议在双方签字后生效，有效期三年。如果一方想续约，应该提前 3 个月通知并得到对方的同意。如果双方都无意续约，协议将在终止日终止。

第二十一条　提前终止

只有在一方违背了协议规定的职责和义务，或者一方侵犯了另一方的利益时，协议才可以提前终止。如果没有达到预定的销售量，或者双方一致认定没有必要在中国继续开拓市场时，协议也可先于最终期限提前中止。

第二十二条　存货的退回

协议期满时，代理商若储有代理产品和备件，应按制造商指示退回，费用由制造商负担。

第二十三条　未完之商务

代理商可以获得全额5%的佣金的情况：协议到期之前得到并执行的所有订单；在协议到期之前得到的可以在60天内预期付款或是以信用证支付的订单。这只适用于那些信用证支付或是预期付款的订单，由制造商以书面形式承认。

第二十四条　赔偿

除协议因一方违约而终止外，由于协议在终止日终止，则双方都不得向另一方提出赔偿。

第二十五条　变更

本协议的变更或附加条款，应以书面形式为准。

第二十六条　禁止转让

本协议未经事先协商不得转让。

第二十七条　留置权

代理商对制造商的财产无留置权。

第二十八条　法律适用

本协议的签订和履行均适用于中国之现行法律。

第二十九条　仲裁

双方在履行本协议发生争议，须经友好协商解决。如果协商不一致，提交有关仲裁委员会按法令规定的程序进行仲裁，仲裁裁决为终局裁决。仲裁费用由败诉方承担。

制造商：　　　　　　　　　　代理商：

授权代表：　　　　　　　　　授权代表：

日期：　　　　　　　　　　　日期：

Chapter 7

国际贸易合同

Section 1 概 述

一、国际贸易合同的定义

《中华人民共和国民法通则》第 85 条规定：合同是当事人之间设立、变更、终止民事关系的协议。《中华人民共和国合同法》第 2 条规定：合同是平等主体的自然人、法人、其他组织之间设立、变更、终止民事权利义务关系的协议。在经济和贸易领域，国际贸易合同是指处于不同国家或地区的当事人就商品买卖所发生的权利和义务关系而达成的书面协议。该类合同受国家法律保护和管辖，是对签约各方都具有同等约束力的法律性文件，也是解决贸易纠纷，进行调解、仲裁与诉讼的法律依据。

二、国际贸易合同的形式

在国际贸易中，合同可以分为口头合同和书面合同两种形式。一般来说，书面形式包括合同（contract）、确认书（confirmation）、协议（agreement）和备忘录（memorandum）。

三、国际贸易合同有效成立的基本条件

（一）发盘与接受

当事人之间达成的国际贸易合同是通过发盘和接受而形成的。一方向另一方提出要约，另一方对该项要约表示承诺，双方的意思表示达成一致，合同即告成立。如果一方有要约，另一方没有承诺，合同则不成立。即使双方相互要约（cross offer），意思表示正好一致，合同仍不成立。要约和承诺在国际贸易实务中分别被称作发盘和接受。在有关国际贸易的法律中，对发盘和接受这两个行为的定义非常严格。判断国际贸易合同是否成立，不仅要看有无发盘和接受，还要看发盘和接受这两个行为是否成立。

（二）实施法律行为的资格和能力

双方当事人应具有实施法律行为的资格和能力。《中华人民共和国对外贸易法》规定，我

国的涉外经济合同当事人必须是企业或者其他经济组织。国际贸易合同一般是在法人之间签订的。法人是由自然人组织起来的，必须通过自然人才能进行活动。因此，代表法人本身的自然人必须具备订立合同的能力。

（三）意思表示一致

当事人应在自愿的基础上达成意思表示一致。合同是双方当事人意思表示一致的结果。根据各国的法律规定，如果由于各种原因或事实，构成当事人表示的意思不是自愿和真实的，合同则不成立。这些原因和事实大致有以下3种。

（1）胁迫（duress）：各国法律都认为，凡在胁迫下订立的合同，受胁迫的一方可以主张合同无效。

（2）欺诈（fraud）：欺诈是指以使他人发生错误为目的的故意行为。各国法律都认为，凡因受欺诈而订立的合同，受到欺诈的一方可以撤销合同。

（3）错误（mistake）：错误是指当事人意思表示错误。错误导致意思表示不真实，从而影响合同有效性。各国法律都认为，任何错误的意思表达都有可能使合同无效。

（四）标准和内容合法

合同的标准和内容必须合法。各国法律均规定，合同不得违反法律，不得违反公共政策和公共秩序。《中华人民共和国合同法》规定：订立合同，必须遵守法律，并不得损害社会公共利益。这包括公众安全、优良习惯和道德规范。在国际贸易中，对违禁品，如毒品、走私物品、严重败坏社会道德风尚的物品等签订贸易合同是不合法的；与敌国或国家明令禁止的贸易对象国签订贸易合同也是不合法的。

（五）符合法律规定的形式

合同必须符合法律规定的形式。大陆法中把合同形式分为要式合同（formal contract）和不要式合同（informal contract）。所谓要式合同是指依照法律规定的形式和程序成立的合同；不要式合同是指可以用口头，或者书面，或者包括人证在内的其他证明形式的合同。《联合国国际货物销售合同公约》（以下简称《公约》）第11条明确规定：销售合同无须以书面订立或书面证明，在形式方面也不受任何其他条件的限制。《公约》的这一规定既兼顾西方国家的习惯做法，又适应了国际贸易发展的特点。因为许多国家的贸易合同是以现代通信的方式订立的，不一定存在书面合同。但《公约》允许缔约国对该条的规定提出声明并予以保留。我国对此做了保留。买卖双方在以函电成交时，任何一方当事人如果要以签订书面合同作为合同成立的依据，都必须在发出要约或在承诺通知中提出这一保留条件。这时，合同的成立不是以双方函电达成协议时成立，而是于签订书面合同时成立。如果任何一方都没有提出以签订书面合同作为合同成立的依据，按合同法的一般原则，合同应于双方的函电达成协议时成立，即当载有承诺内容的信件、电报或电传生效时，合同即告成立。

（六）对价和约因

对价（consideration）是英美法中有关合同成立所必须具备的一个要素。按照英美法解释，合同当事人之间存在着"我给你是为了你给我"的关系。这种通过相互给付，从对方那里获得利益的关系称作对价。例如，在货物买卖合同中，买方付款是为了获得卖方的货物，而卖方交货是为了获得买方的货款。约因（cause）是大陆法中提出的合同成立要素之一，是指当事人签订合同所追求的直接目的。例如，在货物买卖合同中，买卖双方签订合同都要有约因。买方的约因是获得货物，卖方的约因是获得货款。在国际贸易合同中，要有对价或约因，法律才承认合同的有效性；否则，合同得不到法律的保障。

四、国际贸易合同的分类

1. 销售或购货合同（sales or purchase contract）

销售合同俗称买卖合同。由生产国直接出口，消费国直接进口，单进单出、逐笔成交的贸易方式称为逐笔售定。在进行这种贸易时，原则上应订立书面合同，明确规定各项条款。

2. 技术转让合同（contract for technology transfer）

以引进专利或转让专利申请权、专有技术和秘密、商标和许可证等为对象的贸易，其使用的合同包括技术转让合同、技术咨询服务合同和许可证贸易合同。这类合同内容烦琐，专业性强，涉及面广，有效期限较长。

3. 合资或合营合同（contract for joint venture or joint production）

投资当事人按一定的法律和法规建立合资经营企业或合作经营企业，共同投资、共同经营、共同管理、合作开采、共负盈亏、共担风险。这类贸易方式的合同内容复杂，涉及诸方面的法律，如土地、资源、工业、设施、税收、外汇、技术引进、专利转让、许可证、劳动等的法令和政策。

4. 国际工程承包合同（contract for international engineering projects）

一般来说，按事先规定的章程和交易条件采用公开竞争的方式——招标进行交易，称为公开竞争贸易方式（open competitive trade form）。这种贸易方式所使用的合同有招标合同和商品交易所成交合同。中标后，签订国际工程承包合同。这类合同具有国际性，其内容十分复杂，技术性强，风险大，承包商和业主（发包人）要遵循不同国家的法律、法规和政策，在操作过程中务必十分谨慎。

五、国际贸易合同的基本结构

一般来说，合同包含标题、前文和正文三大部分（当事人根据实际情况可作适当调整），具体说明如下。

1. 标题（title）

标题一般标明合同的性质和合同号（contract number）。合同号一般在标题的后面或者右下方，在相应的位置上写上"No._____"，如No.35-777、No.AG318等。

2. 前文（preamble）

前文一般包括订约日期和地点（signing date/place）、合同当事人及其国籍、主要营业场所或住所（signing parties and their nationalities, principal place of business or residence address）、当事人合法的权威依据（each party's authority）、说明条款（WHEREAS clause）。

3. 正文（body）

正文一般包括定义条款、基本条款、一般条款和结尾条款。

（1）定义条款（definition clause）：对合同中重复出现的关键名词术语进行明确定义，给出明确解释。

（2）基本条款（basic clause）：包括当事人的名称/姓名和住所（name and address）；标的（object）——合同的客体，即当事人权利和义务共同指向的对象；数量与质量（quantity and quality）；价款和支付（price and payment）；履行的期限（duration）；履行的地点和方式。

（3）一般条款（general terms and conditions）：包括合同有效期（duration）；合同的终止（termination）；不可抗力（force majeure）；合同的让与（assignment）；仲裁（arbitration）；适用的法律（governing law）；诉讼管辖（jurisdiction）；通知手续（notice）；合同修改（amendment）；其他（others）。

（4）结尾条款（WITNESS clause）：包括合同的份数（copies of the contract）；使用的文字和效力（language used and effectiveness）；签名（signature）；盖章（seal）等。

六、国际贸易合同的主要内容

国际贸易合同的内容一般由当事人约定，主要包含以下内容：

(1) Titles or names of the parties and the domiciles thereof;
(2) Date and place of signature of the contract;
(3) Type of the contract and the kind and scope of the subject matter of the contract;
(4) Technical conditions, quality, standard, specifications and quantities of the subject matter of the contract;
(5) Time limit, place and method of performance;
(6) Terms of price, amount, way of payment and various additional charges;
(7) Whether the contract could be assigned or conditions for assignment;
(8) Compensation and other liabilities for breach of the contract;
(9) Ways of settlement of disputes in case of disputes arising from the contract;
(10) Languages to be used in the contract and their effectiveness.

七、国际贸易合同样本

SALES CONTRACT

CONTRACT NO.　ABC171102
DATE　NOV. 2, 2017

BUYER
Arrabon Trading, Unit 9, Central Office Park, 257 Jean Ave, Centurion
TEL: +357 27 664 0587
FAX: +357 27 664 0586

SELLER
ABC Garments & Accessories Co., Ltd, Hongxing Road, Hangzhou, Zhejiang, China

TEL: +853 24 632 0823

FAX: +853 24 632 0822

The Buyer agrees to buy and the Seller agrees to sell the following goods on terms and conditions as set forth below:

(1) Name	(2) Quality	(3) Unit Price	(4) Total Amount
boy's denim long pant	1,000PCS	USD9.50	USD9,500.00
boy's twill long pant	1,000PCs	USD10.00	USD10,000.00
TOTAL: USD19,500.00			

(5) Packing

One poly bag per pc, 10 pcs a carton-box, solid color per carton-box, 5 moisture-proofing agent per carton-box, an inner-cover-cardboard per carton-box

(6) Mark

MAIN MARK: SIDE MARK:

ARRABON   ARR

(7) Time of Shipment

50 DAYS AFTER THE SELLER RECEIVES THE L/C

(8) Port of Loading

SHANGHAI

(9) Port of Destination

LIMASSOL, CYPRUS

(10) Insurance

ALL RISK AND WAR RISK COVERED BY THE BUYER

(11) Terms of Payment

IRREVOCABLE L/C AT SIGHT

The covering letter of credit must reach the Seller 45 days prior to the shipment date and is to remain valid in above indicated port of loading 15 days after the date of shipment, failing which the Seller reserves the right to cancel this sales contract and to claim from the Buyer compensation for losses resulting therefrom.

OTHER TERMS

(1) Quality/quantity discrepancy: In case of quality discrepancy, claim should be filed by the Buyer within 30 days after the arrival of the goods at port of destination, while for quantity discrepancy, claim should be filed by the Buyer within 15 days after the arrival of the goods at port of destination. In all cases, claims must be accompanied by survey reports of recognized public surveyors agreed to by the Seller. Should the responsibility of the subject under claim be found to rest on part of the Seller, the Seller shall, within 20 days after receipt of the claim, send his reply to the Buyer together with suggestion for settlement. The Seller reserves the option of shipping the indicated percentage more or less than the quantity hereby contracted, and the covering letter of credit shall be negotiated for the amount covering the value of quantity actually shipped. (The Buyer is requested to establish the L/C in accordance with the indicated percentage over the total value of order as per this sales contract.) The contents of the covering letter of credit shall be in strict accordance with stipulations of the sales contract; in case of any variation thereof necessitating amendment of the L/C, the Buyer shall bear the expenses for effecting the amendment. The Seller shall not be held responsible for possible delay of shipment resulting from awaiting the amendment of the L/C, and reserves the right to claim from the Buyer compensation for the losses resulting therefrom. Except in case where the insurance is covered by the Buyer as arranged, insurance is to be covered by the Seller with a Chinese insurance company. If insurance for additional amount and/or for other insurance terms is required by the Buyer, prior notice to this effect mush reach the Seller before shipment and is subject to the Seller's agreement, and the extra insurance premium shall be for the Buyer's account.

The Buyer is requested to send to the Seller authentic copy of the license-application (endorsed by the relative bank) filed by the Buyer and to advise the Seller by fax immediately when the said license is obtained. Should the Buyer intend to file reapplication for license in cases of rejection of the original application, the Buyer shall contact the Seller and obtain the latter's consent before filing reapplication.

(2) Inspection: The certificate of origin and/or the inspection certification of quality/quantity/weight issued by the relative institute shall be taken as the basis for the shipping. The Seller shall not be held responsible if they owing to force majeure cause or causes fail to make delivery within the time stipulated in this sales contract or cannot deliver the goods. However, the Seller shall inform immediately the Buyer by fax. The Seller shall deliver to the Buyer by registered letter, if it is requested by the Buyer, a certificate issued by China Council for the Promotion of International Trade or by any competent authority, certifying to the existence of the said cause or causes. The Buyer's failure to obtain the relative import license is not to be treated as force majeure.

(3) Arbitration: All disputes arising in connection with the sales contract of the execution thereof shall be settled amicably by negotiation. In case no settlement can be reached, the case under dispute shall then be submitted for arbitration to the Foreign Trade Arbitration Commission of China Council for the Promotion of International Trade in accordance with the provisional rules of procedure of the Foreign Trade Arbitration Commission of China Council for the Promotion of International Trade. The decision of the Commission shall be accepted as final and binding upon both parties.

THE BUYER　　　　　　　　　　　　　　THE SELLER

Section 2 译 例 分 析

>> *Passage One*

PURCHASE CONTRACT

This contract is made on the ___ day of _____, by and between[1] _____ Company (hereinafter[2] referred to as the Seller) and _____ Company (hereinafter referred to as the Buyer). Through friendly negotiation, both parties have hereby agreed on the terms and conditions stipulated hereunder:

1. **Contract Products:** _____
2. **Specification:** _____
3. **Quantity:** _____
4. **Unit Price:** _____
5. **Total Value:** _____ FOB[3]
6. **Country of Origin:** _____
7. **Shipping Marks:** _____
8. **Shipment:** _____

To be shipped on or before _____ subject to acceptable Letter of Credit (L/C) reached the Seller before the end of _____, and partial shipments allowed, transshipment allowed.

9. **Grace Period:**

Should[4] last shipment have to be extended for fulfilment of this contract, the Buyer shall give the Seller a grace period of 30 days upon submitting evidence by the Seller.

10. **Insurance:**

To be effected by the Buyer.

11. **Packing:**

In new kraft paper bags of _____ kg/bag or in wooden cases of _____ kg/case, free of charge.

12. **Payment:**

The Buyer shall open a 100% confirmed, irrevocable, divisible and negotiable and partial shipment permitted Letter of Credit in favor of the Seller within 5 calendar days from the date of the agreement through the Issuing Bank. The L/C[5] shall be drawn against draft at sight upon first presentation of the following documents:

(1) Full set of the Seller's Commercial Invoices;

(2) Full set of clean, blank, endorsed Bill of Lading[6];

(3) Inspection Certificates of quality and weight.

13. **Notice of Readiness:**

The Buyer shall advise the Seller by telex the scheduled time of arrival of cargo vessel at least seven days prior to the arrival of the vessel at the loading port.

14. Performance Guarantee:

(1) Upon receipt of the Buyer's irrevocable L/C by the Advising Bank, the Seller shall perform a Performance Guarantee representing _____ % of the L/C value.

(2) The Performance Guarantee shall be returned in full to the Seller after completion of shipment and delivery of the contracted goods. In case of non-delivery (all or part) of the goods for reasons other than those specified in Clause 12, the Performance Guarantee shall be forfeited in favor of the Buyer in proportion to the quantity in default.

(3) Should the Buyer breach the contract or fail to open the L/C in favor of the Seller within the period specified in Clause 9 (except for Clause 12), the Buyer has to pay the Seller the same value as the Performance Guarantee.

(4) The Letter of Credit must fulfill all the terms and conditions of this contract. The terms of the L/C should be clear, fair and made payable to the Seller. Upon acceptance of L/C by the Advising Bank, the Advising Bank shall send the Performance Guarantee to the Issuing Bank.

15. Force Majeure[7]:

The Seller or the Buyer shall not be responsible for non-delivery or breach of contract for any reason due to Force Majeure incidents.

In case the time of delivery or shipment has to be extended, the Seller or the Buyer shall have to provide evidence for such event.

16. Arbitration:

All disputes or divergences arising from the execution of the contract shall be settled through friendly discussion between both parties. In case no settlement can be reached, the case at issue shall then be submitted for arbitration to the China International Economic and Trade Arbitration Commission[8] in accordance with the provisions of the said Commission.

The award by the said Commission shall be deemed as final and binding upon both parties. The Arbitration fee shall be borne by the losing party. In course of arbitration, the contract shall continuously be executed by both parties except for the part under arbitration.

17. Currency Devaluation:

In the event of any official devaluation of U.S. Currency, the Seller reserves the right to readjust the contract price in proportion to the devaluation ratio.

18. Valid Period:

This contract will automatically become null and void should the Buyer fail to open a L/C in favor of the Seller within seven days after signing this contract. However, the Buyer shall still be responsible for the payment of compensation in accordance with the terms in Clause 12, items 2 and 3.

This contract is made in duplicate; both parties have read carefully and agreed to abide by all the terms and conditions stipulated. The contract is signed by both parties in the presence of witnesses.

Seller:
Buyer:
Witnesses:

Key Words

hereinafter	在下文
stipulate	规定
specification	规格
confirm	确认，保兑
kraft	牛皮纸
irrevocable	不可撤销的
divisible	可分割的
negotiable	可转让的
in favor of...	以……为受益人
endorse	背书，为……代言
guarantee	保证金
non-delivery	无法交货
forfeit	没收
in proportion to	按……比例
default	不履行，违约
breach	违反，不履行
arbitration	仲裁
dispute	纠纷，争端
divergence	分歧，歧异
in accordance with	依据，按照
provision	规定
award	裁决，授予，判给
arbitration award	仲裁裁决
statute	法令，法规
ratio	比率
valid	有效的
null	无效的
void	无效的
compensation	补偿
unit price	单价
shipping mark	收发货标志，唛头
letter of credit (L/C)	信用证
grace period	优惠期限
issuing bank	开证银行
advising bank	通知银行
bill of lading (B/L)	货运提单

be drawn against draft at sight	见票即付
commercial invoice	商业发票
inspection certificate	检验证明
performance guarantee	履约保证金
force majeure	不可抗力
losing party	败诉方

▶ Notes

1. By and between，译为"由……和……间"。英文中常用并列短语来使意思的表达更为正式和严谨。再如，第 14（4）中的 terms and conditions 表示"合同条款"，第 18 中的 null and void 表示"无效"。

2. 英文合同常常采用部分古词来增强其文体的正式程度，这样不仅能使句子结构紧凑，而且增强了语义衔接和连贯。该句使用的 hereinafter、hereby、hereunder 在法律文本中经常出现，可分别译为"在下文中""特此"和"如下的"。

3. FOB 为 Free on Board 的缩写。现代国际贸易中最常用的三种价格术语除 FOB（装运港船上交货价）外，还有 Cost and Freight（目的港成本加运费价，CFR）和 Cost, Insurance and Freight（目的港成本加保险费运费价，CIF）。这三种术语规定卖方交货地点为装运港，以越过船舷作为划分双方风险的界限。

4. Should 引导的状语从句，相当于 in case，汉译时一般翻译成"若……（发生）"。

5. L/C 为当今国际贸易中的主要货款支付方式，即信用证结算。

6. Clean Bill of Lading，清洁提单，是指货物在装船后承运人（船运公司）在提单上未加任何有关货物受损或包装不良等批注的提单。

7. Force Majeure，不可抗力，是指合同签订后，因为一些无法预料且人力无法控制的事件导致合同某一方当事人不能履行合同，或者无法如期履行合同，包括严重自然灾害及战争、封锁、冲突、暴乱等社会原因。

8. China International Economic and Trade Arbitration Commission，中国国际经济贸易仲裁委员会，下设于中国国际贸易促进委员会（CCPIT），为中国常设的仲裁机构。

 参考译文

购 货 合 同

本合同由_____公司（以下简称售方）和_____公司（以下简称购方）于_____年_____月_____日签订。双方通过友好协商，特此同意下列条款。

1. 合同货物：_____
2. 规　　格：_____
3. 数　　量：_____

4. 单　　价：_____
5. 总　　值：_____FOB
6. 原产国：_____
7. 唛　　头：_____
8. 装　　船：_____年_____月_____日前装运,但要以卖方_____年_____月_____日前收到可接受的信用证为条件,允许分批装运和转运。
9. 优惠期限：为了履行合同,若最后一次装船时发生延迟,售方提出凭证,购方可向售方提供 30 天的优惠期限。
10. 保险：由购方办理。
11. 包装：用新牛皮纸袋装,每袋为_____公斤或用木箱装,每箱为_____公斤,予以免费包装。
12. 付款条件：签订合同后 5 天（公历日）内购方通过开证行开出以售方为受益人的、100%保兑的、不可撤销的、可分割的、可转让的、允许分批装运的信用证,见票即付并出示下列单证：
    （1）全套售方商业发票；
    （2）全套清洁、不记名、背书货运提单；
    （3）质量、重量检验证明。
13. 装卸准备就绪通知：购方至少在装货船到达装货港的 7 天前,将装货船到达的时间用电传通知售方。
14. 履约保证金：
    （1）通知银行收到购方开具的不可撤销的信用证时,售方必须开具信用证_____% 金额的保证金。
    （2）合同货物装船和交货后,保证金将原数退回给售方。若出于任何原因,本合同规定的第 12 条除外,发生无法交货（全部或部分）的情况,保证金将按数量比例作为违约予以没收并支付给购方。
    （3）若由于购方违约或购方不按照本合同第 9 条规定的时间内（第 12 条规定除外）开具以售方为受益人的信用证,购方必须按照保证金相同的金额付给售方。
    （4）开具的信用证必须满足合同规定的条款内容。信用证所列条款应准确、公道,售方能予以承兑。通知银行收到信用证后,应给开证银行提供保证金。
15. 不可抗力：由于不可抗力的任何原因所造成的无法交货或违约,售方或购方均不承担责任。如交货或装船时间可能出现延迟,购方或售方应提出证明予以说明实情。
16. 仲裁：凡因执行本合同所发生的一切争执和分歧,双方应通过友好协商方式解决。如经协商不能达成协议时,应提交中国国际经济贸易仲裁委员会,按其仲裁规则进行仲裁。仲裁委员会的裁决是终局裁决,对双方都有约束力。仲裁费用应由败诉方承担。除进行仲裁的部分外,在仲裁进行的同时,双方将继续执行合同的其余部分。
17. 货币贬值：若美元货币发生法定贬值,售方保留按贬值比率对合同价格予以调整的核定权力。
18. 有效期限：本合同签字后,购方若在 7 天内不能开出以售方为受益人的信用证,本合同将自动失效。但购方仍然对第 12 条中第（2）、（3）项规定的内容负责支付补偿。

本合同一式两份,双方认真审阅并遵守其规定的全部条款,在见证人出席下经双方签字。

售方：
购方：
见证人：

Passage Two

授权许可协议

LE Fans 特此向被许可方授予非独家、不可转让且不可撤销(本协议第 8 条另有规定除外[1])的个人许可,授权被许可方使用附件 A 中规定的电脑程序组(以下[2]简称"程序")。附件 A 构成本协议的一部分。

根据本协议授予的许可,被许可方有权在本协议附件 A 指定的地点和机器形式上安装此程序。被许可方和 LE Fans 有责任遵守《出口管制法规(EAR)》[3]及任何与被许可方及其海外子公司间的贸易相关的当地进出口规定。LE Fans 将向被许可方提供必要的信息和协助,确保其遵守相关规定。

1. 权利

被许可方承认,本协议转让的仅为本协议明确规定的程序使用权,程序的所有其他权利、所有权和权益仍由 LE Fans 及其供应商所有。对于程序的所有修改或衍生作品,不论其衍生方式和资金来源如何,其所有权利和所有权均由 LE Fans 独家拥有。

2. 保密

被许可方确认,LE Fans 向其披露的所有信息对 LE Fans 而言均具有专有价值,应被视为高度保密信息;此外,被许可方同意,第 5 条规定的所有形式的程序均可能包含 LE Fans 的商业秘密;被许可方承诺其自身将促使其所有员工和代理将所有形式的程序作为保密信息对待,防止向第三方披露任何及所有保密信息,已取得 LE Fans 事先书面同意的除外。LE Fans 不得无理拒绝或迟延做出同意。

LE Fans 承认,被许可方向 LE Fans 披露的所有信息对被许可方而言均具有专有价值,应被视为高度保密信息。未经被许可方明确书面许可,LE Fans 不得使用或向其他人披露该保密信息(但为本协议之目的而合理需要该保密信息且受相当保密义务约束的 LE Fans 员工除外)。

本条款的规定不适用于下述信息:

(1) 有书面记录可以证明在接收之时已经从第三方处获取的信息;

(2) 接收后从有独立披露权的第三方处另行合法获取的信息;

(3) 非因发现方或信息接收方违反本协议而现已或之后成为公众知悉的信息。

LE Fans 和被许可方仅可向直接参与程序许可或使用的相关员工披露保密信息,且应尽力确保该员工了解并遵守保密义务。

对于未经授权而占有、使用或获知本协议项下提供的任何材料的情形,一方应立即通知对方。披露和保密相关义务自《授权许可协议》签署之日起生效,并在本协议终止之后继续有效。对于政府机关或司法命令[4]要求披露的信息,不适用披露和保密的相关义务。被许可方不得基于本协议向被许可方授予的操作目标程序创设或试图创设,或允许他人创设或试图创设源代码计算机程序或其任何部分。

3. 许可费及其支付

被许可人同意按附件 A 规定的时间和数额向 LE Fans 支付相应费用,作为其在本协议项下获取的权利之对价。许可费之外的应付税费,亦由被许可人承担。

4. 支持和加强

被许可方承诺将在程序安装开始之时签订一份《软件支持和加强协议》。

5. 条款标题

本协议中条款标题仅为引用方便而设,对本协议进行解释时不构成本协议的一部分。

6. 终止

本协议授予的许可自本协议签署之日起生效,并可在一方实质违反本协议项下的义务之时终止;但一方实质违反义务时,另一方应以挂号信发出通知,违约方应拥有三十(30)天的时间对此进行补救。违约方未能在规定期间内补救违约的,另一方有权据此终止许可。一方丧失偿债能力或进入清算的,另一方有权以书面通知的形式立即终止本许可。许可的终止不损害任一方在终止日或终止日之前的既得权利。

在许可终止后十四(14)天内,如果被许可方违反其义务,则其应根据 LE Fans 的选择,返还或销毁本许可项下的程序及相关文件的所有复本、形式和部分,并应向 LE Fans 提供(全部文件和程序)已被销毁或返还的书面证明。

7. 赔偿

对于因 LE Fans 及其员工或代理履行许可义务中的行为、过错或过失而导致任何人身伤亡或财产(包括程序)损害的,以及因此而产生任何索赔、主张、程序、赔偿金、成本、费用和支出的,LE Fans 应对被许可人进行赔偿;但对于因被许可人或其员工或承包方(LE Fans 及其员工除外)的行为、过错或过失而导致的人身伤亡和财产损害,LE Fans 没有向被许可人提供补偿或赔偿金的义务。

对于因被许可人及其员工或代理履行许可义务中的行为、过错或过失而导致任何人身伤亡或财产(包括程序)损害的,以及因此而产生任何索赔、主张、程序、赔偿金、成本、费用和支出的,被许可人应对 LE Fans 进行赔偿;但对于因 LE Fans 或其员工或承包方的行为、过错或过失而导致的人身伤亡和财产损害,被许可人没有向 LE Fans 提供补偿或赔偿金的义务。

8. 间接损失 [5]

除非许可中另有明确规定,任一方均不就后续、间接、特殊、惩罚性损失或赔偿金(包括使用损失、利润损失、合同损失或数据丢失)向另一方承担责任,即使该方已被告知该等损失发生的可能性。

9. 运行

LE Fans 保证程序将按照使用手册和预期目的运行,但本协议、使用手册或任何文件、宣传册、说明书或 LE Fans 或其员工、代理所做的任何声明中的任何内容,均不构成程序将适用于特殊目的的担保或条件。

10. 变更

非经书面形式做出并经 LE Fans 和被许可方或其代表签署和注明日期的,对本协议所做的修正或变更均属无效。

11. 通知

本协议要求或允许发出的所有通知和其他通信往来均应采取书面形式,并在以专人送达,或注册、挂号或认证邮件发送至收件方的注册办公场所时视为已正式发出和送达。任何一方均有权按本条关于通知发送的规定,向另一方发出通知变更其收信地址。

12. 知识产权赔偿

对于第三方主张本协议项下提供的程序侵害了任何专利、版权、商标、商号或其他专有权利而针对被许可方及其子公司、关联方、董事、管理人员、员工、代理和独立缔约方而提起的任何索赔或诉讼,LE Fans 应自负费用提供辩护,并应就被许可方因该等索赔而合理支出的所有成本、赔偿金和费用,包括但不限于事务律师和出庭律师费,向被许可方提供赔偿。程序被认定侵害第三方专有权利的,LE Fans 有权选择向被许可方提供不侵权的程序,或将程序的购买费用返还给被许可方,且被许可方应立即将程序返还给 LE Fans。

13. 适用法

本协议依据宾夕法尼亚州法律解释,协议双方之间的法律关系亦按宾夕法尼亚州法律确定。

Key Words

不可撤销的	irrevocable
不可转让的	non-transferable
以下，在下文中	hereinafter
到此为止，关于这个	hereto
即得权利	vested right
保密	confidentiality
被许可方	licensee
泄露，暴露	divulge
书面同意	written consent
授权许可协议	license agreement
出口管制法规	Export Administration Regulations
专有价值	proprietary value
商业机密	trade secret
依照，按照，依据	pursuant to
规定期限	prescribed period
清算	liquidation
赔偿金	damages
间接损失	consequential loss
损失或损坏	loss or damage
知识产权赔偿	intellectual property indemnification

Notes

1. 本句可译为 except as provided for under Clause 8 of this Agreement。under 类似于 in accordance with 或者 according to。

2. 英文协议中常常采用部分古词来增强其文体的正式程度，使得句子结构更加紧凑，而且增强了语义衔接和连贯。此协议中多次使用的"在下文中""于此""依此"和"对此"等在法律文本中经常出现，分别译为 hereinafter、hereby、hereunder、hereto。

3. 《出口管制法规》译为 *Export Administration Regulations*。本法规由美国商务部工业与安全局（BIS）依据控制出口、再出口及其出口活动相关的法律出台。除此之外，本法规还涉及反抵制法律条款，这些条款禁止美国公民做出会推动某个国家对美国的抵制运动表示支持的行为。

4. "司法命令"译为 judicial order，是指法院做出的判决命令、指示或其他决定。

5. "间接损失"译为 consequential loss，是指民事主体因不法行为遭受的可得财产利益的损失。

参考译文

LICENSE AGREEMENT

LE Fans hereby grants to the Licensee a personal, non-exclusive, non-transferable, irrevocable (except as provided for under Clause 8 of this Agreement) License to use the computer program suite defined in the attached Schedule A (hereinafter called "the Programs"), which Schedule shall form part of the Agreement.

The License granted herein authorizes the Licensee to install the Programs in machine form at the site designated in Schedule A hereto. Licensee and LE Fans will be responsible for compliance with the Export Administration Regulations (EAR) and any local import and export regulations in respect of trading between the Licensee and any of its overseas subsidiaries. LE Fans will provide reasonable assistance and information to the Licensee in respect of ensuring compliance with the appropriate regulations.

1. RIGHTS

The Licensee acknowledges that this Agreement conveys only the right to use the Programs as set out herein and that all other rights, title and interest in the Programs remain vested in LE Fans and its suppliers. All rights and title to any modifications or derivatives of the Programs, howsoever derived or funded shall be vested solely in LE Fans.

2. CONFIDENTIALITY

The Licensee recognizes that any information disclosed by LE Fans to the Licensee and designated as confidential is of proprietary value to LE Fans and is to be considered highly confidential information; further, the Licensee agrees that all forms of the Programs as described in Clause 5 may contain confidential trade secrets of LE Fans, and undertakes to treat, and to have its employees and agents treat, all forms of the Programs as confidential and to prevent disclosure of any and all details of the Programs, without obtaining the prior written consent of LE Fans, to any third party, such consent not to be unreasonably withheld or delayed.

LE Fans recognizes that any information disclosed by Licensee to LE Fans is of proprietary value to Licensee and is to be considered highly confidential information. LE Fans shall not use or disclose such confidential information to others (except its employees who reasonably require same for the purposes hereof and who are bound to it by a like obligation as to confidentiality) without the express written permission of Licensee.

The provisions of this Clause shall not apply to any information that:

(1) can be demonstrated by written records to have been previously acquired from a third party at the time of receipt;

(2) was subsequently otherwise legally acquired from a third party having an independent right to disclose the information;

(3) is now or later becomes publicly known without breach of this Agreement by the discovery party or any party that received such confidential information from the disclosing party.

LE Fans and Licensee shall divulge confidential information only to those employees who are directly involved in the License or use of the Program and shall use their best endeavors to ensure that such employees are aware of and comply with these obligations as to confidentiality.

Prompt notification shall be given to the other party of the unauthorized possession, use or knowledge of any item supplied pursuant to this Agreement. The obligations as to disclosure and confidentiality shall come into effect on the signing of the License Agreement and shall continue in force notwithstanding the termination of the Agreement.

The obligations as to disclosure and confidentiality shall not apply to information to the extent such information is required to be disclosed by governmental authority or judicial order.

Licensee shall not create or attempt to create, nor permit others to create or attempt to create, the source computer programs or any part thereof from operational object programs licensed to Licensee hereunder.

3. LICENSE FEE AND PAYMENT

In consideration of the rights received under this Agreement the Licensee undertakes to pay LE Fans the sums defined in the attached Schedule A at the times so specified. The Licensee will pay any taxes and duties necessary to be added to the specified sums.

4. SUPPORT AND ENHANCEMENT

The Licensee undertakes to enter into a *Software Support and Enhancement Agreement* commencing on installation of the Programs.

5. CLAUSE HEADINGS

Clause headings are inserted in this Agreement for ease of reference only and do not form part of the Agreement for purpose of interpretation.

6. TERMINATION

The License granted herein shall be effective as of the date hereof and may be terminated in the event of the Licensee or LE Fans defaulting in its material obligations under this Agreement; provided that notice of such default shall be served by registered mail whereupon the Licensee or LE Fans shall have a period of thirty (30) days to correct such default. Failure to correct such default within the prescribed period may cause the License to be terminated. Either party may terminate the License forthwith on written notice if the other party shall become insolvent or go into liquidation. Termination of the License shall not prejudice any rights of either party which have arisen on or before the date of termination.

Within fourteen (14) days following the date of termination the License, if the Licensee is in default of its obligations, it shall at the option of LE Fans return or destroy all copies, forms and parts of the Programs and related documentation which are covered by this License and shall certify to LE Fans in writing that this has been done.

7. INDEMNITY AND INSURANCE

LE Fans shall indemnify and keep indemnified the Licensee, against injury (including death) to any persons or loss of or damage to any property (including the Programs) which may arise out of the act, default or negligence of LE Fans, their employees or agents in consequence of LE Fans's obligations under the License and against all claims, demands, proceedings, damages, costs, charges and expenses whatsoever in respect thereof or in relation thereto, provided that LE Fans shall not be liable for nor be required to indemnify the Licensee against any compensation or damages for or with respect to injuries or damage to persons or property to the extent that such injuries or damage result from any act, default or negligence on the part of the Licensee, his employees or contractors (not being LE Fans or employed by LE Fans).

The Licensee shall indemnify and keep indemnified LE Fans against injury (including death) to any persons or loss of or damage to any property (including the Programs) which may arise out of the act, default or negligence of the Licensee, his employees or agents in consequence of the Licensee's obligations under the License and against all claims, demands, proceedings, damages, costs, charges and expense whatsoever in respect thereof or in relation thereto, provided that the Licensee shall not be liable for nor be required to indemnify LE Fans against any compensation or damages for or with respect to injuries or damage to persons or property to the extent that such injuries or damage result from any act, default or negligence on the part of LE Fans, his employees or contractors.

8. CONSEQUENTIAL LOSS

Save as expressly stated elsewhere in the License, neither party shall be liable to the other party for consequential, indirect, special, exemplary, or punitive losses or damages including loss of use or of profit or of contracts or of data, even if such party had been advised of the possibility thereof.

9. PERFORMANCE

LE Fans warrants that the Programs will perform in accordance with the user manual and as intended, but nothing contained in this Agreement, in the user manual or in any document, literature or specification of, nor any statement made at the time by LE Fans or its employees or agents, amounts to a warranty on condition that the Programs are suitable for any particular purpose.

10. VARIATIONS

No amendment or variation to the Agreement shall be effective unless it is in writing, is dated and is signed by or on behalf of LE Fans and the Licensee.

11. NOTICES

All notices and other communications required or permitted under this Agreement shall be in writing and shall be deemed to have been duly made and received when personally served, or when mailed by registered, recorded or certified mail, to the party to whom it is addressed at the party's registered office. Any party may alter the address to which communications are to be sent by giving notice of such change of address in conformity with the provisions of this Clause providing for the giving of notice.

12. INTELLECTUAL PROPERTY INDEMNIFICATION

LE Fans shall, at its sole expense, defend any claim or action brought against Licensee and Licensee's subsidiaries, affiliates, directors, officers, employees, agents and independent contractors, to the extent it is based on a claim that the Programs provided under this License infringe or violate any patent, copyright, trademark, trade name, or other proprietary right of a third party, and LE Fans shall indemnify Licensee against all costs, damages and fees reasonably incurred by Licensee, including but not limited to solicitor or attorney fees, that are attributable to such claim, provided that: Should the Programs be found to infringe a third party's proprietary right, LE Fans shall at its option provide the Licensee with non-infringing programs or reimburse the Licensee for the purchase price for the Programs and the Licensee shall return the Programs to LE Fans forthwith.

13. APPLICABLE LAW

This Agreement shall be construed and the legal relations between the parties shall be determined in accordance with the laws of the Commonwealth of Pennsylvania.

Section 3　实　践　总　结

一、翻译技巧

随着中国对外经济贸易的飞速发展，国际贸易合同也在对外经济贸易活动中使用得越来越广泛。一旦合同对权利、义务规范得不够明确，或因合同措辞不当、词义含混不清、文义松散宽泛等，使合同一方有意或无意地利用合同漏洞逃避责任和义务，就有可能导致合同纠纷。因此，国际贸易合同的翻译显得越来越重要。国际贸易合同作为一种法律性文件，行文正式、用语严谨，对语言有严格的要求，强调措辞准确、结构严谨、格式规范。在翻译国际贸易合同时，把握合同语言的特殊性是翻译的关键。

（一）合同的用词特点

1. 用词准确

1）in、after

在英译合同中的"……天之后"时，这里往往是指确切的一天，所以必须用介词 in，而不能用 after。例如：

原文：The goods shall be shipped per M.V. "Dong Feng" on November 10 and are due to arrive at Rotterdam in 41 days. (M.V.= motor vessel)

译文：该货于 11 月 10 日由"东风"轮运出，41 天后抵达鹿特丹港。

2）by、before

在英译合同中的"在……月……日之前"时，如果包括所写的日期，就用介词 by；如果不包括所写的日期，即指到所写日期的前一天为止，就要用介词 before。例如：

原文：The vendor shall deliver the goods to the vendee before June 15.

译文：卖方须在 6 月 15 日前将货交给买方。

3）may、shall、must、may not

may、shall、must、may not 在国际贸易合同中使用要尤其谨慎。由于合同中权利和义务的约定部分构成了合同的主体，这些词如果选用不当，可能会引起纠纷。may 旨在约定当事人的权利（可以做什么），shall 旨在约定当事人的义务（应当做什么），must 用于强制性义务（必须做什么），may not（或 shall not）用于禁止性义务（不得做什么）。may do 不等于 can do、shall do 和 should do；may not do 在美国一些法律文件中可以等同于 shall not。

2. 用词正式

相较于其他英语文本，国际贸易合同属于一种法律性文件，为了体现其法律性，国际贸易合同中通常使用正式的词语。例如：

① 原文：Hereafter it is called the "purchaser".

　　译文：以下称"买方"。

② 原文：Either party reserves the right to terminate this agreement upon negotiation.

译文：任何一方需终止合同都必须经过与对方协商。

上述两句中使用了 purchase、party、reserve、terminate 等正式用词，而未使用常见的 buy、side、keep、end 等。此外，还有其他的常用词汇在合同中可以替换为正式词语，具体如下。

assist 替换 help
render 替换 make
desire 替换 wish
require 替换 want
residence 替换 home
function 替换 work/act
state 替换 say
inform 替换 tell
commence 替换 begin
terminate 替换 end
initiate 替换 start
proceed 替换 go

3. 使用古英语

在英文合同中，使用古英语最为突出的特点是较多使用 here、there、where 加后缀 in、by、after、from 等介词构成的词。在法律文件中，这些词可以有效避免重复和歧义，使行文准确、简洁。英文合同中常使用的古英语词汇如下：hereafter、hereby、herein、hereof、hereto、hereunder、hereupon、herewith、hereinbefore、hereinafter、thereafter、thereby、therein、thereinafter、thereinbefore、thereon、thereof、thereunder、thereupon、therewith、whereas、whereby、wherein、whereof、whereon。

① 原文：Therefore, it is hereby agreed and understood as follows.

译文：因此，双方特此协商如下。

② 原文：Whereas, the purchaser is desirous of importing the said goods for sale in the said territory.

译文：而买方欲进口所述货物在所述地点出售。

4. 用词专业

国际贸易合同用词不以大众是否理解和接受为转移，它是合同语言准确表达的保障。例如，合同中出现的"瑕疵""救济""不可抗力""管辖""损毁""灭失"等部分词汇可能让非专业人士费解，这些词在英文合同中分别表达为 defect、remedy、force majeure、jurisdiction、damage、loss。另外，几乎每个合同都少不了 hereinafter referred to as、whereas、in witness whereof、for and on behalf of、hereby、thereof 等虚词。其他例子还有："不动产转让"用 conveyance；"房屋出租"用 tenancy；"财产出租"用 lease of property；"停业"用 wind up a business 或 cease a business；"根据合同相关规定"一般用 pursuant to provisions contained herein 或 as provided herein。

5. 同义词或近义词并列使用

同义词或近义词并列使用在英文合同中十分普遍，这是出于严谨和杜绝漏洞的考虑。例如：

① 原文：This agreement is made and entered into by and between Party A and Party B.

译文：该协议由甲方和乙方订立。

② 原文：The parties have agreed to vary the Management on the terms and subject to the conditions contained herein.

译文：双方同意根据下述条件变更管理办法。

例①中的 made and entered into 和 by and between 两组分别属于同义词和近义词并列使用。例②中的 on the terms 和 subject to the conditions 是同一个意思，都表示"依照本协议的条款规定"。合同中的"条款"的固定翻译是 terms and conditions。

6. 使用外来词

英文合同中也会使用一些外来词汇，常见的有拉丁语和法语。例如："按比例"用 pro rata；"从事慈善性服务的律师"用 pro bono lawyer；"诉讼代理人"用 agent ad litem。

（二）合同的句法特点

1. 结构复杂的长句

与普通英文相比较而言，国际贸易英文合同中的句子结构就其长度和使用从句的连续性方面要复杂得多。分析英文合同长句的基本方法是：首先，要找出全句的主语、谓语和宾语，即句子的主干结构；其次，要找出句子中所有的谓语结构、非谓语结构、介词短语和从句的引导词；再次，分析从句和短句的功能，判断其是否是主语从句、宾语从句、表语从句或状语从句等，以及词、短语和从句之间的关系；最后，分析句子中是否有固定搭配、插入语等其他成分。例如：

原文：All profits paid by the company to Party C, all salaries and allowances paid by the company to foreign personnel, all direct expenses incurred as a result of the technology transfer and which must be paid by the company to Party C in foreign currency and all other payments that must be made by the company in foreign currency shall be made in United States Dollars or some other freely convertible currency that is mutually agreed upon.

译文：该公司支付给C方的利润，外来人员的工资、津贴和因技术转让而发生的应以外币支付的直接费用，以及所有其他应以外币支付的款项，应以美元或相互同意的可自由兑换的货币支付。

2. 高频次的被动句

国际贸易英文合同中常使用被动句，使用被动句的频率远高于汉语。为了更符合汉语的表达习惯，在翻译英文合同的被动句时，往往是将英文被动句译成汉语主动句。例如：

原文：If the contract shall be terminated as aforesaid the contractor shall be paid by the employer.

译文：如果合同如前所述被终止，发包方应向承包方支付款项。

3. 常用条件句

国际贸易合同主要约定合同各方应享有的权利和应履行的义务，但由于这种权利的行使和义务的履行均赋有各种条件，所以条件句的使用成为国际贸易合同的一个特点。英文合同中的条件句多由下列连接词引导：if、in the event of、in case (of)、should、provided (that)、subject to、unless otherwise 等。例如：

① 原文：In the event of any loss caused by the delay in the delivery, the Representative can claim a compensation from the Manufacturer with a certificate and detailed list registered by the administrative authorities of the Representative's site.

译文：若因任何交货延误导致的代理方损失，代理方可凭代理方所在地主管部门登记的损失清单向制造方索赔，但须出具证明。

② 原文：Should all or part of the contract be unable to be fulfilled owing to the fault of one party, the breaching party shall bear the responsibilities thus caused. Should it be the fault of both parties, they shall bear their respective responsibilities according to actual situations.

译文：由于一方的过失，造成本合同不能履行或不能完全履行时，由过失一方承担违约责任。若属双方过失，则根据实际情况，由双方分别承担各自应负的违约责任。

③ 原文：Either side can replace the representatives it has appointed provided that it submits a written notice to the other side.

译文：任何一方都可更换自己指派的代表，但须书面通知对方。

由上面的例子可以看出，例①和例②的条件句均置于主句之前，英译汉时译成"如果"或"若"即可。而当条件句置于主句之后时，在翻译时可按动态等值理论视具体情况而定，切勿生搬硬套。例③中的 provided that 表示合同该条款需作进一步规定，语气上有转折意义，因而应译为"但是"，使译文过渡自然，符合汉语的表达规范，也达到了功能对等的效果。

二、常用术语和表达

（一）常用术语

execution of contract	履行合同
breach of contract	违反合同
cancellation of contract	撤销合同
completion of contract	完成合同
termination of contract	解除合同
contractor	订约人，承包人
originals of contract	合同正本
copies of contract	合同副本
expiration of contract	合同期满
contract price	合约价格
force majeure	不可抗力
settlement of disputes	解决争议
contract for international sale of goods	国际货物销售合同
contract for international technology transfer	国际技术转让合同
contract for Sino-foreign joint venture	中外合资经营企业合同
contract for Sino-foreign contractual joint venture	中外合作经营企业合同
contract for international engineering projects	国际工程承包合同
contract for compensation trade	补偿贸易合同
contract for foreign labor services	涉外劳务合同

contract for international leasing affairs　　　国际租赁合同
contract for Sino-foreign credits and loans　　　涉外信贷合同
contract for international build-operate-transfer　　　国际 BOT 合同

（二）常用表达

① This contract is made out by and between the Buyer and the Seller, whereby the Buyer agrees to buy and the Seller agrees to sell the under-mentioned commodity according to the terms and conditions stipulated below.

合同由买方和卖方签订，根据下面规定的条款，买方同意购买并且卖方同意销售如下商品。

② This contract shall come into force immediately after signature by representative of both parties and upon approval by the relevant authority of both parties.

本合同在双方代表签字后及双方有关部门批准后立即生效。

③ The Seller shall mark on each package the package number, gross weight, net weight, measurement and the shipping mark.

卖方应在每件包装箱上注明箱号、毛重、净重、尺码和唛头。

④ Insurance is to be covered by the Seller for 110% of total contract value against ALL RISKS.

保险由卖方按合同价的 110%投保一切险。

⑤ 仲裁委员会的仲裁裁决是终局的，对双方都有约束力。

The award of the Arbitration Commission shall be final and binding upon both parties.

⑥ 由于严重的火灾、水灾、台风、地震及双方同意的其他不可抗力事故，致使卖方交货延迟或不能交货时，卖方可不负责任。

The Seller shall not be held responsible for the delay in shipment or non-delivery of the goods due to force majeure, such as war, serious fire, flood, typhoon and earthquake, or other events agreed upon between both parties, which might occur during the process of manufacturing or in the course of loading or transit.

⑦ 卖方在收到买方的索赔 30 天内没有答复将被认为接受上述索赔。

The claims mentioned above shall be regarded as being accepted if the Seller fails to reply within 30 days after receiving the Buyer's claim.

⑧ 本合同采用中文、英文书写，具有同等法律效力。合同正本两份，签字后双方各持一份。

This contract is made out in English and Chinese, both versions being equally authentic. The original contracts are in two copies; each part keeps one of two original copies after signature.

Section 4 巩固练习

一、翻译以下英文合同。

CONTRACT FOR PROCESSING & ASSEMBLY

Contract No.: _____
Conclusion Date: _____
Conclusion Place: _____

Party A: _____ Company (Party of Processing & Assembling)
Legal Address: _____
Tel: _____ Fax: _____ E-mail: _____

Party B: _____ Company (Party of Supplying Materials and Parts)
Legal Address: _____
Tel: _____ Fax: _____ E-mail: _____

Party A and Party B, according to the laws and policies of the People's Republic of China and the relevant regulations and the principles of equality and mutual benefit, have held discussions relating to the processing and assembling of _____ and have reached agreement on the following contractual clauses:

1. Responsibilities of Both Parties

Responsibilities of Party A

(1) Party A shall provide factory space consisting of _____ square meters, field of _____ square meters without covering, _____ factory management personnel and _____ workers for the first phase. The number of workers shall be increased to _____ twelve months after operation. Within the Contract term, Party A shall process the products for Party B which shall be re-exported to _____.

(2) The water supply and utility equipment required for processing shall be provided by Party A. If additional installations of water and electric facilities are required, the expenses thereof shall be borne by Party B.

(3) Party A shall arrange all the necessary import and export approvals required for processing and assembling and provide administration and accounting management for the processing plant. Party A cannot assign Party A's responsibilities to any other party or individual in any way.

Responsibilities of Party B

(1) To provide the equipment with the total value of _____.

(2) To provide the raw materials, auxiliary materials and packaging materials for processing the products. Quantities and specifications are to be specified in separate processing contracts.

(3) In the event that any personnel, including management shows substandard performance and makes no improvement after retraining, Party B shall have the right to request Party A to replace such persons. However, any physical search of the workers shall be regarded as illegal and prohibited.

2. Quantity of Products

During the first year, the total processing fee shall amount to _____. From the second year, the quantity shall be increased. Details shall be specified in separate processing contracts.

3. Salary

(1) The trial production (including training) period shall be _____. During such a period, the workers shall be paid _____ per month on the basis of _____ working days per month and _____ working hours per day.

(2) After the trial production period, the worker's payment shall be calculated according to actual production quantities. On the basis of mutual benefit, both parties shall consider the processing fee, which shall be specified in separate processing contracts, according to different kinds of products, specifications, styles and engineering procedures. In order to ensure the reasonable income of the workers, the worker's monthly salary shall be maintained no lower than _____. If overtime work is required, payment shall be calculated separately. However, overtime shall not exceed _____ hours a day.

(3) Expenses for water and electricity in Party A's plant shall be borne by Party B.

(4) Every month Party B shall pay _____ to Party A for management expenses.

4. Proportion of Products Damaged

(1) During the trial production period, Party B shall absorb the cost of products damaged.

(2) After the trial production period, the proportion of damaged products shall be mutually considered and decided by both parties and specified in separate processing contracts.

5. Shipment of Raw Materials & Finished Products

(1) Every month, Party B shall provide sufficient raw materials and packaging materials according to the contracted processing volume. To ensure the normal production of Party A's plant, Party B shall ship such materials to the plant _____ days before the production of each lot of products. Except for reason of force majeure, the plant shall operate for more than _____ days in a month. In case production is held up for _____ days to insufficient supply of raw materials, Party B shall calculate the actual days when production is shut down and pay to Party A the workers' living expenses at the rate of _____ per person per day.

(2) To ensure the normal operation of Party B's business activities, Party A shall deliver the finished products to Party B in accordance with the time of delivery, quality and quantity. Except for reason of force majeure, in case losses to Party B are caused due to Party A's failure to make delivery as mentioned above, Party A shall be responsible for the compensation. Details of such compensation shall be mutually agreed upon in separate processing contracts.

(3) Both parties shall mutually inspect and document the equipment and materials provided by Party B, such as machinery, ventilation and lighting equipment and raw materials. After the finished products are inspected and shipped from the plant by Party B, Party A shall be free of any responsibility in regard to specifications, quality and quantity, etc.

6. Terms of Payment

Payment of workers' salary and management fee shall be settled once a month by D/P, which shall be conducted through Bank of China Shenzhen Branch by Party B's bank in Hong Kong (＿＿＿Bank, Account No.＿＿＿) in accordance with the invoices issued by Party A and ＿＿＿ Trade Company (authorized by the local government to be in charge of affairs of processing and assembling and with foreign trade authority, hereinafter referred to as the Authorized Trade Company). In case Party B's payment is delayed for ＿＿＿ days, Party B shall be responsible for the interest incurred according to the bank's interest rate; in case payment is not settled for ＿＿＿ consecutive months, Party A shall have the right to suspend delivery of the finished products or take other measures.

7. Labour Protection & Insurance

(1) The plant shall take safety measures and protect the workers from dirt, smoke and poisonous materials. The factory shall be maintained ventilated and bright, and the surroundings clean and tidy.

(2) The transportation expenses for the machinery, ventilation and lighting equipment, raw materials, indirect materials, packaging materials and the finished products shall be paid for by Party B.

(3) All insurance for the transportation and storage of the above materials, machinery and equipment and coverage of the workers operating the machinery shall be arranged through the ＿＿＿ Insurance Company.

8. Technical Exchange

After the arrival of the equipment in the plant, Party B shall dispatch personnel to install such equipment, while Party A shall arrange personnel to assist the installation. When the trial production begins, Party B shall provide technical personnel to carry out the training until the workers have mastered the technology and the production operates normally. Party B shall be responsible for the technical personnel's salary and all related expenses, and Party A shall provide daily necessities.

9. Valid Period

After this contract is signed and approved, Party B shall present to Party A its commercial registration and bank credit certificate for Party A to arrange business license and customs registration. The term of this contract shall be ＿＿＿ year(s), e.g. from ＿＿＿ to ＿＿＿. If either party wishes to terminate in advance or extend the contract, the responsible party shall inform the other party three months in advance so that both parties can discuss and settle such a termination or extension. If either party terminates the contact before the term expires, the responsible party shall compensate the other party for the losses. In such case, the responsible party shall pay the other party as compensation the amount of ＿＿＿ times the monthly processing fee. The fee will be based on the average monthly fee of the previous ＿＿＿ months.

After the contract term expires, the real estate such as the factory building and dormitory building shall return to Party A and the machinery and equipment delivered by Party B shall be returned to Party B. Customs clearance procedures shall be gone through according to relevant regulations.

Both parties agree that, within ＿＿＿ days after the contract is signed and approved, Party B shall pay Party A the amount of ＿＿＿ as its guarantee to carry out the contract. If, within ＿＿＿ months after Party A's receipt of such amount, Party B still cannot arrange to start production, the amount shall be forfeited to Party A unconditionally and Party A shall have the right to cancel the contract. If Party B can start production on time, the amount will be deducted from the processing fee.

10. Arbitration

Any dispute arising from or in connection with this Contract (and including all the separate processing contracts) shall be settled through amicable negotiation. Should no settlement be reached through negotiation, the case shall then be submitted to the China International Economic and Trade Arbitration Commission (CIETAC), Shenzhen Commission for arbitration that shall be conducted in Shenzhen in accordance with the CIETAC's arbitration rules in effect at the time of applying for arbitration. The arbitral award is final and binding upon both parties.

11. Language

The present contract is drawn in Chinese and English as well, both texts being equally authentic. In case of any divergence of interpretation, the Chinese text shall prevail.

12. Copies and Amendment

This contact is made out in _____ copies respectively held by the parties, the customs, vehicle authority and the authorized trade company. They shall have the same force.

If there are other issues not covered in the contract, both parties can discuss to supplement or amend the contract and submit the results to relevant departments for approval.

Party A: _____   Party B: _____
Authorized Representative: _____   Authorized Representative: _____
Signature_____   Signature _____
The Authorized Trade Company: _____

二、翻译以下中文合同。

进 口 合 同

合同编号：_____

签订日期：_____

签订地点：_____

买方：_____

地址：_____

电话：_____ 传真：_____

电子邮箱：_____

卖方：_____

地址：_____

电话：_____ 传真：_____

电子邮箱：_____

买卖双方同意按照下列条款签订本合同：

1. 货物名称、规格和质量：_____

2. 数量：_____（允许_____%的溢短装）

3. 单价：_____

4. 总值：_____

5. 交货条件（离岸价/成本加运费/到岸价）：_____

6. 原产地国与制造商：_____
7. 包装及标准：_____

货物应具有防潮、防锈蚀、防震并适合于远洋运输的包装，由于货物包装不良而造成的货物残损、灭失应由卖方负责。卖方应在每个包装箱上用不褪色的颜色标明尺码、包装箱号码、毛重、净重及"此端向上""防潮""小心轻放"等标记。

8. 唛头：_____
9. 装运期限：_____
10. 装运口岸：_____
11. 目的口岸：_____
12. 保险：

由_____按发票金额的110%投保_____险和_____附加险。

13. 付款条件：

（1）信用证：买方应在装运期前/合同生效后____日，开出以卖方为受益人的不可撤销的议付信用证，信用证在装船完毕后____日内到期。

（2）付款交单：货物发运后，卖方出具以买方为付款人的付款即期汇票，按即期付款交单（D/P）方式，通过卖方银行及_____银行向买方转交单证。买方在首次出具汇票时应及时付款。

（3）承兑交单：货物发运后，卖方出具以买方为付款人的付款跟单汇票，付款期限为____后____日，按即期承兑交单（D/A____日）方式，通过卖方银行及_____银行，经买方承兑后，向买方转交单证，买方在汇票期限到期时支付货款。

（4）货到付款：买方在收到货物后____天内将全部货款支付卖方（不适用于离岸价、成本加运费、到岸价术语）。

14. 单据：

卖方应将下列单据提交银行议付/托收：

（1）标明通知收货人/收货代理人的全套清洁的、已装船的、空白抬头、空白背书并注明运费已付/到付的海运/联运/陆运提单。

（2）标有合同编号、信用证号（信用证支付条件下）及装运唛头的商业发票一式____份；

（3）由_____出具的装箱单或重量单一式____份；

（4）由_____出具的质量证明书一式____份；

（5）由_____出具的数量证明书一式____份；

（6）保险单正本一式____份（到岸价交货条件）；

（7）_____签发的产地证一式____份；

（8）卖方应在交运后____小时内以特快专递方式邮寄给买方上述第____项单据副本一式____份。

15. 装运条款：

（1）离岸价交货方式

卖方应在合同规定的装运日期前30天，以_____方式通知买方合同号、品名、数量、金额、包装件、毛重、尺码及装运港可装日期，以便买方安排租船/订舱。装运船只按期到达装运港后，如卖方不能按时装船，导致的空船费或滞期费等所有费用应由卖方负担。

（2）到岸价或成本加保险和运费交货方式

卖方须按时在装运期限内将货物由装运港装船至目的港。根据成本加保险和运费术语，卖方应在装船前 2 天以_____方式通知买方合同号、品名、发票价值及开船日期，以便买方及时安排保险。

16. 装运通知：

一旦装载完毕，卖方应在____小时内以_____方式通知买方合同编号、品名、已发运数量、发票金额、毛重、船名/车名/机号及装运日期等。

17. 质量保证：

卖方应保证货物必须符合本合同及质量保证书中规定的品质、规格和数量，保证期为货物到达目的港后的____个月内。在保证期内，因制造商在设计制造过程中的缺陷造成的货物损害应由卖方负责。

18. 检验（以下两项任选一项）：

（1）卖方须在装运前____日委托_____检验机构对货物进行检验并出具检验证书，货物到达目的港后，买方可委托_____检验机构对货物进行检验。

（2）发货前，制造商应对货物的质量、规格、性能和数量/重量作精密全面的检验，出具检验证明书，并出具检验证书证明技术数据和结论。货物到达目的港后，买方将申请中国商品检验局（以下简称商检局）对货物的规格和数量/重量进行进一步检验，如发现货物损坏或规格、数量与合同规定不符，除保险公司或航运公司的责任外，买方应在货物到达目的港后____日内凭商检局出具的检验证书向卖方索赔或拒收该货。在保证期内，如货物由于设计或制造上的缺陷而发生损坏或品质和性能与合同规定不符时，买方应委托商检局进行调查。

19. 索赔：

买方凭进一步的检验证书向卖方提出索赔（包括换货），由此引起的全部费用应由卖方负担。若卖方收到上述索赔后_____天未予答复，则认为卖方已接受买方索赔。

20. 延迟发货与罚款：

除合同第 21 条规定的不可抗力因素之外，如卖方不能按合同规定的时间交货，买方应同意在卖方同意支付罚款的条件下延期交货。罚款可由付款行从议付款中扣除，罚款率按每____天收取____%，奇数日不足____天时以____天计算。但罚款不得超过迟交货物总价的____%。如卖方延期交货超过合同规定装运时间____天时，买方有权撤销合同。尽管如此，卖方仍应按上述规定向买方支付罚款，不得延误。

买方有权对因此遭受的损失向卖方提出索赔。

21. 不可抗力：

凡在制造或装船运输的过程中，因不可抗力致使卖方不能或延迟交货时，卖方不负责任。发生上述情况时，卖方应立即通知买方，并在____天内给买方特快专递一份由有关政府部门签发的事故证明书以征求其同意。在此情况下，卖方仍有责任采取一切必要措施加快交货。如事故持续____天以上，买方有权撤销合同。

22. 仲裁：

凡因本合同引起的或与本合同有关的任何争议应友好协商解决。若不能解决，应提交中国国际经济贸易仲裁委员会，按照申请时该会当时施行的仲裁规则进行仲裁，仲裁地点在中国深圳。仲裁裁决是终局的，对双方均有约束力。

23. 通知：
所有通知用_____文写成，并按照如下地址用传真/快件送达给各方。地址如有变更，一方应在变更后____日内通知另一方。

24. 本合同使用的离岸价、成本加保险费和运费、到岸价术语的根据是国际商会《国际贸易术语解释通则2000》。

25. 附加条款：
本合同上述条款与本附加条款抵触时，以本附加条款为准。

26. 本合同用中英文两种文字写成，两种文字具有同等效力。本合同共____份，自双方代表签字（盖章）之日起生效。

买方代表人（签字）：

卖方代表人（签字）：

Chapter 8

国际贸易单证

Section 1 概　述

一、国际贸易单证的概念

国际贸易单证是指在国际贸易业务中所应用的单据、文件和证书，并凭以处理国际货物的交付、运输、保险、检验检疫、清关与结汇等。就出口贸易而言，出口单证是出口货物推定交付的证明，是结算的工具，贸易最终完成往往是以单证交流形式来实现的。因此，对出口企业而言，在完成了货物的交付后，正确、完整、及时、清晰地完成全套单证缮制，是企业安全、顺利结汇的关键。

二、国际贸易单证的分类

根据不同的分类标准，国际贸易单证可分为不同的类别。

（一）根据单证的性质划分

根据单证的性质划分，国际贸易单证可分为金融单据和商业单据。
（1）金融单据：包括汇票、支票、本票或其他类似用以取得款项的凭证。
（2）商业单据：包括发票、运输单据、物权凭证或其他类似单据及任何非金融单据。

（二）根据单证的用途划分

根据单证的用途划分，国际贸易单证可分为资金单据、商业单据、货运单据、保险单据、官方单据、附属单据。
（1）资金单据：汇票、支票、本票等。
（2）商业单据：商业发票、海关发票、装箱单、重量单等。
（3）货运单据：海运提单；不可转让海运单；租船合同提单；空运单；公路、铁路、内河运输单据；快递（邮政）收据；七大运输方式的单据等。
（4）保险单据：保险单、保险凭证、预约保险单等国际货物运输保险单据。
（5）官方单据：领事发票、原产地证书、检验检疫证书、配额许可证等官方出具的单据和证明。

（6）附属单据：寄单证明、寄样证明、船长收据、船公司证明、船航证明、装运通知等。

（三）根据贸易双方涉及的单证划分

根据贸易双方涉及的单证划分，国际贸易单证可分为出口单证和进口单证。

（1）出口单证：出口许可证、出口货物报关单、包装单据、出口货物单据、商业发票、保险单、汇票、检验检疫证书、原产地证书等。

（2）进口单证：进口许可证、信用证、进口货物报关单、进口检验检疫证书、保险单等。

（四）根据不同结算方式的结汇单据划分

根据不同结算方式的结汇单据划分，国际贸易单证可分为信用证单据、托收单据和汇付单据。

（1）信用证单据：商业发票、保险单、提单、装箱单、重量单、原产地证明等。

（2）托收单据：汇票、提单、商业发票、保险单等。

（3）汇付单据：汇票、提单等。

Section 2　译例分析

Passage One

BILL OF EXCHANGE

Drawn Under[1] UNITED MALAYAN BANKING CORP. BHD
Irrevocable L/C[2] No. 3654DYN36
Date[3] OCT. 26, 2017
No.　　GKI-7
Exchange for[4] USD 32,040.00　　HAIKOU, CHINA NOV.25, 2017
At 30 DAYS AFTER sight of this FIRST of Exchange (Second of Exchange Being unpaid)[5], pay to the order of[6] BANK OF CHINA HAINAN BRANCH[7]
the sum of SAY U.S. DOLLARS THIRTY-TWO THOUSAND AND FORTY ONLY[8]
To: UNITED MALAYAN BANKING CORP. BHD

　　　　　　　　　　　　　　　　　　HAINAN TIANHUA TRADE CORP.
　　　　　　　　　　　　　　　　　　　　　　×××
　　　　　　　　　　　　　　　　　　　　（SIGNATURE）

Key Words

bill of exchange	汇票
drawn under	凭
irrevocable	不可撤销的
L/C	信用证
at sight	见票即付
first of exchange	第一正本汇票
second of exchange	第二正本汇票/副本
sum	金额

Notes

1. Drawn under 为汇票字样，译为"凭"。

2. Irrevocable L/C 译为"不可撤销信用证"。信用证一经开出，必须经受益人、申请人、开证行三方同意才可撤销，否则不可撤销。

3. Date 后面跟的日期即为信用证的开证日期。

4. Exchange for 后填写的为金额，翻译时可以将动词译为名词"汇票金额"。

5. 本句译为"见票 30 日后（本汇票之副本未付）"。同一汇票有时可以开出两张或者多张，其效力相同，只要收到其中一张，其他就自动失效。

6. 汇票中的无条件支付语句，用英文动词 pay 表示。pay to the order of 译为"付交"。

7. 汇票当事人的名称或者单位名称，在英文中通常用大写表示，尽量不要简写或者缩写，以免造成误会。出票地点、付款地点等专有名词，在英文中也通常用大写表示。

8. 金额可以按原文用阿拉伯数字或文字同时翻译，两者所表示的数额必须一致。数字金额前用 Exchange for 表示，文字金额在句首加上 SAY，在句末加上 ONLY，表示"整"的意思。

参考译文

汇 票

凭马来亚银行   不可撤销信用证：3654DYN36
开证日期：2017 年 10 月 26 日
发票号：GKI-7
汇票 32 040.00 美元   2017 年 11 月 25 日，海口，中国
见票 30 日后（本汇票之副本未付）付交中国银行海南支行或其指定人叁万贰仟肆拾美元整。

此致
马来亚银行

　　　　　　　　　　　　　　　　　　　　　　　　　海南天华贸易公司
　　　　　　　　　　　　　　　　　　　　　　　　　　　×××
　　　　　　　　　　　　　　　　　　　　　　　　　　（签名）

Passage Two

Shipper SHANGHAI CHEMICAL IMPORT AND EXPORT CORPORATION 16 YANJIANG ROAD, PUDONG DISTRICT, SHANGHAI, CHINA		B/L No. **09C0-BHY 0709** ## PACIFIC INTERNATIONAL LINES LTD COMBINED TRANSPORT BILL OF LADING		
Consignee **TO ORDER OF COMMERCIAL BANK OF ETHIOPIA**		SHIPPED on board in apparent good order and condition (unless otherwise indicated) the goods or packages specified herein and to be discharged at the above mentioned port of discharge or as near thereto as the vessel may safely get and be always afloat. The weight, measure, marks, numbers, quality, contents and value, being particulars furnished by the shipper, are not checked by the carrier on loading. The shipper, consignee and the holder of this bill of lading hereby expressly accept and agree to all printed, written or stamped provisions, exceptions and conditions of this bill of lading, including those on the back hereof.		
Notify Party[1] **MAGIC INTERNATIONAL PLC**				
Pre-carriage by				
Vessel and Voyage Number **GUANGHANG V.312**		Port of Loading **SHANGHAI**	Port of Discharge **ASSAB**	
Place of Receipt **NANJING**		Place of Delivery **NANJING**	Number of Original[2] **THREE**	
Container[3] No., Seal No., Marks[4] and Nos.	Number and Kind of Packages	Description of Goods	Gross Weight (kgs)	Measurement (m³)
MAGIC INTL PLC, P.O.BOX147140, ADDIS ABABA ETHIOPIA VIA ASSAB	**75 PACKAGES**	**TRANSMISSION BELT**	**8,820KGS**	**20CBM**
Total No. of Containers of Packages (In Words)		**SAY TOTALLY: ONE CONTAINER ONLY**		
ABOVE PARTICULARS FURNISHED BY SHIPPER				
Freight & Charges **FREIGHT PREPAID**		IN WITNESS whereof the carrier or his agents have signed the above stated number of bill of lading, all of this tenor and date, one of which being accomplished, the others to stand void.		
		Place and Date of Issue **SHANGHAI, MAR. 19, 2017**		
		Sign for or on Behalf of the Carrier **PACIFIC INTERNATIONAL LINES(CHINA) LTD** **NANJING BRANCH** **AS AGENT**		

Key Words

consignee	收货人
notify party	被通知人
original	正本
container	集装箱
seal No.	铅封号
combined transport	联合运输
Assab	阿萨布（埃塞俄比亚北部港口城市）
Ethiopia	埃塞俄比亚
PLC（public limited company）	公共有限公司

Notes

1. Notify Party 是指船到达指定目的港后，接收承运人发出的通知的人，通常译为"被通知人"。

2. Origin 原意为"起源，原点"，在海运提单中，表示海运提单的"正本"。描述正本提单份数，通常采用大写的形式。

3. Container 原意为"容器"，在海运提单中，表示"集装箱"，所以 Container No.可以翻译成"集装箱号"。

4. Marks 原意为"标志，标记"，在国际贸易中，marks 是由简单的几何图形和几个字母组合而成，是用于区别其他货物的标志，可译为"唛头"。

参考译文

托运人： 上海化工进出口有限公司 中国上海市浦东区沿江路16号	提单号：09C0-BHY 0709		
收货人： 凭埃塞俄比亚商业银行指示	**太平洋船务（中国）有限公司** **联运提单**		
被通知人： 魔力国际公共有限公司	上述外表情况良好的货物（另有说明者除外）已装在上列船上并应在上列卸货港或该船所能安全到达并保持浮泊的附近地点卸货。重量、尺码、标志、号数、品质、内容和价值由托运人提供，承运人在装船时并未核对。 托运人、收货人和本提单的持有人明确表示接受并同意本提单和它背面所载的一切印刷、书写或打印的规定、免责事项和条件。		
前程运输：			
海运船名及航次： 广航312号	装运港： 上海		卸货港： 阿萨布
接货地点： 南京	交货地点： 南京		正本提单份数： 3
集装箱号、铅封号与唛头：	包装件数及种类：	货物描述：	毛重（公斤）：	尺码（立方米）：
MAGIC INTI PLC P.O.BOX147140 ADDIS ABABA ETHIOPIA VIA ASSAB	75包	传动皮带	8 820千克	20立方米
包装总件数（大写）： 一集装箱整			
以上细目由托运人提供			
运费支付 运费已付	为证明以上各节，承运人或其代理人已签署提单一式三份，其中一份经完成提货手续后，其余各份失效。		
	提单签发地点与日期： 上海，2017年3月19日		
	代表承运人签字： 　　　　　　　　　　　太平洋船务（中国）有限公司南京分公司 　　　　　　　　　　　　　　　　代理		

Passage Three

CERTIFICATE OF ORIGIN[1]

Exporter WUHU SHANSHAN NEW MINGDA MANUFACTURE CLOTHING CO., LTD. NANNING INDUSTRIAL PARK, WUHU, ANHUI, CHINA	Certificate No. AH 686/WHC/0033 **CERTIFICATE OF ORIGIN OF THE PEOPLE'S REPUBLIC OF CHINA**
Consignee GEMEYER INTL CO., LTD 3152, TOWN ROAD, TORTOLA	
Means of Transport and Route FROM SHANGHAI, CHINA TO SEATTLE, USA BY SEA	For certifying authority use only
Country/Region of Destination UNITED STATES	

Marks and Numbers	Number and Kind of Packages	HS Code[2]	Quantity	Number and Date of Invoices
PORT AUTHORITY ISSAQUAH WA USA G.W. KGS N.W. KGS	THREE HUNDRED (300) CTNS OF MEN'S SHELL JACKET	62.10	7,200PCS	960329ST Mar. 23, 2017

Declaration by the Exporter The undersigned hereby declares that the above details and statements are correct, that all the goods were produced in China and that they comply with the rules of origin of the People's Republic of China. WUHU, ANHUI, CHINA, Mar. 29, 2017 Place and Date, Signature and Stamp of Authorized Signature	Certification It is hereby certified that the declaration by the exporter is correct. WUHU Apr. 2, 2017 Place and Date, Signature and Stamp of Certifying Authority

Key Words

HS Code	海关商品编码
CTNS (cartons)	纸板箱
undersigned	下面签名的
rules of origin	原产地规则

Notes

1. 原产地证书是用以证明货物原产地或制造地的单据，是进口国海关计征税率的依据。
2. HS Code，海关商品编码。在海关的操作中，会将每一种商品由8位数的代码来表示，每一个代码都有相应的关税对应依循。

参考译文

原产地证书	
出口商： 芜湖姗姗新明达制衣有限公司 中国安徽省芜湖南宁工业园区	证书号：AH 686/WHC/0033
收货人： GEMEYER 国际有限公司 托托拉岛城镇路3152号	**中华人民共和国原产地证书**
运输方式和路线： 从中国上海至美国西雅图 海运	仅用于认证授权
目的地国家/地区： 美国	

唛头：	包装件数及种类：	海关商品编码：	数量：	发票号码及日期：
PORT AUTHORITY ISSAQUAH WA USA G.W. KGS N.W. KGS	300箱男士防风衣	62.10	7 200件	960329ST 2017年3月23日

出口商声明： 以下签字人特此声明，上述细节和声明正确，所有货物均在中国生产，符合中华人民共和国原产地规则。 中国安徽芜湖，2017年3月29日 授权签字人的地点和日期，签名和印章	证明： 特此证明，出口商的声明是正确的。 芜湖，2017年4月2日 认证机构的地点和日期，签名和印章

Passage Four

常州宝药制药有限公司

中国江苏省常州市天宁区和平路 132 号[1]，邮编：213004

商 业 发 票

收货人：	日期：2017 年 3 月 16 日
加拿大奥贝泰克制药股份有限公司	合同号：CHBY17316
加拿大安大略省多伦多市	发票号：CH17010
塞尼路 105 号，M9L1T9	信用证号：BMT0629292IM

起运地[2]：中国宁波市　　　　　　　　运抵地：加拿大安大略省多伦多市

付款方式：信用证见票即付

出票人：常州宝药制药有限公司，中国江苏省常州市天宁区和平路 132 号，邮编：213004

唛头	商品描述	数量	单价	总价
APOTEX 4500189719 TORONTO	加拿大安大略省多伦多市，到岸价 5 千克一罐头包装 2 罐头一纸箱包装	500 千克	57.84 美元/千克	28 920 美元

共计：500 千克

总价：贰万捌仟玖佰贰拾美元整[3]

常州宝药制药有限公司

×××

Key Words

商业发票	commercial invoice
销售合同	sales contract (S/C)
信用证	letter of credit (L/C)
见票即付	at sight
到岸价	cost, insurance and freight (CIF)
罐，罐头	tin
纸箱	carton

1. 翻译地址时要注意英文地址与中文地址格式的不同。英文地址通常按地址单元从小到大书写，并且地址单元间以半角逗号分隔，同时邮政编码可以直接写到地址中，其位置通常位于国家和省（州）之间。而中文格式则是从大到小的顺序。

2. 在商务文本中，为了体现商务英语的简洁性，"起运地""运抵地"不必译成 departure 和 destination，只需译成 from 和 to 即可。

3. 用文字表示金额时，可以在句首加上 SAY，表示"大写"的意思；在句末加上 ONLY，表示"整"的意思。

参考译文

CHANGZHOU BAOYAO PHARMACEUTICALS CO. LTD

NO.132, HEPING ROAD, TIANNING DISTRICT, CHANGHZHOU, JIANGSU, 213004, CHINA

COMMERCIAL INVOICE

TO:
APOTEX INC.
105 SIGNET ROAD
TORONTO, ONTARIO M9L1T9 CA

DATE: 16 MARCH 2017
S/C NO.: CHBY17316
NO.: CH17010
L/C NO.: BMT0629292IM

FROM: NINGBO, CHINA   **TO:** TORONTO, ONTARIO, CANADA
TERMS OF PAYMENT: BY L/C AT SIGHT
ISSUER: CHANGZHOU BAOYAO PHARMACEUTICALS CO. LTD
NO.132, HEPING ROAD, TIANNING DISTRICT, CHANGHZHOU, JIANGSU, 213004, CHINA

SHIPPING MARK	DESCRIPTIONS OF GOODS	QUANTITIES	UNITED PRICE	AMOUNT
APOTEX 4500189719 TORONTO	CIF TORONTO, ONTARIO, CANADA			
	PACKED 5KG PER TIN AND 2 TINS IN ONE CARTON	500KGS	USD57.84/KG	USD28,920.00

TOTAL: 500KGS
SAY TOTAL: U.S. DOLLARS TWENTY-EIGHT THOUSAND NINE HUNDRED AND TWENTY ONLY.

CHANGZHOU BAOYAO PHARMACEUTICALS CO. LTD
×××

Passage Five

<table>
<tr><td colspan="4" align="center">货物运输险投保单</td></tr>
<tr><td colspan="4" align="right">投保单号：MI001931</td></tr>
<tr><td colspan="4">被保险人：江苏苏赛斯公司</td></tr>
<tr><td>发票号（合同号）：</td><td>包装/件数：</td><td>货物名称：</td><td>发票金额：
JYP 3,078,075.00</td></tr>
<tr><td rowspan="2">252022-J</td><td rowspan="2">70 纸箱</td><td rowspan="2">中国皇家果冻</td><td>加成：
10%</td></tr>
<tr><td>保额：
JPY 3,385,882.50</td></tr>
<tr><td>运输工具名称：
空运 CA1508</td><td colspan="2">开航日期：
2017 年 3 月 30 日</td><td>赔款偿付地点：
日本</td></tr>
<tr><td>运输路径：</td><td colspan="2">自 南京 经 到 成田机场</td><td></td></tr>
<tr><td colspan="3" rowspan="2">被保险别：

协会货物保险条款（一切险）
协会战争险条款
协会罢工、暴乱、平民动乱险条款</td><td>投保人盖章：
江苏苏赛斯公司</td></tr>
<tr><td>日期：
2017 年 3 月 28 日</td></tr>
</table>

Key Words

加成	adding
保额	insured amount
成田机场	NARITA
一切险	All Risks
罢工、暴乱、平民动乱险	Strikes, Riots and Civil Commotions (SRCC)

参考译文

APPLICATION FORM FOR EXPORTING CARGO TRANSPORTATION INSURANCE

No. MI001931

INSURED: JIANGSU SUCCESS COMPANY			
INVOICE (CONTRACT) NO.	QUANTITY	DESCRIPTION OF GOODS	INVOICE VALUE JYP 3,078,075.00
252022-J	70 CTNS	CHINESE ROYAL JELLY	ADDING 10%
			AMOUNT INSURED JPY 3,385,882.50
PER CONVEYANCE S.S. BY AIRCRAFT CA1508	SLG. ON OR ABT MARCH 30, 2017		CLAIMS PAYABLE AT JAPAN
VOYAGE	FROM VIA TO NANJING NARITA		
CONDITIONS INSTITUTE CARGO CLAUSES (ALL RISKS) INSTITUTE WAR CLAUSES INSTITUTE SRCC CLAUSES			SIGNATURE JIANGSU SUCCESS COMPANY DATE: MARCH 28, 2017

Passage Six

中华人民共和国出入境检验检疫
健康证书

编号：460100206000021

发货人名称及地址	广东省镇江市徐闻县东方2号路132号徐闻中宏酵母有限公司	
收货人名称及地址	孟加拉吉大港班达尔班区FAKIRHAT路213号 S.A.贸易公司	
品名	即溶干酵母	
加工种类或状态		唛头 S.A.T. W09001A GHITTAGONG C/NO:1-2000
报检数量/重量	2 000 纸箱 20 600 千克	
包装种类及数量	纸箱 2 000 纸箱	
贮藏和运输温度	大约4度	
加工厂名称、地址及编号（如果适用）	广东省镇江市徐闻县东方2号路132号徐闻中宏酵母有限公司	
启运地	中国镇江	到达国家及地点	孟加拉吉大港
运输工具	船运	发货日期	2017年11月16日

检验结果：

所有商品适合人类食用

信用证号：1014/17/011323
信用证日期：2017年8月23日

签证地点：镇江　　　　　　　　　　签证日期：2017年11月20日
签字人：×××　　　　　　　　　　签名

Key Words

检验	inspection
检疫	quarantine
即溶干酵母	instant active dry yeast
报检	declare
孟加拉	Bangladesh
吉大港	Chittagong

 参考译文

ENTRY-EXIT INSPECTION AND QUARANTINE OF THE PEOPLE'S REPUBLIC OF CHINA HEALTH CERTIFICATE

No.460100206000021

Name and Address of Consignor	XUWEN ZHONGHONG YEAST CO. LTD., NO.132, DONG FANG 2ND ROAD, XUWEN COUNTY, ZHENJIANG CITY, GUANGDONG PROVINCE, CHINA		
Name and Address of Consignee	S.A.TRADING, NO. 213, FAKIRHAT ROAD, BANDARBA, GHITTAGONG, BANGLADESH		
Description of Goods	INSTANT ACTIVE DRY YEAST		
State or Type of Processing		Mark & No.	
Quantity/Weight Declared	2,000 CARTONS 20,600 KGS	S.A.T. W09001A GHITTAGONG C/NO:1-2000	
Number and Type of Packages	CARTON TOTAL 2,000 CARTONS		
Temperature during Storage and Transport	ABOUT 4℃		
Name, Address and Approval No. (if applicable)	XUWEN ZHONGHONG YEAST CO. LTD., NO.132, DONG FANG 2ND ROAD, XUWEN COUNTY, ZHENJIANG CITY, GUANGDONG PROVINCE, CHINA		
Place of Dispatch	ZHENJIANG, CHINA	Country and Place of Destination	GHITTAGONG, BANGLADESH
Means of Conveyance	BY VESSEL	Date of Dispatch	Nov. 16, 2017

Results of Inspections:

THE GOODS ARE FIT FOR HUMAN CONSUMPTION
****

L/C NO: 1014/17/011323
L/C DATE: Aug. 23, 2017

Place of Issue   ZHENJIANG   Date of Issue   Nov. 20, 2017
Authorized Officer   ×××   Signature

Section 3　实践总结

一、翻译技巧

（一）国际贸易单证的语言特点

国际贸易单证英语属于专门用途英语，其文体特色鲜明，词句特点独特。了解国际贸易单证英语的词句特征，掌握国际贸易单证的翻译技巧，有助于外贸工作的顺利进行。

1. 国际贸易单证的词汇特点

国际贸易单证英语作为一种特殊的文体，有其独特的词汇特点，主要表现在以下三个方面。

1）用词正式规范

国际贸易单证具有国际通用性，其用词规范并且符合约定俗成的含义。在国际上，常使用《国际贸易术语解释通则》对单证用语进行统一规范，以避免因各国不同的解释而出现的不统一。例如：

① 原文：The amount and date of negotiation of each draft must be endorsed on reverse hereof by the negotiating bank.

译文：每份汇票的议付金额和日期都必须由议付行在本证背面背书。

② 原文：Please arrange shipment as per the terms and conditions of our contract.

译文：请根据合同条款安排装船。

2）使用大量的专业术语

为了描述进出口流程的各个环节，国际贸易单证常使用大量的专业术语，如 invoice（发票）、packing list（装箱单）、bill of lading（提单）、inspection certificate（检验证书）、insurance policy（保险单）、beneficiary certificate（受益人证明）等。

值得注意的是，单证中也有许多术语是由普通词汇转化而来，但是其采用的词义并非常见的意义，而是某一领域的术语。例如，documents 的常见词义为"文档、文件"，而在单证中指的是各类单据；draft 的常见词义为"草稿、稿纸"，而在单证中译为"汇票"；condition 在海洋货物运输保险单据中不译为"条件"，而应译为"险别"；free on board 译为"船上交货"，其中的 free 不是"空闲、自由"的意思；bill of lading 译为"提单"，其中的 lading 是"装载、船货"的意思，在单证中词义拓展为"提运"；general average 中的 average 原意是指"平均数、中等、一般水平、普通"等，该术语在报关中指海损的公平分担或商船支付的引水费、拖船费等杂费，所以应译为"共同海损"。

3）使用较多的名词及名词短语

大多数国际贸易单证的主体部分都是由统一的格式和固定的填写栏目组成，以便于信息筛查和数据统计，这些固定的栏目常使用名词或名词短语。如 unit price（单价）、description of goods（货物描述）、consignee（收货人）、port of loading（装运港）等均采用名词或名词短语。

2. 国际贸易单证的句式特点

与一般的商务英语书信相比，国际贸易单证具有较强的规约性和法律特性，在表述时多采用陈述句式及各种复合句式，并常使用被动语态、状语（从句）和定语（从句）。

1）多使用陈述句

在英语中，陈述句用于阐述、解释说明、规定和判断，语言客观、平实，感情色彩较少。国际贸易单证多用于商务场合，要求准确、客观地描述交易过程的相关事项，因此陈述句的使用频率非常高。例如：

① 原文：We hereby certify that the above mentioned goods are of Chinese origin.

译文：我们特此证明，上述货品原产于中国。（原产地证书）

② 原文：The goods under the above mentioned letter of credit have been shipped. The details of the shipment are stated below.

译文：上述信用证项下的货品已发运。装船细节具体如下。（装船通知）

上述例句均使用了陈述句语序，以平实、客观的语言清晰地阐述单据的要求及所需注明的事项。

2）采用较多的复合句

与普通英语相比，国际贸易单证中的英语句子结构长度和连贯性更复杂，存在较多的状语（从句）和定语（从句），对主句的意义起着解释、修饰与限定的作用。例如：

① 原文：Transshipment is allowed on condition that the entire voyage be covered by B/L.

译文：只要提供直达提单，允许转船。

本句使用 on condition that 引导的状语从句，清晰地表述了运输单据中的转船条件。

② 原文：One original bill of lading must be surrendered duly endorsed in exchange for the goods or delivery order. In witness whereof the number of original bill of lading stated under have been signed, all of this tenor and date, one of which being accomplished, the other to stand void.

译文：承运人签发的正本提单份数，具有相同的法律效力，提取货物时必须交出经背书的一份正本提单，其中一份完成提货后，其余各份自行失效。

本句使用了 one of which 的定语结构，既避免了用词的重复，又对其所修饰的 bill of lading 进行了解释与限定，说明了提单的使用要求及失效条件。

3）常使用被动语态

被动语态是英语中常见的语法现象。被动语态能避免给人主观臆断的感觉，使文本表现得更客观、正式。在国际贸易单证中，被动语态常用来提供建议、表达愿望、提醒对方应尽的责任和义务等。例如：

原文：Discrepant document fee of USD 50.00 or equal currency will be deducted from drawing if documents with discrepancies are accepted.

译文：如果（开证行）接受含有不符点的单据，将会扣减50美元或等价的其他币值的不符点费用。

本句使用了两个被动结构，这种结构在正式的单证文体中较常出现，体现了客观、委婉的语气。本句中的被动结构还适用于提醒买方在修改信用证的不符点时需要注意的事项。

（二）国际贸易单证的翻译方法

1. 国际贸易单证的具体栏目翻译方法

国际贸易单证词汇具有规范性、术语化和使用较短名词短语的特点。国际贸易单证的基本栏目通常由一些专业性很强的术语、词语或短语构成，一般情况下，单证的具体栏目内容采用套译法及惯用译法。

在翻译单证的具体栏目时，首先应找到与之相对应的专业术语或习惯用语，这些术语或用语一般都有已被国际惯例认可的翻译方法。例如，可以在《国际贸易术语解释通则》的资料中找到相应项目的译名，然后套译。例如：free on board 译为"离岸价"；terms of payment 译为"付款方式"；500 pieces 译为"500件"；150 cartons 译成"150箱"；mark 译为"唛头"。

2. 国际贸易单证的句型翻译方法

在国际贸易单证中，为了更清晰、全面地界定买卖双方及相关银行的权利和义务，制单人员往往通过在长句中添加较多的定语（从句）或状语（从句）等附加成分，对各项条款进行解释、限定或补充，以避免漏洞和争议。在对国际贸易单证的句子进行翻译时，应注重对整个句子的理解和把握，正确处理好句子中各成分之间的逻辑关系。总的来说，国际贸易单证中的句型可采用以下3种方法翻译。

1）顺译法

国际贸易单证中有不少条款使用陈述语序，按一连串动作、逻辑关系或发生的时间先后进行陈述，这与汉语的表达方式一致。在对这类条款进行翻译时，可以按照原文的顺序，使用顺译法进行翻译。例如：

原文：Full set of marine insurance policy endorsed in blank for 110% of invoice value covering the ICC(A) with claims payable in Canada in the currency of draft.

译文：全套海运保险单，空白背书，按发票总值的110%投保协会货物条款(A)，以汇票上的币种在加拿大办理赔付。

本句是按照出单、承保、索赔等连贯动作进行陈述的，同时整句话也是按时间进度推进的，因此，在翻译时可以采用顺译法，按原文顺序进行翻译。

2）拆译法

汉语和英语在语言上的一个重要区别是，两种语言对构建句子的要求不同：英语注重句子形式的完整，汉语则注重意境的表达。在翻译国际贸易单证中的英文长句时，可以适时打破原句的结构，按汉语的造句规律重新安排，即采用拆译法，将原句拆分成几个短句进行翻译。例如：

原文：Certificate issued by the shipping company/carrier or their agent stating the B/L No(s) and the vessel's name certifying that the carrying vessel is…

译文：由船公司/承运人或其代理人出具的、注明提单号和船只名称的证明，其应能够证明该船只……

该长句如果直译，则译文会显得生涩难懂。该长句宜拆分成两个短句进行翻译，既保持了句子的结构平衡,又便于读者理解。

3)重组法

在进行国际贸易单证主体内容的翻译时,经常会遇到一些由结构复杂的短语和句子组合而成的条款。翻译时,应该在理解英语原文的基础上,打破原文的句群、段落和语言框架,对句子进行重组。例如:

原文:The seller shall not be held responsible for late delivery or non-delivery of the goods owing to generally recognized force majeure causes.

译文:由一般公认的不可抗力所造成的延迟交货或无法交货,卖方不负责任。

此句把原文的被动语态 the seller shall not be held 按原句的语序翻译成了主动语态,在不改变原文主语的前提下,将被动变成主动,并且对语序进行重组,使译文符合单证文体的汉译习惯。

通过以上例句及分析不难看出,对国际贸易单证的重点词汇与难点句型的正确理解和准确翻译,是外贸工作中安全交货、及时收货和结汇的重要因素。因此,译者应掌握一定的翻译技巧,学会针对不同的情况,运用合适的翻译方法,准确恰当地表达国际贸易单证中各种项目和条款所承载的信息。

二、常用术语和表达

(一)汇票常用词汇

出票人	drawer
受票人	drawee/payer
收款人	payee
出票	issue/draw
限制性抬头	restrictive order
指示性抬头	demonstrative order
持票人抬头	bearer order
提示	presentation
承兑	acceptance
付款	payment
背书	endorsement
拒付	dishonour
追索权	recourse
委托人	principal
托收行	remitting bank
代收行	collecting bank

(二)运输单据常用词汇

| 承运人 | carrier |
| 托运人 | shipper |

发货人	consignor
收货人	consignee
被通知人	notify party
前程运输	pre-carriage
收货地点	place of receipt
海运船名及航次	name of vessel and voy. No.
装运港	port of loading
卸货港	port of discharge
交货地点	place of delivery
集装箱号	container No.
铅封号	seal No.
唛头	marks
包装与件数	number and kind of packages
货物描述	description of goods
毛重	gross weight
尺码	measurement
正本提单份数	No. of original B/L
运费支付	payment of freight
运费已付	freight paid
运费预付	freight prepaid
签发地点和时间	place and date of issue
承运人签字	signed for the carrier

（三）商业单据常用词汇

商业发票	commercial invoice
销售合同号	S/C No.
信用证号	L/C No.
发票编号	invoice No.
规格	specification
数量	quantity
包装	packing
重量	weight
单价	unit price
总值	total value

Section 4　巩 固 练 习

一、翻译以下短语。

1. 付款交单
2. 承兑交单
3. 电汇
4. 跟单托收
5. 支付条件
6. airway bill
7. net weight
8. ocean vessel
9. tariff barrier
10. cost and freight

二、翻译以下句子。

1. Each payment to be made hereunder shall be made in American currency.
2. We agree that payment is made by documentary draft at sight drawn in favor of you on collection basis instead of L/C.
3. Full set of clean on board ocean bills of lading issued on the order of shipper and blank endorsed, marked "Notify XYZ Corporation, and Freight Collect."
4. The date of receipt issued by transportation company concerned shall be regarded as the date of delivery of goods.
5. The relevant negotiating documents for the contracted goods are now with us and you are expected to collect them upon the advice.
6. 保质期为2～3星期的袋装饼干。
7. 所有主要箱子必须注明原产地名称。
8. 先以备用L/C预付30%的定金，余款在出货前T/T到付。
9. 我方声明运输此批货物的船舶并没有不良记录。
10. 持票人应在汇票到期前交由付款人承兑。

Chapter 9

信 用 证

Section 1 概 述

信用证是具有法律效力的文件。买卖合同是进出口商之间的契约,而信用证则是开证行与收益人之间的契约,对双方都有约束力。信用证的语言具有法律文书的特点,行文严谨,用词准确规范,有很强的专业性。在国际贸易中,起草、审核信用证的人员应当熟悉国际贸易业务,同时应具备良好的英语水平,了解信用证的语言特点。信用证是由银行发行的证书,授权持证者可从开证行、其支行或其他有关银行或机构提取所述款项。信用证作为贸易上最重要的信用保证方法,代表买方的外汇银行,接受买方的委托,保证其货款的支付。万一买方付不出货款,根据契约规定,银行必须履行向卖方付款的责任。

信用证是保证卖方收到汇票后即可收取货款的信用文件。在卖方将货物装船后,外汇银行代替买方开立汇票给卖方;卖方带着汇票和装船单据,到自己往来的外汇银行办理结算而取得货款。

一、信用证的概念

国际商会制定的《跟单信用证统一惯例》第 600 号出版物(UCP 600)规定:信用证意指一项约定,无论其如何命名或描述,该约定不可撤销并因此构成开证行对于相符提示予以兑付的确定承诺。

二、信用证开立的形式

(1) 信开信用证。
(2) 电开信用证:简电本(brief cable)、全电本(full cable)、SWIFT 信用证(最常用的形式)。

三、信用证的内容

完整的信用证通常包括当事人(申请人、受益人、开证行、议付行和保兑行等)、汇票条款(出票人、受票人、汇票金额等)、单据条款(单据种类、份数及其列明的信息等)、货物描述、运输条款、特别条款、开证行的保证及 UCP 600 的统一文句。

四、信用证的特点

(1) 信用证不依附于买卖合同，银行在审单时强调的是信用证与基础贸易相分离的书面形式上的认证。

(2) 信用证是凭单付款，不以货物为准。只要单据相符，开证行就应无条件付款。

(3) 信用证是一种银行信用，它是银行的一种担保文件。

五、信用证的作用

(1) 担保付款作用：由于一国的卖方不了解另一国买方的信誉和支付能力，只有在先付货款或有银行信用证的条件下才会发货。

(2) 融资作用：卖方在信用证到期前急需用款时，可以将该信用证质押，从第三方处（或者银行）取得贷款。买方也可以申请银行垫款。

(3) 便利作用：信用证除了有担保付款和提供融资的作用外，还对买卖双方有一定的便利作用。双方的资信调查、担保登记、质押办理、付款安排等都可以被信用证简化。

六、信用证当事人的权利和义务

(1) 申请人（applicant）：开证申请人是向银行提交申请书申请开立信用证的人，它一般为进出口贸易业务中的进口商。

权利：对货物进行检验

义务：及时申请开证；及时付款赎单；承担信用证的最终责任。

(2) 开证行（issuing bank）：开证行是应申请人（进口商）的要求向受益人（出口商）开立信用证的银行，该银行一般是申请人的开户银行。

权利：收取开证押金或取得质押；审单及拒付；控制单据及货物。

义务：根据申请人的指示开立信用证；承担第一付款责任。

(3) 受益人（beneficiary）：受益人是开证行在信用证中授权使用和执行信用证并享受信用证所赋予的权益的人，受益人一般为出口商。

权利：决定是否接受信用证；取得货款；在特殊情况下将货物转卖他人。

义务：装运出单。

(4) 通知行（advising bank）：通知行是受开证行的委托，将信用证通知给受益人的银行，它一般为开证行在出口地的代理行或分行。

权利：决定是否接受开证行关于通知信用证或修改的委托；验明信用证的真实性；收取通知费或因通知而产生的其他费用。

义务：无法鉴别信用证的表面真实性时需告知申请人或开证行。

(5) 付款行（paying bank/drawee bank）：付款行是开证行在承兑信用证中指定并授权向受益人承担（无追索权）付款责任的银行。

权利：选择是否付款。

义务：履行付款责任。

(6) 保兑行（confirming bank）：保兑行是应开证行或信用证受益人的请求，在开证行的付款保证之外对信用证进行保证付款的银行。

权利：选择权；审单权。

义务：不可撤销的责任。

（7）议付行（negotiating bank）：议付行又称押汇银行或贴现银行，是开证行指定的或自由议付信用证项下受益人请求的、对信用证项下汇票及单据承担议付或贴现义务的银行。

权利：当发现单证不一致时，有权拒绝议付；追索权；质押权。

义务：在信用证到期日内（有效期）和交单日内，接受受益人提交的单据，进行审单并垫付款项（押汇）。

（8）偿付行（reimbursing bank）：偿付行是受开证行指示或由开证行授权，对信用证的付款行、承兑行、保兑行或议付行进行付款的银行。

权利：选择权；追索权；收取偿付费用。

义务：接受开证行的委托和要求为其偿还索偿款项。

七、其他的结算方式：汇付和托收

在国际贸易中，常用的结算方式有三种：汇付（remittance）、托收（collection）、信用证（letter of credit）。汇付和托收属于商业信用，信用证属于银行信用。

（一）汇付

汇付，也叫汇款，是付款人通过银行或其他途径将款项汇交收款人的结算方式。汇付的当事人有四个：汇款人（remitter）、收款人（payee）、汇出行（remitting bank）、汇入行（receiving bank）。

汇付方式包括信汇、电汇、票汇。

1. 信汇（mail transfer，M/T）

信汇是指汇出行应汇款人的申请，将信汇委托书寄给汇入行，授权解付一定金额给收款人的一种付款方式。信汇的成本较低，但速度较慢。

2. 电汇（telegraphic transfer，T/T）

电汇是指汇出行应汇款人的申请，电报通知另一国家的代理行指示解付一定金额给收款人的一种汇款方式。电汇方式下收款人可以迅速收到汇款，但由于是电报发送，费用较高。

3. 票汇（demand draft，D/D）

票汇是指汇出行应汇款人的申请，代汇款人开立以其分行或代理行为解付行的银行即期汇票，支付一定金额给收款人的一种汇款方式。票汇可以转让，这点与信汇和电汇不同。

（二）托收

托收（collection）是出口方在货物装运后，开具以进口方为付款人的汇票（随付或不随附货运单据），委托出口地银行通过其在进口地的分行或代理行代收取货款的一种结算方式。托收的当事人主要包括：委托人（principal）、托收银行（remitting bank）、代收银行（collecting bank）、提示行（presenting bank）。

托收分为光票托收和跟单托收。

1. 光票托收（clean collection）

光票托收是指资金单据的托收不附有商业单据。资金单据是指汇票、期票、支票、付款收据或其他用于取得付款的类似凭证；商业单据是指发票、装运单据、所有权单据或其他类似的单据，或一切不属于资金单据的其他单据。

2. 跟单托收（documentary collection）

跟单托收是指附有商业单据的金融单据的托收和不附有金融单据的商业单据的托收。在国际贸易中所讲的托收多指前一种。

跟单托收又分为付款交单和承兑交单两种。付款交单要求转交货运单据即付货款，而承兑交单要求买方承兑卖方开具的汇票，才转交货运单据。

1）付款交单（documents against payment，D/P）

在付款交单支付方式下，卖方交出单据后指示托收行和代收行在国外的买方付清货款后才交出单据。根据付款时间不同，付款交单可分为即期付款交单和远期付款交单。

（1）即期付款交单（D/P at sight）：卖方开具即期汇票并通过银行向买方提示，买方见票后立即付款，只有付款清货后才能领取单据。这种方式也称"凭单据付款"。

（2）远期付款交单（D/P after sight）：卖方开具远期汇票。代收行向买方提示汇票和货运单据。买方见票后仅需承兑汇票，等汇票到期时支付货款。代收行收到货款后交付单据。

2）承兑交单（documents against acceptance，D/A）

这种付款方式仅用于跟单托收中的远期汇票。在此方式下，代收行向买方交付单据不以后者付款为条件，仅以后者承兑为条件，即买方做出的在买卖双方同意的某个将来的日期保证支付汇票款项的书面承诺。也即承兑交单是指卖方的交单以买方在汇票上承兑为条件。卖方在装运货物后开具远期汇票连同货运单据，通过银行向买方提示，买方承兑汇票后，代收行即将货运单据交给买方，买方在汇票到期时才履行付款义务。

八、信用证操作流程

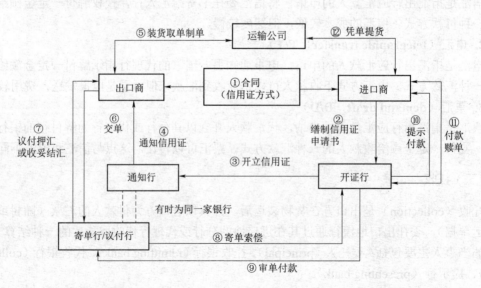

九、信用证样本

*27:	SEQUENCE OF TOTAL	
	1/1	
*40A:	TYPE OF DOCUMENTARY CREDIT	
	IRREVOCABLE	
*20:	LETTER OF CREDIT NUMBER	
	LC84E0081/99	
*31G:	DATE OF ISSUE	
	140916	
*31D:	DATE AND PLACE OF EXPIRY	
	141015 KOREA	
*50:	APPLICANT	
	DALIAN WEIDA TRADING CO., LTD.	
*59:	BENEFICIARY	
	SSANGYONG CORPORATION	
*32B:	CURRENCY CODE, AMOUNT	
	USD 1,146,725.04	
*41D:	AVAILABLE WITH... BY...	
	ANY BANK BY NEGOTIATION	
*42C:	DRAFTS AT	
	45 DAYS AFTER SIGHT	
*42D:	DRAWEE	
	BANK OF CHINA LIAONING BRANCH	
*43P:	PARTIAL SHIPMENTS	
	NOT ALLOWED	
*43T:	TRANSSHIPMENT	
	NOT ALLOWED	
*44A:	SHIPPING ON BOARD	
	BUSAN PORT, KOREA	
*44B:	TRANSPORTATION TO	
	DALIAN PORT, CHINA	
*44C:	LATEST DATE OF SHIPMENT	
	140918	
*45A:	DESCRIPTION OF GOODS OR SERVICES:	
	FROZEN YELLOW FIN SOLE WHOLE ROUND (WITH WHITE BELLY)	
	USD 770/MT CFR DALIAN	
	QUANTITY: 200 MT	

ALASKA PLAICE (WITH YELLOW BELLY)
USD 600/MT CFR DALIAN
QUANTITY: 300 MT

*46A: DOCUMENTS REQUIRED:

1. SIGNED COMMERCIAL INVOICE IN 5 COPIES.

2. FULL SET OF CLEAN ON BOARD OCEAN BILLS OF LADING MADE OUT TO ORDER AND BLANK ENDORSED, MARKED "FREIGHT PREPAID" NOTIFYING LIAONING OCEAN FISHING CO., LTD.

3. PACKING LIST/WEIGHT MEMO IN 4 COPIES INDICATING QUANTITY/GROSS AND NET WEIGHTS OF EACH PACKAGE AND PACKING CONDITIONS AS CALLED FOR BY THE L/C.

4. CERTIFICATE OF QUALITY IN 3 COPIES ISSUED BY PUBLIC RECOGNIZED SURVEYOR.

5. BENEFICIARY'S CERTIFIED COPY OF FAX DISPATCHED TO THE ACCOUNTEE WITHIN 3 DAYS AFTER SHIPMENT ADVISING NAME OF VESSEL, DATE, QUANTITY, WEIGHT, VALUE OF SHIPMENT, L/C NUMBER AND CONTRACT NUMBER.

6. CERTIFICATE OF ORIGIN IN 3 COPIES ISSUED BY AUTHORIZED INSTITUTION.

7. CERTIFICATE OF HEALTH IN 3 COPIES ISSUED BY AUTHORIZED INSTITUTION.

*47A: ADDITIONAL INSTRUCTIONS:

1. CHARTER PARTY B/L AND THIRD PARTY DOCUMENTS ARE ACCEPTABLE.

2. SHIPMENT PRIOR TO L/C ISSUING DATE IS ACCEPTABLE.

3. BOTH QUANTITY AND AMOUNT 10 PERCENT MORE OR LESS ARE ALLOWED.

*71B: CHARGES

ALL BANKING CHARGES OUTSIDE THE OPENING BANK ARE FOR BENEFICIARY'S ACCOUNT.

*48: PERIOD FOR PRESENTATION

DOCUMENTS MUST BE PRESENTED WITHIN 15 DAYS AFTER THE DATE OF ISSUANCE OF THE TRANSPORT DOCUMENTS BUT WITHIN THE VALIDITY OF THE CREDIT.

*49: CONFIRMATION INSTRUCTIONS

WITHOUT

*78: INSTRUCTIONS TO THE PAYING/ACCEPTING/NEGOTIATING BANK

1. ALL DOCUMENTS TO BE FORWARDED IN ONE COVER, UNLESS OTHERWISE STATED ABOVE.

2. DISCREPANT DOCUMENT FEE OF USD 50.00 OR EQUAL CURRENCY WILL BE DEDUCTED FROM DRAWING IF DOCUMENTS WITH DISCREPANCIES ARE ACCEPTED.

Section 2　译例分析

>> Passage One

*27:	SEQUENCE OF TOTAL
	1/1
*40:	FORM OF DOCUMENTARY CREDIT
	IRREVOCABLE
*20:	DOCUMENTARY CREDIT NUMBER
	ABLE-AN1075
*31C:	DATE OF ISSUE
	20170405
*31D:	EXPIRY DATE AND PLACE
	20170615 CHINA
*50:	APPLICANT
	ITOCHU CORPORATION, OSAKA, JAPAN
*59:	BENEFICIARY
	SHANGHAI TEXTILES IMP. AND EXP. CORP.
	E1, NO. 127 ZHONGSHAN ROAD, SHANGHAI, CHINA
*32B:	CURRENCY CODE, AMOUNT
	USD 9,665.00
*41D:	AVAILABLE WITH…BY…
	BANK OF COMMUNICATIONS IN SHANGHAI, CHINA
	BY NEGOTIATION
*42C:	DRAFTS AT
	60 DAYS AFTER SIGHT FOR FULL INVOICE VALUE
*42A:	DRAWEE
	ASAHI BANK LTD., TOKYO
*43P:	PARTIAL SHIPMENT
	PROHIBITED
*43T:	TRANSSHIPMENT
	PROHIBITED
*44A:	LOADING IN CHARGE
	CHINESE PORT(S)
*44B:	FOR TRANSPORT TO

	OSAKA, JAPAN
*44C:	LATEST DATE OF SHIP
	20170531
*45A:	DESCRIPTION OF GOODS
	80% COTTON APRON

ARTICLE NO.	QUANTITY	UNIT PRICE
4031（01425）	3,250 PIECES	USD 1.20
5052（01426）	2,700 PIECES	USD 1.30
5210（01427）	2,050 PIECES	USD 1.10

PRICE TERM: CIF OSAKA

*46A: DOCUMENTS REQUIRED

+ SIGNED COMMERCIAL INVOICE[1] IN TRIPLICATE[2] INDICATING "WE HEREBY CERTIFY THAT THE GOODS HEREIN OF INVOICE CONFIRM WITH S/C NO. AHM-1356, ORDER NO. 23051".

+ FULL SET OF CLEAN ON BOARD BILLS OF LADING[3] MADE OUT TO ORDER OF SHIPPER AND BLANK ENDORSED[4], MARKED "FREIGHT PREPAID[5] TO OSAKA" NOTIFYING APPLICANT (WITH FULL NAME AND ADDRESS) AND INDICATING FREIGHT CHARGES.

+ INSURANCE POLICY OR CERTIFICATE IN DUPLICATE ENDORSED IN BLANK, FOR 120% OF THE INVOICE VALUE[6] INCLUDING: INSTITUTE CARGO CLAUSES (A),[7] INSTITUTE WAR CLAUSES, INSURANCE CLAIMS TO BE PAYABLE IN JAPAN IN THE CURRENCY OF THE DRAFTS INDICATING INSURANCE CHARGES.

+ CERTIFICATE OF ORIGIN.[8]

+ PACKING LIST IN 3 FOLD.

*47A: ADDITIONAL CONDITIONS

+ T/T[9] REIMBURSEMENT PROHIBITED.

+ THE GOODS TO BE PACKED IN EXPORT CARTONS.

+ SHIPPING MARK:[10]

SUNARA

WSC-4320A

OSAKA

NO. 1-UP

*71B: DETAILS OF CHARGES

ALL CHARGES OUTSIDE JAPAN INCLUDING REIMBURSEMENT COMMISSIONS ARE FOR ACCOUNT OF BENEFICIARY.

*48: PRESENTATION PERIOD

DOCUMENTS TO BE PRESENTED WITHIN 15 DAYS AFTER THE DATE OF ISSUANCE OF THE SHIPPING DOCUMENTS BUT WITHIN THE VALIDITY OF THE CREDIT.

*49: CONFIRMATION INSTRUCTIONS

WITHOUT

Key Words

applicant	申请人
beneficiary	受益人
drawee	受票人
loading in charge	起运港
price term	价格条款
commercial invoice	商业发票
insurance policy	保险单
certificate of origin	原产地证书
T/T (telegraphic transfer)	电汇

Notes

1. signed commercial invoice：已签署的商业发票。如果信用证没有特殊规定，用于对外收汇的商业发票不需要签署，但用于报关、退税等国内管理环节的发票必须签署。当信用证规定 signed commercial invoice 时，发票需要签署，有时信用证会要求 manually signed invoice，这种情况下必须根据要求手签商业发票。

2. in triplicate：一式三份。在国际贸易中，为方便客户清关，需要提交三份正本发票，但有时也会看到两份，其表达为 in duplicate。

3. clean on board bills of lading：清洁已装船提单。清洁表明货物在装船时状态良好，没有破损，所谓清洁已装船提单，即提单上注明 on board（已装船）字样，且没有不良批注。这实质上是船公司的一项免责条款。

4. made out to order of shipper and blank endorsed：凭收货人指示空白背书。背书通常分为空白背书和记名背书。空白背书，又称无记名背书，指不记载被背书人名称而仅由背书人签章的背书，在信用证中对应的英文是 blank endorsed。空白背书主要是贸易中间商避免厂家和买家直接联系而使用的一种手段。记名背书指记载被背书人的名称、背书日期及背书人的签名的背书。

5. freight prepaid：运费预付。运费预付是指国际贸易中运费在启运港由出口商支付，与之相对应的是 freight collect（运费到付）。运费到底是预付还是到付主要与进口商和出口商所协定的贸易术语有关，FOB 价格术语下显示 freight collect，而 CFR 和 CIF 价格术语下显示 freight prepaid。

6. for 120% of the invoice value：按发票金额的 120%。这是保险中的投保金额条款，投保金额一般按发票金额的 110%投保，但如果买方提出额外要求（如 120%），那么多出的费用由买方负责。

7. Institute Cargo Clauses(A)：英国伦敦保险协会 A 险，ICC(A)相当于投保 All Risks（一切险）。在国际贸易中有三种基本险别，除了上述的一切险外，另外两个分别是平安险（free from particular average，FPA）和水渍险（with particular average，WPA）。

8. certificate of origin：原产地证明。原产地证明即出口商应进口商要求由公证机构、政府或出口商出具的证明货物原产地或制造地的一种证明文件。它是贸易关系人交接货物、结算货款、索赔理赔、通关验收、征收关税的重要凭证，还是出口国享受配额待遇等优惠贸易政策的凭证。

9. T/T：电汇。国际贸易中的支付方式主要有三种，分别是汇付（remittance）、托收（collection）和信用证（letter of credit，L/C），其中汇付又可以分成信汇（mail transfer，M/T）、电汇（telegraphic transfer，T/T）和票汇（demand draft，D/D）。

10. shipping mark：唛头。国际贸易中的唛头是一种运输标志，其目的是识别货物，避免发错货，唛头通常由型号、收货单位名称或标志、目的港（地）名称、件数或批号组成。

 参考译文

*27:	报文页次
	1/1
*40:	信用证类型
	不可撤销
*20:	信用证编号
	ABLE-AN1075
*31C:	开立日期
	2017年4月5日
*31D:	有效期及地点
	2017年6月15日在中国到期
*50:	申请人
	日本大阪伊藤忠商事株式会社
*59:	受益人
	上海纺织进出口公司
	中国上海市中山路127号E1座
*32B:	币种及金额
	9 665美元
*41D:	议付
	由中国上海交通银行议付
*42C:	汇票
	按发票金额总值开具60天的远期汇票
*42A:	受票人
	东京朝日银行
*43P:	分批装运
	禁止
*43T:	转运

禁止

*44A：启运港
中国港口

*44B：目的港
日本大阪

*44C：最迟装运期
2017年5月31日

*45A：货物描述
80%棉围裙

货号	数量	单价
4031（01425）	3 250 件	1.20 美元
5052（01426）	2 700 件	1.30 美元
5210（01427）	2 050 件	1.10 美元

价格术语：CIF 大阪

*46A：所需单据
+ 注明"我们特证明发票上的货物与第 AHM-1356 号销售合同中第 23051 号订单一致"字样的已签署商业发票一式三份。
+ 全套凭收货人指示空白背书的清洁已装船提单，提单标注"运费预付，到大阪"字样，通知申请人（注明全称和地址）并标明运费。
+ 保险单或保险证明一式两份，由银行背书，按发票金额的 120%投保，包括伦敦保险协会（A）条款和战争险。保险可在日本以汇票中规定的货币进行索赔，标明保险费用。
+ 原产地证明。
+ 装箱单一式三份。

*47A：附加条款
+ 禁止电索。
+ 货物用出口纸箱包装。
+ 唛头：
SUNARA
WSC-4320A
OSAKA
NO.1-UP

*71B：费用详情
一切非日本境内产生的费用（包括偿付和佣金）均由受益人承担。

*48：交单期限
所有单据应在装船单据开立后十五天但在信用证有效期内提示。

*49：保兑
无

Passage Two

在国际贸易活动中,买卖双方可能互不信任,买方担心预付款后卖方不按合同要求发货;卖方也担心在发货或提交货运单据后买方不付款。因此需要两家银行作为买卖双方的保证人,代为收款交单,以银行信用代替商业信用。那么银行在商业活动中所使用的工具就是信用证。

1. 原则

(1) 独立抽象原则:该原则是贯穿信用证法律关系始终,对信用证各方当事人的行为具有普遍指导意义的基本法律原则。该原则包含两方面的内容:① 独立性或无因性,即开证行与受益人间的法律关系、开证行与开证申请人间的法律关系及开证申请人与受益人间的法律关系相分离,不受这些关系中所产生的权利请求与抗辩的影响。② 文义性或单证相符,即信用证项下的单据必须在表面上与信用证条款的规定相符,不论基础合同是否履行或完全履行,只要单证之间、单单之间相互一致,开证行就必须付款或承兑,银行无须考虑基础合同中的具体履约行为有无违约或违法,也无义务对相关单据的真实性进行审核。

(2) 严格相符原则:亦称单证相符原则,是指卖方在向银行提交单据要求付款时,这些单据必须在表面上完全符合信用证的要求,银行才予以付款。

(3) 欺诈例外原则:即在肯定信用证独立抽象原则的基础上,如果有证据证明存在欺诈,银行有权拒付,受欺诈的买方也可以请求银行不予付款或要求法院发出止付令,禁止银行对信用证付款或承兑。

2. 特点

(1) 信用证是一项自足文件。信用证不依附于买卖合同,银行在审单时强调的是信用证与基础贸易相分离的书面形式上的认证。

(2) 信用证方式是纯单据业务。信用证是凭单付款,不以货物为准。只要单据相符,开证行就应无条件付款。

(3) 开证银行负首要付款责任。信用证是一种银行信用,它是银行的一种担保文件。

3. 种类

以信用证项下的汇票是否附有货运单据为依据,信用证可分为:

(1) 跟单信用证:是指凭跟单汇票或仅凭单据付款的信用证。此处的单据指代表货物所有权的单据(如海运提单等),或证明货物已交运的单据(如铁路运单、航空运单、邮包收据)。

(2) 光票信用证:是指凭不随附货运单据的光票付款的信用证。银行凭光票信用证付款,也可要求受益人附交一些非货运单据,如发票、垫款清单等。

在国际贸易的货款结算中,绝大部分使用跟单信用证。

以开证行所负的责任为标准,信用证可分为:

(1) 不可撤销信用证:信用证一经开出,在有效期内,未经受益人及有关当事人的同意,开证行不能片面修改和撤销,只要受益人提供的单据符合信用证规定,开证行必须履行付款义务。

(2) 可撤销信用证:开证行不必征得受益人或有关当事人同意,有权随时撤销信用证,信用证上会注明"可撤销"字样。但《跟单信用证统一惯例》第500号出版物(UCP500)规定:只要受益人依信用证条款规定已得到了议付、承兑或延期付款保证时,该信用证即不能被撤销或修改。它还规定，如信用证中未注明是否可撤销，应视为不可撤销信用证。最新的UCP600规定，银行不再开立可撤销信用证，常用的都是不可撤销信用证。

以有无另一银行加以保证兑付为依据，信用证可分为：

（1）保兑信用证（confirmed L/C）：开证行开出的信用证由另一银行保证对符合信用证条款规定的单据履行付款义务。

（2）不保兑信用证（unconfirmed L/C）：开证行开出的信用证没有经另一家银行保兑。

以付款期限不同，信用证可分为：

（1）即期信用证：开证行或付款行收到符合信用证条款的跟单汇票或装运单据后立即履行付款义务的信用证。

（2）远期信用证：开证行或付款行收到信用证的单据时在规定期限内履行付款义务的信用证。

4. 当事人

（1）申请人：根据合同规定向银行申请开立信用证的人，即进口商。

（2）受益人：信用证上指定的有权使用信用证的人，即出口商。

（3）开证行：接受开证申请人的要求和指示或根据其自身的需要，开立信用证的银行。一般为进口商所在地银行。

（4）通知行：受开证行的委托，将信用证通知转交给受益人的银行，一般为开证行在出口地的联行、分行或代理行。

（5）议付行：根据开证行的授权买入或贴现受益人开立和提交的符合信用证规定的汇票或单据的银行。

（6）偿付行：被指示及/或被授权按照开证行发出的偿付授权书提供偿付的银行。

（7）保兑行：出口国的某一银行应开证行的请求，在信用证上加注条款，表明该行与开证行一样，对受益人所提示的符合信用证规定的汇票和单据负有付款或承兑的责任。

5. 操作流程

（1）开证申请人根据合同填写开证申请书并交纳押金或提供其他保证，请开证行开证。

（2）开证行根据申请书内容，向受益人开出信用证并寄交出口人所在地通知行。

（3）通知行核对印鉴无误后，将信用证交给受益人。

（4）受益人审核信用证内容与合同规定相符后，按信用证规定装运货物、备妥单据并开出汇票，在信用证有效期内，送议付行议付。

（5）议付行按信用证条款审核单据无误后，把货款垫付给受益人。

（6）议付行将汇票和货运单据寄给开证行或其特定的付款行索偿。

（7）开证行核对单据无误后，付款给议付行。

（8）开证行通知开证人付款赎单。

▶ Key Words

发货	delivery
货运单据	transportation documents
保证人	guarantor

交单	presentation of documents
银行信用	bank credit
商业信用	commercial credit
严格相符	strict compliance
自足文件	self-sufficient instrument
审单	examination of documents
纯单据业务	pure documentary transaction
首要付款责任	primary liabilities for payment
押金	deposit
开证行	issuing bank
跟单信用证	documentary L/C
光票信用证	clean L/C
可撤销信用证	revocable L/C
不可撤销信用证	irrevocable L/C
保兑信用证	confirmed L/C
不保兑信用证	unconfirmed L/C
提单	bill of lading
通知行	advising bank
议付行	negotiation bank
即期信用证	sight L/C
远期信用证	usance L/C
申请人	applicant
邮包收据	parcel postal receipt

 参考译文

In the international trade, the buyer and the seller may not trust each other. For the buyer, he or she worries that the seller will not deliver the goods in accordance with the contract. For the seller, however, he or she is also concerned that the buyer will not make payment after he or she delivers the goods or presents shipping documents. Consequently, two banks must be required to receive payments and present documents respectively as guarantors of the buyer and the seller, substituting the bank credit for the commercial credit. Then the letter of credit becomes a tool that the bank uses in business activities.

1. Principles

(1) Principle of independent abstraction: It is the basic legal principle that offers a universal guidance for behaviors of parties involved in the letter of credit throughout the legal relations of the letter of credit. It can be divided into two parts: ① independence or non-causation, namely legal relations between the issuing bank and the beneficiary, the legal relations between the issuing bank and the applicant as well as the legal relations between the applicant and the beneficiary separate

from each other, not being influenced by rights of pledge and defense that arise from these relations. ② literacy or documents in compliance with L/C terms, namely documents under the letter of credit must be in conformity with the stipulations in the terms of the letter of credit. No matter whether the basic contract is executed or completely executed, the issuing bank must pay or honor as long as it is consistent between documents and the letter of credit or between documents. It is unnecessary for the bank to consider whether the specific acts of honor are legal or not, nor is it obligatory to examine the authenticity of related documents.

(2) Principle of strict compliance: Also named as principle of consistence between documents and the letter of credit. It represents that when the seller asks for payments after he or she presents the documents to the bank, the bank will honor to pay for it provided that these documents are in complete compliance with the requirements of the letter of credit.

(3) Principle of fraud exception: On the basis of affirming the principle of independent abstraction, the bank is entitled to dishonor only if there is evidence showing fraud exists, and the buyer who is deceived can also request for non-payment of the bank or demand that the court decree a payment bar which forbids that the bank pays or dishonors the letter of credit.

2. Characteristics

(1) The letter of credit is a self-sufficient instrument. It does not depend on the business contract, and the bank puts an emphasis on the written certification that the letter of credit separates from basic trade when examining the documents.

(2) The method of the letter of credit is a pure documentary transaction. The letter of credit is payment against documents, instead of being in line with the goods. Only if it is consistent between documents the issuing bank ought to pay in an unconditional way.

(3) The issuing bank bears the liabilities for payment. The letter of credit is the commercial credit and it is a kind of letter of indemnity.

3. Types

According to whether the draft is attached with shipping documents, L/C can be divided into:

(1) Documentary L/C: It refers to the letter of credit that is paid by documentary drafts or documents alone. Documents herein include documents that stand for the ownership of the goods (e.g. bill of lading) or that can be as certifications for the delivered and shipped goods (such as railway bill of lading, air bill of lading and parcel postal receipt).

(2) Clean L/C: It refers to the letter of credit that is paid without the attached shipping documents. When the bank makes payments through clean credit, it is able to make a request that the beneficiary send some other documents like the commercial invoice and the list of advances, etc.

During the settlement for loans in the international trade, the documentary credit is widely used in most cases.

According to the liabilities that the issuing bank bears, L/C can be divided into:

(1) Irrevocable L/C: It means that once the irrevocable credit is opened, the issuing bank cannot make a one-sided amendment to or withdraw it without the permission of the beneficiary and the related parties within the validity date of it. Provided that documents presented by the

beneficiary are consistent with the stipulations of the letter of credit, the issuing bank must carry out its obligations to pay.

(2) Revocable L/C: The issuing bank is entitled to withdraw the letter of credit at any time without the permission of the beneficiary or the related parties involved and ought to indicate "revocable" on the letter of credit. However, according to the stipulation in UCP 500, as long as the beneficiary has obtained the guarantee for negotiation, acceptance or deferred payment, the letter of credit cannot be withdrawn. UCP 500 also stipulates that if it does not indicate whether it can be withdrawn or not, the letter of credit ought to be regarded as an irrevocable letter of credit. In accordance with the latest UCP 600, the bank does not open a revocable credit. (The irrevocable credit is usually used.)

According to whether there is a bank confirming to pay, L/C can be divided into:

(1) Confirmed L/C: The letter of credit that is opened by the issuing bank is confirmed by another bank which will carry out its obligations for payment provided that documents are in consistence with the terms under the letter of credit.

(2) Unconfirmed L/C: The letter of credit that is issued by the issuing bank is not confirmed by another bank.

According to different time of payment, L/C can be divided into:

(1) Sight L/C: It represents that the issuing bank or the paying bank carries out its obligations for payment immediately on receipt of the documentary draft or shipping documents.

(2) Usance L/C: It means that the issuing bank or the paying bank carries out its obligations for payment within a stipulated period when receiving documents that the letter of credit requires.

4. Parties involved

(1) Applicant: The person applies for opening a letter of credit to the bank in accordance with the stipulations in the contract, namely the importer.

(2) Beneficiary: The person is entitled to use the letter of credit, namely the exporter.

(3) Issuing bank: The bank opens a letter of credit after accepting the request and indication of the applicant or meeting its own needs.

(4) Advising bank: The bank hands over the notification of the letter of credit to the beneficiary's bank after accepting entrustment from the issuing bank. It in general refers to the correspondents, branches or agents that are set up in the export place by the issuing bank.

(5) Negotiating bank: The bank purchases or discounts the draft or documents issued and submitted by the beneficiary with the authorization of the issuing bank.

(6) Reimbursing bank: The bank provides a reimbursement in accordance with the authorization of reimbursement.

(7) Confirming bank: A bank in the exporter's country adds a term on the letter of credit, suggesting that it, being the same as the issuing bank, will bear the liabilities for payment or honor the draft and documents that are consistent with stipulations in the letter of credit presented by the beneficiary.

5. Procedures

(1) The applicant fills out the application for opening a letter of credit according to the contract and pays deposits, or offers other guarantees to pledge for a letter of credit by the issuing bank.

(2) The issuing bank opens a letter of credit on the basis of the application and sends it to the advising bank in the exporter's country.

(3) The advising bank sends the letter of credit to the beneficiary after examining that the seal is true and valid.

(4) The beneficiary ships the cargo, prepares documents, draws a draft and negotiates within the valid date of the letter of credit after ensuring that the contents of the letter of credit are in consistence with the stipulations in the contract.

(5) The negotiating bank pays to the beneficiary when examining that the documents are correct.

(6) The negotiating bank sends the draft and shipping documents to the issuing bank or its specific paying bank for reimbursement.

(7) The issuing bank pays to the negotiating bank after ensuring that the documents are correct.

(8) The issuing bank notifies that the applicant pays to redeem the documents.

Section 3 实践总结

一、翻译技巧

信用证是具有法律效力的文件。信用证的语言具有法律文书的特点，行文严谨，用词准确规范，有很强的专业性。在国际贸易中，起草、审核信用证的人员应当熟悉国际贸易业务，同时应具备良好的英语水平，了解信用证的语言特点。

（一）信用证的用词特点

1. 格式统一规范，用词简练

（1）信用证中的日期采用"YYMMDD"的格式。例如：2018 年 10 月 8 日，在信用证中显示为"181008"。

（2）被动语态省略 be 动词。例如："允许转运"在信用证中表示为"Transshipment allowed"。

（3）用分词短语做定语。例如：Full set of clean on board bill of lading made out to order.（凭指示作出全套的清洁已装船提单）。

2. 用词专业性强

1）多使用特定专业词汇

专业术语和缩略语具有国际通用性，意义精确、无歧义，不带个人感情色彩。信用证一般使用国际通用的专业术语，大多具有贸易实务的内涵，所以在翻译时要符合国际贸易实务的习惯，且必须熟悉该专业的知识，否则会贻笑大方。例如：

（1）表示信用证类别的词汇：

documentary L/C	跟单信用证
clean L/C	光票信用证
reciprocal L/C	对开信用证
irrevocable L/C	不可撤销信用证
back-to-back letter of credit	背对背信用证

（2）表示当事人的词汇：

party	当事人
applicant	开证申请人
beneficiary	受益人
issuing bank	开证行
advising/notifying bank	通知行
negotiating bank	议付行
reimbursing bank	偿付行

（3）表示运输的词汇：

partial shipment	分批装运
transshipment	转运
carrier	承运人
consignor/shipper	发货人
consignee	收货人

（4）表示单据的词汇：

invoice	发票
draft	汇票
packing list	装箱单
bill of lading (B/L)	提单
inspection certificate	检验证书
bona fide holder	善意持有人
proforma invoice	形式发票

2）多使用常见单词的生僻含义

英语的很多词语在不同情景中常具有不同的含义，信用证中的英语更是如此。许多常见的词语，在信用证中往往具有特定的专业意义，对此应从专业的角度来明确其含义，而不能将其作为普通词来理解，否则会导致信用证意思模糊不清。例如：

原文：We hereby engage with drawers and/or bona fide holders that drafts drawn in conformity with the terms of this credit will be duly accepted on presentation and duly honored at maturity.

译文：我们特此承诺，出票人和/或善意持票人只要提交根据本信用证条款开具的汇票，我们就及时承兑，而且一到期我们就及时支付。

本句中的 acceptance 不是"接受"之意，而是"承兑"；engage 意为"承诺"；honor 在信用证中的意义是指"兑现""承付"，而非"荣誉"。

3）多使用正式用语

信用证属于法律文书，文体较正式，经常使用一些书面用语以显得严谨、庄重。例如，在一般文体中，我们用 be going to do 或 be about to do 来表示将来。但在信用证中，这种方式几乎不会出现，而是用 shall/will 或 be to do。

4）多使用古体词语

古体词的使用在信用证中也是很常见的，其主要原因是为了避免重复，突出其严谨性，使得句子更加简练、正规、严肃。古体词是由 here、there 和 where 加上 after、by、from、in、on、to、under、upon、with 等词构成，例如：hereby=by means of（以此方式，特此）；herein=in this document（此中，在此文件中）；thereby=by that means（因此，在那方面）；therein=in that/in that particular（在那里，在那点上）。这些古体词虽然可以在词典上查到与之相对应的汉语含义，但实际运用起来却比较困难。因此，翻译时要弄清此类词的结构与语意之间的联系，在实际翻译中，具体的译文需灵活处理，不能完全依照对等原则翻译。例如：

① 原文：We hereby certify to the best of our knowledge that the foregoing statement is true and correct and all available information and date have been supplied herein, and that we agree to provide documentary proof upon your request.

译文：特此证明，据我们所知，上述声明内容真实，正确无误，并提供了全部现有的资料和数据。应贵方要求我们同意出具证明文件。

该句中的 hereby 译为"特此"，herein 未译出。再如：

② 原文：Now therefore, under the consideration of the mutual promises made by the parties of this agreement, the parties hereto agree the contents herein as follows.

译文：据此，以本协议双方相互承诺为对价，就下述内容达成一致。

该句中的 therefore 译为"据此"，hereto 和 herein 并未译出。

5）同义词并列使用

同义词在信用证中并列使用，其目的在于使原文所表达的含义不被曲解。因为并列成分之间通常意义交叉，可以在内容上互相补充，从而使表述更全面，更缜密严谨。例如：

原文：The seller agrees to sell and the buyer agrees to purchase the undermentioned commodity according to the terms and conditions stipulated below.

译文：买卖双方同意按下列条款买卖以下货物。

terms 在贸易文本中一般指付款、手续费、佣金等有关金钱的条件，而 conditions 则指其他条件，两者合译成"条款"。

6）多使用名词

信用证英语的名词性风格体现在采用"介词+抽象名词+介词"的结构中。这一结构能起到简洁和强调的作用，更符合外贸用语的风格。这类结构在句中作修饰成分，常充当状语，有时也可作表语或定语。翻译这类结构时，同样应根据上下文把握好其中名词的翻译；至于介词，可参照上下文和汉英间的差异，做出合适的翻译，一般转译成汉语的动词。例如：

① 原文：The content of the covering letter of credit shall be in strict conformity with the stipulations of the sales contract. In case of any variation thereof necessitating amendment of the L/C, the buyers shall bear the expenses for effecting the amendment.

译文：信用证内容须严格<u>符合</u>本售货合同的规定，否则修改信用证的费用由买方负担。

该句中"介词+名词+介词"结构在句中充当表语。再如：

② 原文：We contacted the beneficiaries <u>after receipt of</u> your amendment and were told that they would accept it provided the validity could be further extended to May 31.

译文：<u>收到</u>你方信用证修改书<u>后</u>，我方已联系受益人，被告知若有效期延至 5 月 31 日，他们将接受上述修改。

该句中的 after receipt of your amendment 相当于 after receiving the amendment，但前者使用名词化结构，更正式，更符合外贸用语的风格。该句中的"介词+抽象名词+介词"结构在句中充当状语。

（二）信用证的句法特点

1. 使用长句

信用证中多使用长句，这也是信用证作为法律文体的一种特点。信用证中的长句修饰成分较多，结构较复杂，大多是复合句，并很少使用标点符号。这种一气呵成、结构复杂的长句使文体显得庄重严谨，以免双方产生误解和纠纷。在翻译时，必须正确理解句子主干与其修饰成分，不能把连贯的意思拆开来译，否则会造成错误的理解。例如：

原文：We hereby agree with the drawers, endorsers and bona fide holders of the drafts drawn under and in compliance with the terms of this credit that such drafts shall be duly honored on due presentation and delivery of documents as herein specified.

译文：凡根据本信用证并按其所列条款而开具的汇票向我行提示并交出本证规定的单据者，我行同意对其出票人、背书人及善意持有人履行付款义务。

这是开证行在自由议付信用证中加列的保证文句。该句 agree with...of...中，drawers、endorsers 和 bona fide holders 是并列成分，为 agree with 的宾语；drafts drawn under and in compliance with the terms of this credit 为 of 的宾语；that such drafts...是 agree 的宾语从句，表述开证行履行付款义务的条件。

2. 使用条件句

在信用证中，需要阐明权利和义务时，必须要明确指出在什么情况下，什么时间和地点，以何种方式进行什么行动，因而会使用较多的条件句。信用证中引导条件句的词语表述方式较丰富。条件句的运用主要是开证行站在自己的角度，对受益人或第二方提出的一些限制。信用证中用来引导条件句的词语主要有：if、only if、in case、provided that 等。

（1）由 in case 引导的条件句，例如：

原文：<u>In case you want to make some amendments on the terms of the L/C</u>, please do not hesitate to communicate with us.

译文：<u>如贵方要修改信用证条款</u>，请立即同我们联系。

（2）由 provided that 引导的条件句，例如：

原文：<u>Provided that a bank uses the services of an advising bank to have the credit advised to the beneficiary</u>, it must also use the services of the same bank for advising an amendment.

译文：如果银行利用某一通知行的服务将信用证通知受益人，则它必须利用同一家银行的服务通知修改书。

通过对信用证英语用词和句型的分析，可以发现，信用证的翻译应遵循准确严谨、规范通顺的翻译原则。这个原则要求在翻译信用证的过程中必须透彻理解原文的精神实质，对原文内容准确把握；再现原文时应忠实、完整地传达原文内容，做到用词准确、术语统一、格式完整，避免出现译文文字上的随意性。

二、常用术语和表达

（一）常用术语

letter of credit (L/C)	信用证
form of credit	信用证形式
date of issue	开证日期
amendment	修改
sight L/C	即期信用证
usance L/C	远期信用证
revocable L/C	可撤销信用证
irrevocable L/C	不可撤销信用证
confirmed L/C	保兑信用证
unconfirmed L/C	不保兑信用证
transferable L/C	可转让信用证
nontransferable L/C	不可转让信用证
revolving L/C	循环信用证
reciprocal L/C	对开信用证
back to back L/C	背对背信用证
red clause L/C	红条款信用证
anticipatory L/C	预支信用证
Uniform Customs and Practice for Documentary Credits	跟单信用证统一惯例
beneficiary	受益人
guarantor	保证人
paying bank	付款行，汇入行
remitting bank	汇出行
opening/issuing bank	开证行
advising bank	通知行
payer	付款人
consignor	委托人，发货人
consignee	受托人，收货人
notifying bank	通知行

negotiating bank	议付行
confirming bank	保兑行
presenting bank	提示行
accepting bank	承兑行
pay bearer	付给持票人
bearer	持票人
drawer	出票人
endorse	背书
endorser	背书人
endorsee	被背书人
discount	贴现
holder	持票人
documents against payment	付款交单
documents against acceptance	承兑交单
letter of guarantee (L/G)	担保书
bank guarantee	银行保函
contract guarantee	合约保函
documents of title to the goods	物权凭证
authority to purchase (A/P)	委托购买证
letter of indication	印鉴证明书
letter of hypothecation	质押书
general letter of hypothecation	总质押书
signed commercial invoice	已签署的商业发票
in duplicate	一式两份
in triplicate	一式三份
in quadruplicate	一式四份
in quintuplicate	一式五份
in sextuplicate	一式六份
in septuplicate	一式七份
in octuplicate	一式八份
in nonuplicate	一式九份
in decuplicate	一式十份

（二）常用表达

① drafts to be accompanied by the documents marked... below
汇票须随附下列注有……的单据

② accompanied by the following documents marked... in duplicate
随附下列注有……的单据一式两份

③ Drafts drawn under this credit must contain the clause "Drafts drawn under the Bank of

China of credit No. 123 dated 180418".

本信用证项下开具的汇票须注明"本汇票系凭中国银行2018年4月18日第123号信用证下开具"的条款。

④ Drafts are to be drawn in duplicate to our order bearing the clause "Drawn under United Malayan Banking Corp. Bhd. irrevocable letter of credit No. 20 dated July 12, 2018".

汇票一式两份，以我行为抬头，并注明"根据马来西亚联合银行2018年7月12日第20号不可撤销信用证项下开立"。

⑤ Beneficiary's original signed commercial invoices at least in 8 copies issued in the name of the buyer indicating (showing/evidencing/specifying) the merchandise, country of origin and any other relevant information.

以买方的名义开具注明商品名称、原产国及其他有关资料并经签署的受益人的商业发票正本至少一式八份。

⑥ Full set of clean on board bill(s) of lading marked "Freight Prepaid" to order of shipper endorsed to… Bank, notifying buyers.

全套清洁已装船提单应注明"运费付讫"，以装船人为抬头，背书给……银行，通知头方。

⑦ 买方应通过卖方可接受的银行于装运月份前30天开立并送达卖方不可撤销的即期信用证，有效期至装运月份后15天在中国议付。

The buyer shall open through a bank acceptable to the seller irrevocable sight letter of credit to reach the seller 30 days before the month of shipment, valid for negotiation in China until the 15th day after the month of shipment.

⑧ 合同价值应由以制造商为受益人100%保兑的不可撤销信用证支付，信用证须在下订单时开具并保兑，并且在递送单据时即可支付。

Payment shall be made by 100% of the contract value out of an irrevocable and confirmed letter of credit, in the principal's favour, opened with and confirmed at the moment of placing the order and payable against sending documents.

⑨ 付款将通过无追索权的保兑的不可撤销信用证支付，60天即期汇票向南京的议付行提交议付。乙方应向甲方支付发票金额的2%作为60天延迟付款的利息费用。每次订单的信用证应在装货期前45天到达甲方。

Payment is to be made by confirmed, irrevocable letter of credit, without recourse, available by 60 days sight draft upon presentation of shipping documents to the negotiating bank in Nanjing. Party B shall pay Party A 2% of invoice value as interest charges for the 60 days delayed payment. The letter of credit for each order shall reach Party A 45 days before the date of shipment.

⑩ 保兑的不可撤销的无追索权的以中国远洋运输集团为受益人的信用证，合同货物全部货款为美元，凭即期汇票并附运输单据向装运港的中国银行议付。

By confirmed, irrevocable L/C without recourse in favour of COSCO for the total value of the contracted goods in USD, payable at sight against presentation of shipping documents to the Bank of China in the port of loading.

⑪ 80%发票金额凭即期光票支付，其余20%即期付款交单。100%发票金额的全套货运单

据随附于托收项下，于申请人付清发票全部金额后交单。

80% of the invoice value is available against clean draft at sight while the remaining 20% of documents shall be held against payment at sight under this credit. The full set of the shipping documents of 100% invoice value shall accompany the collection item and shall only be released after full payment of the invoice value.

⑫ 货款 60%以不可撤销即期信用证支付。其余 40%托收，见票后 30 天付款交单，按发票金额全部付款后，全套货运单据到达买方。

60% of the value of goods by irrevocable sight L/C at sight and remaining 40% on collection basis, D/P at 30 days after sight. The full set of shipping documents are to be delivered to the buyer until full payment of invoice value is made.

Section 4 巩 固 练 习

一、翻译以下短语。

1. telegraphic transfer
2. bona fide holder
3. issuing bank
4. acceptance
5. clean L/C
6. presentation
7. sight draft
8. bill of lading
9. letter of guarantee
10. date of expiry
11. 跟单信用证
12. 装箱单
13. 托收
14. 委托人
15. 汇付
16. 保险单
17. 议付行
18. 商业发票
19. 清洁已装船提单
20. 原产地证明

二、翻译以下句子。

1. Signed commercial invoice in triplicate and goods specified on the invoice are in strict conformity with the goods mentioned in proforma invoice.

2. Full set of clean on board ocean bills of lading made out to order and blank endorsed.

3. By confirmed, irrevocable L/C without recourse in favour of COSCO for the total value of the contracted goods in USD, payable at sight against presentation of shipping documents to the Bank of China in the port of loading.

4. Certificate of origin issued by the chamber of commerce of the exporting country submitted with the original shipping documents.

5. The buyers shall pay 10% of the total value of the contract as deposit within 7 days after conclusion of the contract. The other payment (that is 90% of the total value of the contract) shall pay by irrevocable documentary sight letter of credit.

6. 按照双方商定，付款是 100%保兑的不可撤销的以我方为受益人的见票即付的信用证。该信用证必须在装运前一个月开到卖方，并在上述装运期后 15 天在香港议付有效。

7. 以买方的名义开具注明商品名称、原产国及其他有关资料并经签署的受益人的商业发票正本至少一式八份。

8. 偿付行的费用应由开证行承担。然而，假如费用系由受益人承担，则开证行有责任在信用证和偿付授权书中予以注明，且该费用应在偿付时从支付索偿行的金额中扣除。

9. 除商业发票外，其他单据中的货物、服务或行为描述若须规定，可使用统称，但不得与信用证规定的描述相矛盾。

10. 付款将通过保兑的不可撤销的无追索权的信用证支付，60 天即期汇票向南京的议付行提交议付。乙方应向甲方支付发票金额的 2%作为 60 天延迟付款的利息费用。每次订单的信用证应在装货期前 45 天到达甲方。

三、翻译以下两段话。

1. An issuing bank is irrevocably bound by an amendment as of the time it issues the amendment. A confirming bank may extend its confirmation to an amendment and will be irrevocably bound as of the time it advises the amendment. A confirming bank may, however, choose to advise an amendment without extending its confirmation and, if so, it must inform the issuing bank without delay and inform the beneficiary in its advice. The terms and conditions of the original credit (or a credit incorporating previously accepted amendments) will remain in force for the beneficiary until the beneficiary communicates its acceptance of the amendment to the bank that advised such amendment. The beneficiary should give notification of acceptance or rejection of an amendment. If the beneficiary fails to give such notification, a presentation that complies with the credit and to any not yet accepted amendment will be deemed to be notification of acceptance by the beneficiary of such amendment. As of that moment the credit will be amended.

2. 倘若规定的单据被提交至被指定银行或开证行并构成相符提示，开证行必须按下述信用证所适用的情形予以兑付：

（1）由开证行即期付款、延期付款或者承兑；

（2）由被指定银行即期付款而该被指定银行未予付款；

（3）由被指定银行延期付款而该被指定银行未承担其延期付款承诺，或者虽已承担延期付款承诺但到期未予付款；

（4）由被指定银行承兑而该被指定银行未予承兑以其为付款人的汇票，或者虽已承兑以其为付款人的汇票但到期未予付款；

（5）由被指定银行议付而该被指定银行未予议付。

自信用证开立之时起，开证行即不可撤销地受到兑付责任的约束。

开证行保证向对于相符提示已经予以兑付或者议付并将单据寄往开证行的被指定银行进行偿付。无论被指定银行是否于到期日前已经对相符提示予以预付或者购买，对于承兑或延期付款信用证项下相符提示的金额的偿付于到期日进行。开证行偿付被指定银行的承诺独立于开证行对于受益人的承诺。

Chapter 10

商 务 索 赔

Section 1 概 述

一、索赔的定义

在执行合同的过程中,签约双方都应该严格遵守合同中的各项规定,履行其义务。任何一方失信违约,都将给对方带来麻烦,更甚之,会给对方造成经济损失。此时,受损方对责任方未能全部或部分履行合同规定的责任和义务,通常有权提出索赔。索赔是指遭受损害的一方在争议后,根据合同或法律,向违约方(责任方)提出赔偿要求。

二、索赔条款

索赔条款,就是索赔条件,即在磋商交易中,对将来发生违约如何索赔的问题作出规定,并订入合同,成为合同的交易条件之一,以便双方遵守。争议与索赔条款的主要内容,是规定买方对于卖方所交货物的品质、数量、包装等方面提出异议或索赔的限期,以及规定卖方对于买方因违约,如不按期开证或付款等,使卖方遭到损失时,有权取消合同并向买方提出索赔。一般进出口合同索赔条款的订法有两种。

(1)买方在目的口岸卸货后90天内,如发现货物的品质及/或数量/重量与合同或发票不符,除属于保险公司及/或船公司应该负责的索赔外,可根据相关出入境商品检验检疫部门出具的证书向卖方提出索赔。如果是FOB价格条件时,重量如有短缺,买方有权同时就短量部分进行索赔。

(2)如买方不能按约开证,卖方有权不通知买方而取消合同的全部或部分,或延迟全部或部分交货,同时有权对因此而造成的任何损失向买方提出索赔。

三、商务索赔信函

索赔信函是合同任何一方,以双方签订的合同条款为依据,具体指出对方违反合同条款的事实,提出要求赔偿损失或者其他权利,同时又为妥善解决问题所写的信函。写好索赔信函是问题得到解决的第一步。商务索赔信函主要由以下几大部分组成。

（1）提及订货日期，装运期及货物名称。
（2）提出对货物不满的原因。
（3）对提出索赔表示抱歉。
（4）提出解决问题的建议。
索赔信函应有理、有节、有证、有据，正当地提出赔偿要求。

四、索赔时应该注意的问题

进行索赔时首先应当证件齐全，并用书面文本正式提出索赔要求。例如：卖方向买方索赔时，如索赔证件不全或不足，对方很可能拒赔；同样，买方向卖方索赔时，如果证件不齐全，卖方亦可不予受理。

索赔证件包括检验证明、索赔清单、有关费用单据，以及该批货物的发票、提单、装箱单等。卖方提出索赔的商检证件或有关证件要合理、科学。当买方向卖方索赔时，卖方不仅要审核检验证件，而且要审核检验方法是否合理、科学。在写索赔函时，要提出具体的索赔项目、要求、金额，凡由于对方违约造成的费用和花销，都应向对方开列清单，全部索取。当发现问题时，可先用函电提出保留索赔权，当索赔证件准备齐全后，再正式书面提出。

五、商务索赔的责任范围

在商务索赔中，为了分清何种损失向卖方索赔，何种损失向运输部门索赔，何种损失向保险公司索赔，就需要了解国际贸易中上述三方责任范围的国际惯例。

1. 卖方的主要责任

（1）数量不足。
（2）质量与合同不符。
（3）规格与合同不符。
（4）包装不良使货物受损。
（5）未按规定时间交货。

上述 5 种情况，除了卖方不按期交货，买方可根据合同收取逾期费用外，其他几项内容都可向卖方提出索赔。若买方提出的理由不充分，卖方可拒赔。

2. 运输部门的主要责任

（1）货物数量少于提货单所列数量，经运输部门负责人（如船长）签认，并非由于托运人短装的。
（2）货物在运输途中发生残损和潮湿。

3. 保险公司的主要责任

（1）在保险的范围内，由于自然灾害或意外事故发生的货物缺损。
（2）在保险的范围内，运输部门不予赔偿的损失或赔偿数额不足，应补偿保险人的损失。

在商务索赔中，某些情况下，卖方也有权向买方提出索赔，如买方拒开或迟开信用证，或属于离岸价，买方不能及时将货物运走，使卖方受到损失时，即会发生卖方向买方索赔。

六、索赔期限

商务索赔必须特别重视索赔期限。

1. 向卖方索赔

要按合同规定的索赔期限提出,因此,合同中必须明确规定索赔期限,否则当买方提出索赔时,卖方可能会抵赖推卸。

2. 向运输部门索赔

按照《1978年联合国海上货物运输公约》规定,交货后两年内提出索赔都是有效的。但买方在提出索赔时,必须持有船长签认的货物短缺证件。有的国家规定,如卸货时发生短缺,应立即取得船长的证件;如卸货时未发现,而后来发现的,必须在三天之内向船长取得短缺证件,这些证件须有理货员、船长、货主三方认可。

3. 向保险公司索赔

应在保险单规定的期限内提出,收货人须特别注意的是,如货物在港口仓库验收时就发现损失,应暂停验收,立即致函保险公司派员查验,出具查验报告;如货物进入收货人仓库后验收发现损失,应立即致函保险公司,并停止继续开验;如货船中途遇险,收货人在接到轮船公司通知后应立即致函保险公司。

七、商务索赔信函样本

Dear Sirs,

150 Cases of Green Tea under Contract No. FD543

We thank you very much for delivering the green tea under our contract No. FD543 so promptly. However, we feel it regrettable that only 147 cases were received by us. Your carrier was unable to explain the shortage, so 3 cases of green tea are missing.

As is evidenced by the clean bill of lading, our shipping order and your mate's receipt, it is obvious that the shortage is due to your fault. In fact, our customers are pressing us for a timely delivery and we are still in need of the full quantity we ordered. We shall be very pleased if you inquire into the matter and arrange to dispatch the remaining 3 cases as soon as possible. Otherwise, we shall reserve the right to claim on you for the shortage.

Your early clarification and settlement of the case will be appreciated.

Yours faithfully,
×××

Section 2 译例分析

Passage One

Dear Sirs,

The goods you shipped per S. S. "Goddess" on 15th last month arrived here yesterday.[1]

On examination, we have found that many of the desk lamps are severely damaged, though the cases themselves show no trace of damage.

Considering this damage was due to the rough handling by the steamship company, we claimed[2] on them for recovery of the loss. But an investigation made by the surveyor has revealed the fact that the damage is attributable to improper packing. For further particulars, we refer you to the surveyor's report enclosed.

We are, therefore, compelled to[3] claim on you to compensate us for the loss, $160, which we have sustained by the damage to the goods.

We trust that you will be kind enough to accept this claim and deduct the sum claimed from the amount of your next invoice to us.[4]

Yours faithfully,

Key Words

examination	验货
claim	索赔
rough handling	粗暴搬运，野蛮装卸
be attributable to	归因于
be compelled to do sth.	被迫做某事
sustain	遭受，经受，蒙受
deduct	扣除
further particulars	详细情况

Notes

1. 商务信函多采用礼貌客气的措辞，所以这里的 you 可以翻译成"贵方"。S. S.是 steamship（轮船）的缩写。

2. lodge a claim against sb. for an amount for a reason on sth 表示对于某物因为某种原因而向某人索赔一笔金额。可用于此句型的动词还有 file、raise、register、lay、put in 等。

表示向某人索赔，一般用介词 against、with 或 on，例如：
a claim against the underwriters 向保险公司索赔
表示索赔的原因，一般用介词 for 或 on，例如：
a claim for/on damaged goods   由于货物损坏而索赔
表示索赔的金额一般用介词 for，例如：
a claim for US$20,000 索赔 2 万美元
accept a claim   接受索赔
entertain a claim   考虑并接受索赔
reject a claim   拒绝索赔
withdraw a claim   撤回索赔
settle a claim   解决索赔，理赔

3. 此处的 be compelled to 译为"不得不"更加委婉且符合习惯。

4. deduct the sum claimed from the amount of your next invoice to us. 从下次给我方的发票金额中扣除该笔索赔费用。the amount of 译为"……的金额"。

 参考译文

敬启者：

贵方上月 15 日由"女神"号货轮运来的货物已于昨日抵达。

我方验货时发现，尽管货箱并无损坏的痕迹，但许多台灯却严重受损。我方以为损坏是由船运公司方面野蛮装卸所致，但公正行调查证实损坏是因包装不当所致。特此附上公证人报告书以供贵方了解详情。

因此，我们不得不要求贵方赔偿我方蒙受的货物损坏费 160 美元。相信贵方会接受这一索赔，并将这笔赔偿金额从下次给我方的发票总额中扣除。

谨上

>> Passage Two

尊敬的×××：

有关第 578 号销售合约的 200 吨面粉问题。[1]

货物已于 4 月 20 日运抵本公司，并已于 5 月 17 日传真告知相关事宜。但我们不得不因短重问题而向你方提出索赔。[2]

检查货物时，我们发现有 180 袋破损，估计损失 900 千克。其后安排进行检验，有关报告与估计的损失相符。该报告指出这次损失是由于包装袋不符合标准所致，故应由贵公司负责此损失。[3]

现按照报告结果向贵公司索偿：

损失面粉：200 美元

检验费：50 美元

合计：250 美元

随函附上第 6724 号检验报告，烦请早日解决赔偿事宜。

谨上

Key Words

销售合约	sales contract
货物	consignment
向你方提出索赔	lodge a claim with you
检查	inspection
短重	short weight
按照	on the strength of
检验费	survey charges
检验报告	survey report

Notes

1. 第一句首先指明订单号或合同交易事项。这句话缺少主语，因此在翻译时，根据商务英文索赔信函的表达习惯，我们可以翻译成 we refer to，而"问题"是范畴词，在这里省略不译。

2. 该句直接、简要说明索赔原因。这一个句子是由三个小分句组成，其中第二个小分句省略了主语"我方"。考虑到前两句与后一句的转折关系，以及商务信函语言的简洁性，我们可以将前两个小分句通过从句巧妙地译到一起，所以可以处理成 We telexed you on May 17 informing you that the consignment arrived on April 20。

3. 索赔通常以官方的鉴定证明为支撑，切不可妄自提出赔偿，给出索赔内容。受损失方可根据损失提出索赔，对方也有权对事情查证后进行理赔，如受损失方的情况不属实或索赔不合理，对方可以拒绝理赔。"该报告指出这次损失是由于包装袋不符合标准所致，故应由贵公司负责此损失"可以译成 The report indicates that the loss was due to the use of substandard bags for which you, the suppliers, are responsible。在翻译"包装袋不符合标准"时，通常会采用动宾搭配的方式来处理，如 do not meet the standards。但是这样的翻译显得啰唆且不地道，所以我们可以将它处理成偏正结构 substandard bags，这是英汉互译中非常常用的技巧。此外，后半句也可以用定语从句来译，这样更加简洁。

 参考译文

Dear Sirs,

We refer to sales contract No. 578 covering the purchase of 200 tons of flour.

We telexed you on May 17 informing you that the consignment arrived on April 20. But we are compelled to lodge a claim with you for the short weight.

On inspection, we found that 180 bags had burst and that the contents estimated at 900 kg had been irretrievably lost. We proceeded to have a survey report made. The report has now confirmed our initial findings. The report indicates that the loss was due to the use of substandard bags for which you, the suppliers, are responsible.

On the strength of the survey report, we hereby register our claim against you as follows:

Short delivered quantity: US$ 200

Survey charges: US$ 50

Total claimed: US$ 250

We enclosed survey report No. TS6724 and look forward to an early settlement of the claim.

Yours truly,

Section 3 实 践 总 结

一、翻译技巧

（一）英语商务索赔信函的语言特点

1. 多采用礼貌客气的措辞

在外贸业务中，每笔业务的达成，无不与贸易双方的密切合作有关。因此，礼貌的用语与客气的措辞不仅能体现外贸工作者自身的文化素质，树立外贸企业的良好形象，还会给贸易双方的合作营造一个友好的氛围，有利于促进贸易往来，建立良好的贸易关系。即使是索赔信函也应注意措辞的礼貌和委婉。

2. 在代词使用方面，多采用"个人参与"模式

英语商务索赔信函的另一个语言特点就是"个人参与"（personal participation），即在信函中经常会出现一些"我方……""贵方……"之类的话。在商务索赔信函中，之所以强调"个人参与"，就是为了使读信人产生亲切感，不至于让信函显得冷冰冰。

"个人参与"的模式具体表现为：在英语商务索赔信函写作中，通常会采取 You-attitude（对方态度）。主语的选择通常为 you，几乎不使用 I-attitude（我方态度），必要时也要用 We-attitude 代替 I-attitude。所谓的 You-attitude，就是将自己置于对方的立场上，充分考虑对方的要求、需要、利益、愿望和感觉，尊重、体谅和赞誉对方。因为从公司发出的每一封信函都代表公司的形象，所以从对方的观点来看问题，看到对方的处境，了解对方的问题和困难，可以使自己的要求显得更加切合实际和可以理解，还可以有助于避免尴尬，促进贸易双方的进一步合作。

3. 多使用书面语、专业术语和专业缩略词

在英语商务索赔信函中，为体现正式、庄重与严肃性，较少使用口语化的介词，而多用较复杂的介词短语，例如：

in view of	考虑到，鉴于
prior to	在……之前
as per	按照
in accordance with	按照，依照

另外，还有一些由 here、there 和 where 加上 after、at、by、from、in、of、to、under、upon、with 等介词共同构成的副词，如 hereafter、hereby、thereby、whereas、whereby 等，虽然在日常英语中很少使用，但由于其带有浓厚的法律语体和正式语体色彩，因而常出现在英语商务索赔信函中，以显示其行文的严肃性和法律意味。此外，这些古体词也可以避免表达上不必要的重复，从而使语言更加简练。例如：

原文：With reference to Clause 18 of the contract, we hereby place our claims before you as follows.

译文：根据合同条款第18条，我方向你方提出如下索赔。

（二）英语商务索赔信函的 7C 原则

（1）Correctness——准确：商务索赔信函要表达准确，不能言过其实；要用正确的语言把信息传递给对方。

（2）Conciseness——简洁：避免使用冗长的表达，尽量使用简洁的表达。

（3）Clearness——清楚：选择简明易懂的词语，避免使用意义不清楚的词语和句子。信函内容应条理清楚，逻辑性强。

（4）Completeness——完整：写信人应该提供给对方所需要的信息，或答复来信所提出的全部问题和要求。

（5）Concreteness——具体：具体的文字能使阅信人产生明确的印象和观念，应避免使用抽象或笼统的词语。

（6）Courtesy——礼貌：一封彬彬有礼的书信可以博取对方的好感，使对方乐意与你合作或者进一步友好解决争议问题。

（7）Consideration——体谅：写信时要多为对方着想，多从对方的角度看问题，把双方的距离缩小，使对方认真考虑信中所言。

一封得体的商务索赔信函不仅应具有上面所提到的 7 个方面的语言特点，而且还要特别注意语气的亲切自然，避免生硬和过分夸张。这是因为，无论是哪一种商务信函，写信人使用的语气可以反映出写信人和收信人之间的关系。在给客户写英语商务索赔信函时，一般采用恭敬礼貌、积极合作的语气。即使在表示不满或责问时，在英语商务索赔信函中也要注重讲究策略。

（三）常见错误辨析实例

【例 1】

原文：买方有权要求替换质量低劣的货物。

The buyers are appointed to ask for replacement of the goods which are found defective. ［错句］

The buyers are entitled to ask for replacement of the goods which are found defective. ［正句］

解析："有权利/有资格做……"可以用 be entitled to do 来表达，也可以用 reserve the right to do 或者 have the right of doing/to do 来表达。例如：

① This office reserves the right to accept any offer it chooses.

招标单位有选定中标单位的权利。

② The buyers have the right to reinspect/of reinspecting the goods upon arrival even though inspection has been made of the goods before shipment.

即使货物在装运前已经检验，买方也有权在货到时复验。

【例 2】

原文：我方用户正就低劣质量向我方提出抱怨。

Our end-users are complaining on the inferior quality against us. ［错句］

Our end-users are complaining of the inferior quality against us. ［正句］

解析：动词 complain 表示"抱怨，申诉"，后接介词 of，而不是 on，有时也可以接 about。另外，需要注意 complain 在下列句子中的搭配结构。例如：

① The buyers complained about the poor packing of this shipment.

买主抱怨这批货包装低劣。

② They have to complain that the seller has not yet made delivery of the goods ordered two months ago.

卖方还没有交付两个月前定购的货物，对此，他们不得不提出抱怨。

③ We have to complain to you of the damage taken place in transit.

我们不得不投诉你方在运输途中的损坏。

【例 3】

原文：公司经理坚持要仔细调查该索赔案件。

The manager of the company insisted that the claim be gone onto carefully. ［错句］

The manager of the company insisted that the claim be gone into carefully. ［正句］

解析："调查，检查"用介词短语 go into 表达，而不是用 go onto，也可以用 investigate 或者 look into 来表达。例如：

① We have investigated the matter and found your claim perfectly justified.

我们已调查了此案，并发现你方提出的索赔确实有道理。

② They have promised to look into the matter.

他们已答应调查此事。

③ The new regulation goes into effect today.

新章程即日生效。

④ We shall go farther into your order after receipt of your detailed specifications.

在接到你方详细规格后，我方再进一步研究你方订单。

【例 4】

原文：我们已开出以你方为受益人的信用证。

We have established a letter of credit for your benefit. ［错句］

We have established a letter of credit in your favor. ［正句］

解析："以……为受益人"翻译成 in one's favor，而 for one's benefit 意思是"为……利益"，二者意思截然不同。例如：

① We assure you of every cooperation and by joint efforts, continue our business for our mutual benefit.

为了双方的利益，我们保证通力合作并通过共同努力继续我们的业务。

② We shall thank you for any favor you can do me.

如蒙关照则不胜感谢。

③ This article not only sells best in Africa, but also meets with great favor in Europe.

这种商品不仅在非洲很畅销，而且在欧洲也很受欢迎。

④ Your goods that you offer us are much in favor on our market.

你方报给我们的货物在我们的市场颇受好评。

⑤ Our bankers have issued an irrevocable L/C No. 2458 in favor of ABC Trading Co, Ltd.

我行已开出 2458 号不可撤销的信用证，受益人是 ABC 贸易公司。

⑥ Our manager is in favor of the suggestion that we accompany the sale of our electric products with a free gift.

我们经理赞成这个建议：在销售电器时随送赠品。

【例 5】

原文：对于不合格的货物，买方有权提出索赔。

The buyer has the right to lodge a claim for the defective goods. ［错句］

The buyer has the right to lodge a claim on the defective goods. ［正句］

解析：表示"对某货物提出索赔"，货物前面应用介词 on，而不是 for，也可以用 against。在表示索赔原因时，原因前面可用介词 for 或者 on。例如：

① The buyer raised a claim against this consignment in respect of quality.

买主就这批货的质量问题提出了索赔。

② We file a claim against you for the short delivery of 250 lbs.

我们向你方提出短交 250 磅的索赔。

③ Your claim on improper packing has been settled.

你方对包装不良所提出的索赔已受理完毕。

④ They have made a claim with the insurance company on account of all the lost incurred in the transit.

对运输途中遭受的全部损失,他们已向保险公司提出了索赔。

⑤ We are therefore putting in a formal claim for the sum of RMB 1,000.

因此,我方正式提出索赔金额人民币 1 000 元。

⑥ We hereby notify you that we reserve the right to register/lay a claim on you for the shortage.

兹通知你方,我们有权对短装之事向你方提出索赔。

⑦ The client has withdrawn the claim he raised last month.

客户已撤回了他上个月提出的索赔。

⑧ You should claim a compensation of US$ 10,000 from the insurance company for the damage.

你方应就损失向保险公司提出 10 000 美元的索赔。

【例 6】

原文:20 箱丢失了。

20 cases were missing. [错句]

Twenty cases were missing. [正句]

解析:一般而言,如果句首出现了数字,通常宜用字母拼写方式。但要注意,如果句首是年份,则用数字为好。例如:

① Four overseas offices of our company received the invitation.

我公司的四个驻外办事处均收到了该邀请。

② 1988 was a good year for business.

1988 年那一年生意非常兴隆。

二、常用术语和表达

(一) 常用术语

claim arising from a defect of the goods	货物瑕疵引起的索赔
inspection certification	检验证书
missing articles	丢失的货物
put the matter right	更正此事
discharge receipt	卸货收据
in connection with	关于,与……有关
be liable for damage	有赔偿损失的责任

on examination	经检验
claim against a person	向某人提出索赔
in no case	在任何情况下都不
short weight	短重
short shipment	短货，短装
short delivery	短交，缺交
short-calculated	少算的
short-delivered	短交，缺交的
short-established	少开的
short-invoiced	发票少开的
short-landed	短卸的
short-opened	少开的
short-paid	少付的
short-shipped	短装的
survey report	检验报告
survey report on quality	品质鉴定证明书
survey report on weight	重量鉴定证明书
statement of claim	索赔清单
have complaints about	对……投诉
settle a complaint/complaints	解决投诉
draw attention	引起注意
sustain losses	蒙受损失
make a claim for damage	要求赔偿损失
take responsibility	负责，承担责任
faulty goods	次品
have no choice but	别无选择只有……
look into the matter	调查此事
claim on sth.	为某货物索赔
put us in no small trouble	给我们造成很大的麻烦
have a thorough investigation of sth.	全面调查某事
meet sb. halfway	各让一半
reserve the right	保留权利

（二）常用表达

（1）提及订单日期、提货日期和所索赔的货物名称，常见的表达有：

① Our order of...

② Referring to the goods we ordered on...

③ As we pointed out, our order...

④ We refer to our letter/telephone call/telegram of...

⑤ We have received the goods of our order for...

写清楚订单日期及相关货物的名称，可以帮助责任方轻易地把握信的内容，也便于责任方调查事情的原因和经过，然后作出相应的补救或补偿措施。

（2）说明（对货物）不满的原因，并要求对方给出解释。一般来说，买方会就以下情况提出索赔。

① The wrong goods may have been sent.
② The quality may not be satisfactory.
③ The goods may have been delivered damaged or late.
④ The prices charged may be excessive, or not as agreed.
⑤ Short weight or short quantities.
⑥ Lack of shipping documents or wrong amount No. in documents.

根据不同的情况，我们通常使用以下表达：

A.
① When unpacking the case, we found that...
② On examination we found that...
③ We were surprised to find that...
④ The color/weight/is unsatisfactory.
⑤ The goods do not agree with the original pattern.
⑥ The quality is inferior to that of the sample.
⑦ The contents do not agree with your advice note/packing note/invoice.
⑧ Some of the goods have been damaged in transit/transport.

B.
① On checking your invoice/statement, we find that...
② When comparing your invoice/statement with our order, we find that...
③ You show an invoice No.... for $200 of which we have no trace.
④ You have listed/shown your invoice No.... with $250 instead of $150.
⑤ You have omitted your credit note No.... for $50.

（3）对提出索赔表示抱歉。常见的表达有：

① Much to our regret...
② We very much regret to...
③ Best regretful to lodge/raise/file/put in/bring up a claim against you for...

（4）就如何处理索赔事宜，向对方提出建议。常见的表达有：

① As the goods are urgently needed/required...
② As these goods/articles/qualities we specially ordered for the spring season...
③ As the demand for these qualities has now ceased...
④ Unless the good can be dispatched/shipped immediately/at once...
⑤ We must request you to dispatch them without further delay.
⑥ We must now insist on immediate delivery/shipment/execution of our order.
⑦ We have to ask you to cancel our order/contract.

⑧ Please give this matter your immediate/urgent attention.
⑨ Please let us know/inform us by return/telegram/by cable when we can expect delivery.
⑩ We are expecting/waiting for your reply/confirmation/advice by return of post.

Section 4 巩 固 练 习

一、翻译以下短语。

1. outturn weight
2. faulty packing
3. inferior quality
4. lodge a claim against sb.
5. at one's disposal

6. 短装
7. 野蛮装卸
8. 装运延误
9. 鉴于
10. 调查

二、翻译以下句子。

1. We were surprised to find that the quality is inferior to that of the sample.

2. Five cases of the shipment were badly damaged when delivered on 8th.

3. We shall lodge a claim against you for all the losses on the last shipment for the amount of £1,000.

4. On the basis of Clause 18 of the contract, we hereby place our claims before you as follows.

5. We enclose a survey report in support of our claim.

6. 由于包装不善，约有 1/3 的玻璃器皿已经破碎，我方客户对此十分失望。

7. 非常遗憾，我们收到的货物尺码、形状与我们所订购的货物不符。我们要求尽快更换为我们所订的产品。

8. 由于贵方装运来的我方第 586 号订单项下的船货质量与商定的规格不符，我们只能向贵方提出索赔。

9. 我们将寄给你证明文件作为我们索赔的依据。

10. 由于你方未能按时交货，我方将向你方提出由此而遭受的全部损失的索赔。

三、翻译以下两封信函。

1.

Dear Sirs,

We are writing to inform you that the toys covered by our order No.519 arrived in such an unsatisfactory condition that we have to lodge a claim against you. It was found upon examination that 10% of them are broken and some are badly scratched, obviously due to the improper packing. Therefore, we cannot offer them for sale at the normal price and suggest that you make us an allowance of 20% on the invoiced cost. This is the amount by which we propose to reduce our selling price. If you cannot accept, I am afraid we shall have to return them for replacement.

Sincerely yours,

2.

敬启者：

事由：短装索赔

第 FA7708 号销售确认书项下 1 500 箱蘑菇罐头，已由"永丰"轮于 4 月 10 日运抵。遗憾的是，我们在提货时发现少了 145 箱。轮船公司告诉我们只有 1 355 箱装船。

由于短装数量大，请在交付最后三个品种时，将这 145 箱补交。请你们核对一下，当时在装运港 1 500 箱是否全都装上了船。

盼早复。

谨上

Chapter 11

商 务 仲 裁

Section 1 概 述

一、仲裁的含义

仲裁是指由双方当事人根据他们之前订立的仲裁协议,自愿将其争议提交由非司法机构的仲裁员组成的仲裁庭进行裁判,并受该裁判约束的一种制度。仲裁活动和法院的审判活动一样,关乎当事人的实体权益,是解决民事争议的方式之一。商业仲裁是指买卖双方在纠纷发生之前或发生之后,签订书面协议,自愿将纠纷提交双方所同意的第三者予以裁决,以解决纠纷的一种方式。

仲裁协议是指合同当事人通过在合同中订明仲裁条款、签订独立仲裁协议或采用其他方式达成的就有关争议提交仲裁的书面协议。它是仲裁得以进行的法定前提。仲裁协议有两种形式:一种是在争议发生之前订立的,它通常作为合同中的一项仲裁条款出现;另一种是在争议之后订立的,它是把已经发生的争议提交给仲裁的协议。这两种形式的仲裁协议,其法律效力是相同的。

二、仲裁的分类

1. 国内仲裁和涉外仲裁

根据所处理的纠纷是否具有涉外因素,仲裁可分为国内仲裁和涉外仲裁。前者是该国当事人之间为解决没有涉外因素的国内民商事纠纷的仲裁;后者是处理涉及外国或外法域的民商事务争议的仲裁。

2. 临时仲裁和机构仲裁

根据是否存在常设的专门仲裁机构,仲裁可以分为临时仲裁和机构仲裁。临时仲裁是当事人根据仲裁协议,将他们之间的争议交给临时组成的仲裁庭而非常设性仲裁机构进行审理并作出裁决意见书的仲裁;机构仲裁是当事人根据其仲裁协议,将他们之间的纠纷提交给某一常设性仲裁机构所进行的仲裁。

3. 依法仲裁和友好仲裁

根据仲裁裁决的依据不同，仲裁可分为依法仲裁和友好仲裁。依法仲裁是指仲裁庭依据一定的法律规定对纠纷进行裁决；友好仲裁是指依当事人的授权，依据他所认为的公平的标准作出对当事有约束力的裁决。

Section 2 译例分析

Passage One

AWARD[1]

PARTIES
1. Claimant/counter-defendant: Seller
2. Defendant/counter-claimant: Buyer

FACTS

In 1996, the parties concluded three contracts for the sale of a product according to certain contract specifications. The buyer paid 90% of the price payable under each of the contracts upon presentation of the shipping documents, as contractually agreed[2].

The product delivered pursuant to the first and third contracts met the contract specifications. The conformity of the second consignment was disputed prior to its shipment. When the product was again inspected upon arrival, it was found that it did not meet the contract specifications. The product was eventually sold by the buyer to third parties at considerable loss, after having undergone a certain treatment to make it more saleable[3].

The seller initiated arbitration proceedings to recover the 10% balance[4] remaining due under the contracts. The buyer filed a counterclaim alleging that the seller's claim should be set off against the amounts which the buyer estimates to be payable to the buyer by the seller, i.e., the direct losses, financing costs, lost profits and interest[5].

APPLICABLE LAW

1. The contract contains no provisions regarding the substantive law. Accordingly that law has to be determined by the arbitrators in accordance with Art. 13 (3) of the ICC rules. Under that article, the arbitrators will apply the law designated as the proper law by the rule of conflicts which they deem appropriate.

2. The contract is between a seller and a buyer of different nationalities for delivery in a third

country. The sale was FOB so that the transfer of risks to the buyer took place (in the country of the seller. The country of the seller accordingly appears as being the jurisdiction to which the sale is most closely related.

3. The *Hague Convention* on the law applicable to international sales of goods dated 15 June 1995 regarding sales contracts, refers as governing law to the law of the seller's current residence[6]. The country of the buyer has adhered to the *Hague Convention*, not the country of the seller. However, the general trend in conflicts of law is to apply the domestic law of the current residence of the debtor of the essential undertaking arising under the contract[7]. That debtor in a sales contract is the seller. Based on those combined findings, the law of the country of the seller appears to be the proper law governing the contract between the seller and the buyer.

4. As regards the applicable rules of the law of the country of the seller, the arbitrators have relied on the parties' respective statements on the subject and on the information obtained by the arbitration from an independent consultant. The arbitrators, in accordance with the last paragraph of Art. 13 of the ICC rules will also take into account the relevant trade usage[8].

Key Words

award	裁决书
claimant	申诉方
counter-defendant	反诉被诉方
defendant	被诉方
counter-claimant	反诉申诉方
shipping document	货运单据
pursuant to	按照
balance	余额
set off	抵销
substantive law	实体法
ICC (International Chamber of Commerce)	国际商会
Hague Convention	海牙公约
debtor	债务人
arbitrator	仲裁人
trade usage	贸易惯例

Notes

1. 在法律英语中，有很多普通词汇具有特殊的法律含义，如 award，它的常用意思是"授予某种奖项，给某人奖励"，但在法律英语中它的含义却大不相同，常使用的意思主要有两个，一是"仲裁裁决，裁决书"，二是"损失赔偿金等的裁定额"，本文使用它的第一种意思。

2. 在翻译这个句子时，可以把 as contractually agreed 提到最前面进行翻译，under 在这里的意思不是"在……之下",而是"根据"。

3. 该句虽然是被动句,但是在翻译成中文时需要翻译成主动句。after having undergone a certain treatment to make it more saleable 这里作非谓语动词修饰 product,在翻译时要提到句首进行翻译。

4. balance 在这里不是"平衡"的意思,在经济学里它特指"余额"。

5. 仲裁文本中存在很多复杂冗长的句子,在翻译时要先分析原文的结构、重心及整个句子的含义,再进行拆解,探析不同层次的意思,最后进行句意整合。例如,这句的第一个层次是 the buyer filed a counterclaim,也是主干成分;alleging that…amounts 是第二个层次,修饰 counterclaim;剩下的是第三个层次,修饰 amounts,在翻译时一定要弄清各部分之间的关系。file a counterclaim 这里等同于 lodge a counterclaim,意思是"提起反诉"。

6. 此句的主语是 the *Hague Convention*,谓语动词是 refer。由于主语修饰的成分太长,在翻译前一定要先找到句子的主干结构。这句可以译成"有关国际货物买卖适用法律的《海牙公约》(1995年6月15日)在涉及销售合同时,将卖方现行居住地法律视为占支配地位的法律。

7. 此句中有很多 of,每一个 of 后面的成分都对前面的词语进行修饰,在翻译时可以从后往前翻,译作"尽管如此,法律冲突法的总趋势是适用合同主要业务的债务人现行所在地的国内法"。

8. trade usage 这里的意思是"贸易惯例"。"贸易惯例"的常用英语表达还包括 trade practice 和 trade custom。

 **参考译文**

裁 决 书

双方当事人

1. 申诉方/反诉被诉方:卖方
2. 被诉方/反诉申诉方:买方

事实

1996年,双方当事人根据某种协议规定签署了3份买卖一种产品的合同。在收到货运单据后,买方即按合同规定,支付了全部合同价的90%。

按第一和第三份合同提供的产品符合协议规格,第二批货物的规格在装运前就有过争议。产品抵达目的地后重新检验,发现其不符合协议规定。为便于脱手,经过某种处理,最终买方将产品卖给了第三方,损失惨重。

卖方提请仲裁,要求收回10%的合同余款。买方提起反诉,声称应从卖方所索费用中扣除买方估计应由卖方赔偿买方的一笔费用,即直接损失费、财务成本费、所损失的利润及利息费。

适用的法律

1. 鉴于合同未含有关实体法的任何条款,故法律问题应根据国际商会仲裁规则第13条第 3 款决定。根据该条规则，仲裁员们应适用他们认为适合的法律冲突规则所规定的准据法则。

2. 这是一个由不同国籍的卖方和买方签署的在第三国交货的合同。交易规定为船上交货，故风险在卖方所在国便转给了买方。由此，卖方所在国似乎就成为与买卖关系最近的管辖地。

3. 有关国际货物买卖适用法律的《海牙公约》(1995 年 6 月 15 日) 在涉及销售合同时，将卖方现行居住地法律视为占支配地位的法律。买方所在国加入了《海牙公约》，卖方所在国则没有。尽管如此，法律冲突法的总趋势是适用合同主要业务的债务人现行所在地的国内法。在销售合同中，此债务人为卖方。基于这些因素，卖方所在国的法律似乎便成了规定买卖双方之间合同的准据法。

4. 至于卖方所在国法律的适用规则，仲裁员们依据的是双方当事人各自陈述的理由，以及仲裁员们从一位独立咨询人处所得的信息。根据国际商会仲裁规则第 13 条最后一段之规定，仲裁员们也将考虑相关的贸易惯例。

Passage Two

中国国际经济贸易仲裁委员会仲裁规则（2015）

（2014 年 11 月 4 日中国国际贸易促进委员会/中国国际商会修订并通过，自 2015 年 1 月 1 日起施行）

第一章 总 则

第一条 仲裁委员会

（一）中国国际经济贸易仲裁委员会（以下简称"仲裁委员会"），原名中国国际贸易促进委员会对外贸易仲裁委员会、中国国际贸易促进委员会对外经济贸易仲裁委员会，同时使用"中国国际商会仲裁院"名称。

（二）当事人在仲裁协议中订明由中国国际贸易促进委员会/中国国际商会仲裁，或由中国国际贸易促进委员会/中国国际商会的仲裁委员会或仲裁院仲裁的，或使用仲裁委员会原名称为仲裁机构的，均视为同意由中国国际经济贸易仲裁委员会仲裁[1]。

……

第五条 仲裁协议

（一）仲裁协议指当事人在合同中订明的仲裁条款或以其他方式达成的提交仲裁的书面协议。

（二）仲裁协议应当采取书面形式。书面形式包括合同书、信件、电报、电传、传真、电子数据交换和电子邮件等可以有形地表现所载内容的形式。在仲裁申请书和仲裁答辩书的交换中，一方当事人声称有仲裁协议而另一方当事人不做否认表示的，视为存在书面仲裁协议。[2]

（三）仲裁协议的适用法对仲裁协议的形式及效力另有规定的，从其规定[3]。

（四）合同中的仲裁条款应视为与合同其他条款分离的、独立存在的条款，附属于合同的仲裁协议也应视为与合同其他条款分离的、独立存在的一个部分；合同的变更、解除、终止、转让、失效、无效、未生效、被撤销以及成立与否，均不影响仲裁条款或仲裁协议的效力。[4]

第六条　对仲裁协议及/或管辖权的异议

（一）仲裁委员会有权对仲裁协议的存在、效力以及仲裁案件的管辖权作出决定。如有必要，仲裁委员会也可以授权仲裁庭作出管辖权决定。

（二）仲裁委员会依表面证据认为存在有效仲裁协议的，可根据表面证据作出仲裁委员会有管辖权的决定，仲裁程序继续进行。仲裁委员会依表面证据作出的管辖权决定[5]并不妨碍其根据仲裁庭在审理过程中发现的与表面证据不一致的事实及/或证据重新作出管辖权决定。

（三）仲裁庭依据仲裁委员会的授权作出管辖权决定时，可以在仲裁程序进行中单独作出，也可以在裁决书中一并作出。

（四）当事人对仲裁协议及/或仲裁案件管辖权的异议，应当在仲裁庭首次开庭前书面提出；书面审理的案件，应当在第一次实体答辩前提出。

（五）对仲裁协议及/或仲裁案件管辖权提出异议不影响仲裁程序的继续进行。[6]

（六）上述[7]管辖权异议及/或决定包括仲裁案件主体资格异议及/或决定。

（七）仲裁委员会或经仲裁委员会授权的仲裁庭作出无管辖权决定的，应当作出撤销案件的决定[8]。撤案决定在仲裁庭组成前由仲裁委员会仲裁院院长作出，在仲裁庭组成后，由仲裁庭作出。

Key Words

中国国际经济贸易仲裁委员会	China International Economic and Trade Arbitration Commission (CIETAC)
中国国际商会	China Chamber of International Commerce (CCOIC)
中国国际贸易促进委员会	China Council for the Promotion of International Trade (CCPIT)
对外经济贸易仲裁委员会	Foreign Economic and Trade Arbitration Commission
仲裁协议	arbitration agreement
电报	telegram
电传	telex
电子数据交换	EDI (electronic data interchange)
答辩书	statement of defense
解除	cancellation
终止	termination
无效	invalidity
管辖权	jurisdiction
仲裁庭	arbitral tribunal
表面证据	prima facie evidence

| 实体答辩 | substantive defense |

Notes

1. 英语重形式关联，中文重意义关联，这意味着中文里的有些逻辑关系不会直接表达出来，但是翻译成英文则需要将其补充完整，即将逻辑关系显性化——化意义关联为形式关联。这句的中文文本没有显性逻辑连词，但它实际上是条件句，所以在译成英文时必须把"如果"翻译出来。由于仲裁条例翻译强调使用规范化的语言，因此"如果"不能译成 if，而要译作 where。注意，在法律英语中，where 的意思是"如果，倘若"。

2. 这句的主干应该是"视为存在书面仲裁协议"，在翻译时要注意将其翻译成被动句，即 An arbitration agreement shall be deemed to exist…。

3. "从其规定"可以翻译成 those provisions shall prevail，此处的 prevail 不是"盛行"之意，而是指 be valid or applicable。

4. 这句话含有大量的法律术语，翻译时应当规范，可译为 The validity of an arbitration clause or an arbitration agreement shall not be affected by any modification, cancellation, termination, transfer, expiry, invalidity, ineffectiveness, rescission or non-existence of the contract.

5. 由于前面已经出现过仲裁委员会依表面证据作出的管辖权决定，所以第二次翻译时不必译出全部，只需译为 such a decision 即可。

6. 这句可以解释为"尽管对仲裁协议及/或仲裁案件管辖权存在异议，但是仲裁程序依然可以继续进行"，译者在翻译成英文时要注意把转折关系翻译出来，可以用 notwithstanding 作介词引导名词性短语，这里的 notwithstanding 意思同 although 相似。

7. "上述"不必译成 above mentioned，用 aforesaid 就能很好地传达意思，也更加简洁。

8. "撤销案件"可以翻译成 dismiss the case。

参考译文

China International Economic and Trade Arbitration Commission (CIETAC)

Arbitration Rules (2015)

(Revised and adopted by the China Council for the Promotion of International Trade/China Chamber of International Commerce on November 4, 2014. Effective as of January 1, 2015)

Chapter I General Provisions

Article 1 The Arbitration Commission

1. The China International Economic and Trade Arbitration Commission (hereinafter referred to as CIETAC), originally named the Foreign Trade Arbitration Commission of the China Council for the Promotion of International Trade and later renamed the Foreign Economic and Trade Arbitration Commission of the China Council for the Promotion of International Trade, concurrently uses as its name the "Arbitration Institute of the China Chamber of International

Commerce".

2. Where an arbitration agreement provides for arbitration by the China Council for the Promotion of International Trade/China Chamber of International Commerce, or by the Arbitration Commission or the Arbitration Institute of the China Council for the Promotion of International Trade/China Chamber of International Commerce, or refers to CIETAC's previous names, it shall be deemed that the parties have agreed to arbitration by CIETAC.

…

Article 5 Arbitration Agreement

1. An arbitration agreement means an arbitration clause in a contract or any other form of a written agreement concluded between the parties providing for the settlement of disputes by arbitration.

2. The arbitration agreement shall be in writing. An arbitration agreement is in writing if it is contained in the tangible form of a document such as a contract, letter, telegram, telex, fax, EDI, or E-mail. An arbitration agreement shall be deemed to exist where its existence is asserted by one party and not denied by the other during the exchange of the request for arbitration and the statement of defense.

3. Where the law applicable to an arbitration agreement has different provisions as to the form and validity of the arbitration agreement, those provisions shall prevail.

4. An arbitration clause contained in a contract shall be treated as a clause independent and separate from all other clauses of the contract, and an arbitration agreement attached to a contract shall also be treated as independent and separate from all other clauses of the contract. The validity of an arbitration clause or an arbitration agreement shall not be affected by any modification, cancellation, termination, transfer, expiry, invalidity, ineffectiveness, rescission or non-existence of the contract.

Article 6 Objection to Arbitration Agreement and/or Jurisdiction

1. CIETAC has the power to determine the existence and validity of an arbitration agreement and its jurisdiction over an arbitration case. CIETAC may, where necessary, delegate such power to the arbitral tribunal.

2. Where CIETAC is satisfied by prima facie evidence that a valid arbitration agreement exists, it may make a decision based on such evidence that it has jurisdiction over the arbitration case, and the arbitration shall proceed. Such a decision shall not prevent CIETAC from making a new decision on jurisdiction based on facts and/or evidence found by the arbitral tribunal during the arbitral proceedings that are inconsistent with the prima facie evidence.

3. Where CIETAC has delegated the power to determine jurisdiction to the arbitral tribunal, the arbitral tribunal may either make a separate decision on jurisdiction during the arbitral proceedings or incorporate the decision in the final arbitral award.

4. An objection to an arbitration agreement and/or jurisdiction over an arbitration case shall be raised in writing before the first oral hearing held by the arbitral tribunal. Where a case is to be decided on the basis of documents only, such an objection shall be raised before the submission of

the first substantive defense.

5. The arbitration shall proceed notwithstanding an objection to the arbitration agreement and/or jurisdiction over the arbitration case.

6. The aforesaid objections to and/or decisions on jurisdiction by CIETAC shall include objections to and/or decisions on a party's standing to participate in the arbitration.

7. CIETAC or its authorized arbitral tribunal shall decide to dismiss the case upon finding that CIETAC has no jurisdiction over an arbitration case. Where a case is to be dismissed before the formation of the arbitral tribunal, the decision shall be made by the President of the Arbitration Court. Where the case is to be dismissed after the formation of the arbitral tribunal, the decision shall be made by the arbitral tribunal.

Section 3　实　践　总　结

一、翻译技巧

（一）商务仲裁用词特点及翻译

1. 专业词汇的使用

商务仲裁文本属于正式的书面文件，文本中有很多专业词汇为其特定使用。这些专业词汇意义精确、单一，具有特定的法律含义，是仲裁文本规范化的一个重要保证。商务仲裁文本中的一些专业词汇，如 arbitration award（仲裁裁决）、arbitral tribunal（仲裁庭）、plaintiff（原告）、defendant（被告）、reasonable doubt（合理怀疑）、damages（赔偿金）、dismiss（撤销）、claim（索赔），等等，译者在翻译时绝不能盲目对译，更不能凭空捏造词语，这也就对译者的专业素养提出了要求。

2. 正式语的使用

仲裁文本用语同其他文本用语不同，前者倾向于用更正式规范的语言，措辞通常正式而严肃，避免口语化。例如："开始"用 commence，不用 begin 或者 start；"表明"用 demonstrate，不用 show；"认为"用 deem，不用 think；"在……之前"用 prior to 或者 preceding，不用 before；"依据"用 pursuant to 或者 in accordance with，不用 according to；"关于"用 as regards，不用 about；"因为"用 by virtue of，不用 because of，等等。因此，译者在翻译仲裁文本时一定要注意措辞，选择那些更加正式的词语，避免日常用语泛滥。

3. 古体词的使用

古体词是一种具有鲜明文体色彩的词汇成分。尽管古体词在现代英语口语和一般书面语中极少使用，但时常出现在商务文本中，仲裁文本也不例外。使用古体词可以使行文更加简洁、准确、正式。英语中的古体词是由自由词素 where、here、there 与 in、by、with、after 等构成的复合词，例如：hereto、hereof、herein、hereinafter、thereto、therein、thereof、whereby、wherein、whereof、whereupon，等等。需要注意的是，在翻译时，here 相当于 this，指本文献或有关文件；hereto（本合同）相当于 to this；there 相当于 that，指句子前面已出现的某个名词或名词词组；thereto（根据那一点）相当于 to that；where 相当于 which 或者 what；whereof（关于它）相当于 of which。

4. 情态动词 shall 的使用

仲裁文本中情态动词的存在也是该文本的一大词汇特征。情态动词在仲裁文本中使用非常频繁，其中以情态动词 shall 最为突出。shall 主要是用来表现法律的约束力，强调某种义务和责任，含有"必须"的强制意义，充分体现法律的权威性和约束性，通常翻译成"应，应当，必须"。例如：

原文：Except as otherwise expressly provided, the law of the People's Republic of China shall apply to this Agreement and to the arbitration conducted under this Agreement.

译文：除非另有规定，否则本协议和据本协议进行的仲裁应适用中华人民共和国法律。

（二）商务仲裁句法特点及翻译

1. 长句的使用

由于仲裁文本涉及的主题较为严肃，涵盖内容较多，逻辑相对复杂，因此为了更好地说明条例，明确责任，仲裁文书通常使用长句。在这些长句中，从句和修饰词相互交错，结构层层递进，往往一个句子就构成了一个长段落。例如：The summary procedure shall apply to any case where the amount in dispute does not exceed RMB 5,000,000 unless otherwise agreed by the parties; or where the amount in dispute exceeds RMB 5,000,000, yet one party applies for arbitration under the summary procedure and the other party agrees in writing; or where both parties have agreed to apply the summary procedure.

翻译长句在步骤上是化整为零，即理解并解构原句，在理解之后，对长句进行句法分析，分清该长句的结构脉络，认清主句、各修饰成分及分句、各修饰成分之间的逻辑关系。仲裁文本中的长句主要包括三种要素：从句、修饰限定成分、连词 and 和 or，这三种成分相互结合最终构成长句，其中条件句以条件状语从句的使用最为突出。以下就三种要素的翻译进行解释。

1）条件状语从句的翻译

原文：如果任何当事人拒绝或未能参加仲裁或仲裁程序的任何阶段，仲裁将继续进行，不受影响。

译文：If any of the parties refuses or fails to take part in the arbitration or any stage thereof, the arbitration will proceed notwithstanding such refusal or failure.

中文中的条件状语从句引导词通常有"如果""若""倘若"等，在英文中除了可以翻译成 if 之外，还可以翻译成 should、in the event of、in case、where、provided that 等。此外，有时中文的句子中没有相关引导词，但它实际上是一个条件状语从句，在翻译成英文时需要译出逻辑词，而在英译中的时候引导词可能会省去不翻。例如：

原文：当事人约定将争议提交仲裁委员会香港仲裁中心仲裁或约定将争议提交仲裁委员会在香港仲裁的，由仲裁委员会香港仲裁中心接受仲裁申请并管理案件。

译文：Where the parties have agreed to submit their disputes to the CIETAC Hong Kong Arbitration Center for arbitration or to CIETAC for arbitration in Hong Kong, the CIETAC Hong

Kong Arbitration Center shall accept the arbitration application and administer the case.

2）修饰限定成分的翻译

除了各类从句之外，修饰限定成分在长句结构中的作用也不容忽视。在翻译时，修饰限定成分往往被放置在所修饰词之后，这是为了能准确地表达意思。一个处在正确位置的限定词可以发挥重要的作用。例如：

原文：当事人以书面协定承允彼此间所发生或可能发生之一切或任何争议，如关涉可以仲裁解决事项之确定法律关系，不论为契约性质与否，提交仲裁时，各缔约国应承认此项协定。

译文：Each contracting state shall recognize an agreement in writing under which the parties undertake to submit to arbitration all or any differences which have arisen or which may arise between them in respect of a defined legal relationship, whether contractual or not, concerning a subject matter capable of settlement by arbitration.

本句的中文"法律关系"有两个修饰成分，一是"关涉可以仲裁解决事项"，二是"不论为契约性质与否"，在翻译成英文时可以把这两个成分跟在其后作限定成分。

3）连词 and 和 or 的使用

连词 and 和 or 在处理一个长句中的几个分句、分句中各种平行及并列成分上发挥着重要的作用，它们往往使逻辑更加通顺。and 的意思是"和"，or 的意思是"或者"。有时，and 和 or 的不同用法对于责任的限定也可能有所不同。例如：

① If a party does A and B, the party shall be liable to punishment.

② If a party does A or B, the party shall be liable to punishment.

在例①中 and 连接 A 和 B，意思是一方受到惩罚的前提是 A 和 B 两种情况同时满足，但是例②中用 or 的话，意思是只要满足一种情况即受到惩罚。所以尽管 and 和 or 连接的成分相同，但是它们对责任的限定却有分别，因此译者一定要小心使用 and 和 or。

2. 被动句的使用

仲裁文本体现的是司法部门的意志，因此需要避免个人主观色彩，强调内容的客观性和公正性。英语被动句的使用正好体现了仲裁文本自身语言的客观性。仲裁文本中的英语被动句在翻译成中文时通常有两种翻译方法，一是保持被动态不变，二是被动变主动。

1）被动态不变

原文：Provision of security by a party to the other party in conformity to the provision in Paragraph 1 of this Clause shall not be taken as admission by him of collision liability.

译文：按照本条例第一款规定，当事人向对方提供担保不被视为其承认碰撞责任。

在该例中，英文的"shall not be taken"在翻译成中文时保持原有被动态，译成了"不被视为"。

2）被动变主动

原文：The product was eventually sold by the buyer to third parties at considerable loss, after having undergone a certain treatment to make it more saleable.

译文：为便于脱手，经过某种处理，最终买方将产品卖给了第三方，损失惨重。

这里的 was eventually sold by the buyer to third parties 直译过来应该是"产品最终被买方卖给了第三方"，但是这么表达不符合中文的语言习惯，所以译为"最终买方将产品卖给了第三方"。需要注意的是，中文仲裁文本里的有些主动句在译成英文时可能需要变成被动句。

二、常用术语和表达

（一）常用术语

arbitrator	仲裁人
arbitration award	仲裁裁决
arbitration clause	仲裁条款
arbitration notice	仲裁通知
arbitration rule	仲裁规则
arbitration agreement	仲裁协议
compulsory arbitration	强制仲裁
enforcement	执行
foreign civil case	涉外民事案件
preservative measures in litigation	诉讼保全
stateless person	无国籍人
plaintiff	原告
defendant	被告
entrusted agent	委托代理人
retrial	重审
notarial act	公证行为
general principle	一般原则
level the playing field	创造公平竞争环境
impartial	公平的，公正的
foreign affairs arbitration agency	涉外仲裁机构
International Chamber of Commerce	国际商会
ad hoc arbitration	临时仲裁
institutional arbitration	机构仲裁
amiable arbitration	友好仲裁

（二）常用表达

① Arbitration participants shall proceed with the arbitration in good faith.
仲裁参与人应遵循诚实信用原则，进行仲裁程序。

② This dispute existing between the plaintiff A and the defendant B was brought about by the defendant's failure to commit itself to…
申诉人 A 和被诉人 B 之间争议的原因在于被诉人没有履行……

③ The claimed amount called for by the plaintiff comes totally to….
申诉人提出总金额为……的索赔主张。

④ In the present case, the main claim and the counterclaim, in accordance with the terms of reference, have been examined together so as to be the subject of a single award, and there is no reason to separate them.

在本案中，按规定说明，主诉和反诉已经进行共同审理，成为一次性裁决事项，故没有理由再将它们分割开。

⑤ The plaintiff hereby requests that it be compensated by the defendant not only with an amount of losses totaling...caused by the defendant's failure to execute the contracts concluded, but also with all costs arising from this arbitration.

申诉人在此除要求被诉人赔偿因违约而造成的总额为……的损失之外，还要求负担此次的全部仲裁费用。

⑥ The plaintiff is therefore applying formally to the China International Economic and Trade Arbitration Commission for arbitration of this dispute.

申诉人现正式向对外经济贸易仲裁委员会提出申请，要求对本争议进行仲裁。

⑦ The parties shall perform the arbitral award within the time period specified in the award. If no time period is specified in the award, the parties shall perform the award immediately.

当事人应依照裁决书写明的期限履行仲裁裁决；裁决书未写明履行期限的，应立即履行。

⑧ If a party has justified reasons to request an extension of the time period, the arbitral tribunal shall decide whether to grant such extension. Where the arbitral tribunal has not yet been formed, such decision shall be made by the arbitration court.

当事人确有正当理由请求延长上述期限的，由仲裁庭决定是否延长；仲裁庭尚未组成的，由仲裁委员会仲裁院作出决定。

Section 4 巩 固 练 习

一、翻译以下短语。

1. foreign civil case   6. 商务仲裁
2. arbitrator   7. 仲裁裁决
3. notarial act   8. 最终裁决
4. oral findings   9. 赔偿金
5. general principle   10. 上诉

二、翻译以下句子。

1. This Law is formulated in order to ensure that economic disputes shall be impartially and promptly arbitrated, to protect the legitimate rights and interests of the relevant parties and to guarantee the healthy development of the socialist market economy.

2. If the said award or agreement is not made in an official language of the country in which the award is relied upon, the party applying for recognition and enforcement of the award shall produce a translation of these documents into such language.

3. When signing, ratifying or acceding to this Convention, or notifying extension under Article X hereof, any state may on the basis of reciprocity declare that it will apply the Convention to the recognition and enforcement of awards made only in the territory of another contracting state.

4. In the circumstances, the buyer had the shipment examined within a reasonable time-span since an expert was requested to inspect the shipment even before the goods had arrived. The buyer should also be deemed to have given notice of the defects within a reasonable period; that is eight days after the expert's report had been published.

5. The arbitral tribunal has the power to decide in the arbitral award, having regard to the circumstances of the case, that the losing party shall compensate the winning party for the expenses reasonably incurred by it in pursuing the case. In deciding whether or not the winning party's expenses incurred in pursuing the case are reasonable, the arbitral tribunal shall take into consideration various factors such as the outcome and complexity of the case, the workload of the winning party and/or its representative(s), the amount in dispute, etc.

6. 仲裁庭裁决如下：卖方应获得其全部所主张的金额，扣除买方在反诉中提出的抵销部分数额。

7. 当事人采用仲裁方式解决纠纷，应当双方自愿，达成仲裁协议。没有仲裁协议，一方申请仲裁的，仲裁委员会不予受理。

8. 被告应在收到仲裁通知后20天内提交答辩书、证据材料及其他证明文件；如有反诉请求，也应在此期限内提交反诉请求书、证据材料及其他证明文件。

9. 仲裁庭认为必要或当事人提出请求并经仲裁庭同意的，仲裁庭可以在作出最终裁决之前，就当事人的某些请求事项先行作出部分裁决。部分裁决是终局的，对双方当事人均有约束力。

10. 对于开庭审理的案件，仲裁庭确定第一次开庭日期后，应不晚于开庭前15天将开庭日期通知双方当事人。当事人有正当理由的，可以请求延期开庭，但应于收到开庭通知后3天内提出书面延期申请；是否延期，由仲裁庭决定。

Chapter 12

国 际 商 法

Section 1 概 述

一、国际商法的定义及法律渊源

国际商法是指调整国际商事主体在从事国际商事交易活动中所形成的各种关系的法律规范的总和。它的调整对象是国际商事关系,这种关系是各国商事组织在跨国经营中所形成的商事关系。其基本原则是尊重国家主权、平等互利、国际合作与共同发展、有约必守、等价有偿等原则,这些原则又充分体现在尊重国际条约和国际惯例的基础上。它是促进国际商务发展的重要因素,也是从事国际商务活动的重要依据。

国际商法的法律渊源主要有三个:一是国际条约,二是国际贸易惯例,三是各国有关商事和国际贸易的国内法。

二、国际商法的特征

(1) 国际商法中的"国际"并非指国家与国家之间,而是指跨越国界。
(2) 从法律渊源看,国际商法包括国际法和国内法,其中国内法占重要地位。
(3) 从法律属性看,国际商法主要属于私法领域,用以规范商事主体及其行为。
(4) 国际商法是组织法与行为法的结合。

三、国际商法的内容

从形式上讲,国际商法体系的确定既要考虑国际商法所调整、涉及的商事关系领域,又要考虑国际商法渊源本身的结构和特点,还要确定体系各组成部分内容之间的关系。在内容上,国际商法体系的确定取决于跨国界的商事关系的发展。从形式和内容两方面的结合和国际商法目前的发展阶段看,我们可以大致确定国际商法体系的主要组成部分。国际商法应包括:商事主体法(包括商事组织、商事代理、商业登记等);商事行为法(包括国际货物买卖法、国际货物运输法、国际货物运输保险法、海商法、国际技术贸易法、产品责任法、票据与国际结算法、国际资金融通法);国际商事争议解决规则(包括国际民事诉讼、国际商事仲裁）。每一组成部分在表现形式上都是由国际法渊源和国内法渊源有机结合而成的。

Section 2 译例分析

Passage One

United Nations Convention on Contracts for the International Sale of Goods, 1980 (CISG)

Chapter II   General Provisions

Article 7

(1) In the interpretation of this Convention, regard is to be had to[1] its international character and to the need to promote uniformity in its application and the observance of good faith in international trade.

(2) Questions concerning matters governed by this Convention which are not expressly settled in it[2] are to be settled in conformity with the general principles on which it is based or, in the absence of such principles, in conformity with the law applicable by virtue of the rules of private international law.

Article 8

(1) For the purposes of this Convention statements made by and other conduct of a party are to be interpreted according to his intent where the other party knew or could not have been unaware what that intent was.

(2) If the preceding paragraph is not applicable, statements made by and other conduct of a party are to be interpreted according to the understanding that a reasonable person of the same kind as the other party[3] would have had in the same circumstances.

(3) In determining the intent of a party or the understanding a reasonable person would have had, due consideration is to be given to[4] all relevant circumstances of the case including the negotiations, any practices which the parties have established between themselves, usages and any subsequent conduct of the parties.

Article 9

(1) The parties are bound by any usage to which they have agreed and by any practices which they have established between themselves.

(2) The parties are considered, unless otherwise agreed, to have impliedly made applicable to their contract or its formation a usage of which the parties knew or ought to have known and which

in international trade is widely known to, and regularly observed by, parties to contracts of the type involved in the particular trade concerned.⁵

Article 10

For the purposes of this Convention:

(1) If a party has more than one place of business, the place of business is that which has the closest relationship to the contract and its performance, having regard to⁶ the circumstances known to or contemplated by the parties at any time before or at the conclusion of the contract;

(2) If a party does not have a place of business, reference is to be made to his habitual residence.

Article 11

A contract of sale need not be concluded in or evidenced by writing and is not subject to⁷ any other requirement as to form. It may be proved by any means, including witnesses.

Article 12

Any provision of Article 11, Article 29 or Part II of this Convention that allows a contract of sale or its modification or termination by agreement or any offer, acceptance or other indication of intention to be made in any form other than in writing does not apply where any party has his place of business in a contracting state which has made a declaration under article 96 of this Convention.⁸ The parties may not derogate from or vary the effect of this article.

Article 13

For the purposes of this Convention "writing" includes telegram and telex.

Key Words

uniformity	统一，一致
observance	遵守
preceding	在前的，前述的
usage	惯例
impliedly	言外地，隐含地
contemplate	设想，深思熟虑
habitual residence	惯常居住地
modification	更改
termination	终止
indication of intention	意旨
derogate	减损
telegram	电报

Notes

1. 英文国际商法中常使用被动句，这是因为被动语态的表达具有客观性，符合国际商法的语言特点。在翻译时，为符合中文的表达习惯，我们常常要把被动句翻译成主动句。该句中的 regard is to be had to…可以翻译成"应该考虑到……"。

2. 本句中有一个很长的后置结构修饰 questions，在这个结构中还要注意 which 引导的定语从句跟在 Convention 之后。在翻译此句时，要注意把英语后置修饰词提到所修饰成分之前，此句可以译成"凡本公约未明确解决的属于本公约范围内的问题……"。

3. a reasonable person of the same kind as the other party 可以译成"一个与另一方当事人同等资格、通情达理的人"。

4. due consideration is to be given to…这里在翻译时也应该化被动为主动，译作"应适当地考虑到……"。

5. 此句是一个长句，主干部分是 the parties are considered to have impliedly made applicable to their contract or its formation a usage。unless otherwise agreed 是插入语，在译成中文时要提到句首，译作"除非另有协议"。两个 which 引导的定语从句在这里修饰 usage，但是在翻译的时候由于修饰成分太长，可以把两个 which 引导的成分分开翻译。

6. 尽管这里的 having regard to…没有转折意味，但是为了行文流畅，在翻译此句是要加上"但是"。

7. is subject to 常出现在英文商务文本中，大部分情况下作表语，意为"根据，按照，如果，受……约束/限制"等，这里取最后一个意思。

8. 国际商法中有很多长句，译者在翻译之前需要剖析句子成分，才能做到准确、完整地传达内容。例如，此句主要可以划分为三个层次：一是主语部分，any provision of Article 11, Article 29 or Part II of this Convention that allows…in writing；二是谓语部分，does not apply；三是状语部分，这里是由 where 引导的条件状语从句。

参考译文

联合国国际货物销售合同公约（1980）

第二章 总 则

第七条

（1）在解释本公约时，应考虑到本公约的国际性质和促进其适用的统一及在国际贸易上遵守诚信的需要。

（2）凡本公约未明确解决的属于本公约范围内的问题，应按照本公约所依据的一般原则来解决，在没有一般原则的情况下，则应按照国际私法规定适用的法律来解决。

第八条

（1）为本公约之目的，一方当事人所作的声明和其他行为，应依照他的意旨解释，并且另一方当事人已知道或者不可能不知道此意旨。

（2）如果上一款的规定不适用，当事人所作的声明和其他行为，应按照一个与另一方当事人同等资格、通情达理的人处于相同情况中时应有的理解来解释。

（3）在确定一方当事人的意旨或一个通情达理的人应有的理解时，应适当地考虑到与事实有关的一切情况,包括谈判情形、当事人之间确立的任何习惯做法、惯例和当事人其后的任何行为。

第九条

(1)双方当事人业已同意的任何惯例和他们之间确立的任何习惯做法,对双方当事人均有约束力。

(2)除非另有协议,双方当事人应视为已默示同意对他们的合同或合同的订立适用双方当事人已知道或理应知道的惯例,而这种惯例,在国际贸易上,已为有关特定贸易所涉同类合同的当事人所广泛知道并为他们所经常遵守。

第十条

为本公约之目的:

(1)如果当事人有一个以上的营业地,则以与合同及合同的履行关系最密切的营业地为其营业地,但要考虑到双方当事人在订立合同前任何时候或订立合同时所知道或所设想的情况;

(2)如果当事人没有营业地,则以其惯常居住地为准。

第十一条

销售合同无须以书面订立或书面证明,在形式方面也不受任何其他条件的限制。销售合同可以用包括人证在内的任何方法证明。

第十二条

本公约第十一条、第二十九条或第二部分准许销售合同或其更改或根据协议终止,或者任何发盘、接受或其他意旨表示得以书面以外任何形式做出的任何规定不适用,如果任何一方当事人的营业地是在已按照本公约第九十六条做出了声明的一个缔约国内,各当事人不得减损本条或改变其效力。

第十三条

为本公约之目的,"书面"包括电报和电传。

Passage Two

中华人民共和国对外贸易法(1994)

第一章 总 则

第一条 为了发展对外贸易,维护对外贸易秩序,促进社会主义市场经济的健康发展,制定本法[1]。

第二条 本法所称对外贸易,是指货物进出口、技术进出口和国际服务贸易[2]。

第三条 国务院对外经济贸易主管部门依照本法主管全国对外贸易工作[3]。

第四条 国家实行统一的对外贸易制度,依法维护公平的、自由的对外贸易秩序。

国家鼓励发展对外贸易,发挥地方的积极性,保障对外贸易经营者的经营自主权。

第五条 中华人民共和国根据平等互利的原则,促进和发展同其他国家和地区的贸易关系。

第六条　中华人民共和国在对外贸易方面根据所缔结或者参加的国际条约、协定，给予其他缔约方、参加方或者根据互惠、对等原则给予对方最惠国待遇、国民待遇[4]。

第七条　任何国家或者地区在贸易方面对中华人民共和国采取歧视性的禁止、限制或者其他类似措施的[5]，中华人民共和国可以根据实际情况对该国家或者该地区采取相应的措施。

....

第十条　国际服务贸易企业和组织的设立及其经营活动，应当遵守本法和其他有关法律、行政法规的规定。

第十一条　对外贸易经营者依法自主经营、自负盈亏。

第十二条　对外贸易经营者从事对外贸易经营活动，应当信守合同，保证商品质量，完善售后服务[6]。

第十三条　没有对外贸易经营许可的组织或者个人，可以在国内委托对外贸易经营者在其经营范围内代为办理其对外贸易业务[7]。

接受委托的对外贸易经营者应当向委托方如实提供市场行情、商品价格、客户情况等有关的经营信息。委托方与被委托方应当签订委托合同，双方的权利义务由合同约定。

第十四条　对外贸易经营者应当按照国务院对外经济贸易主管部门的规定，向有关部门提交与其对外贸易经营活动有关的文件及资料。有关部门应当为提供者保守商业秘密[8]。

Key Words

对外贸易	foreign trade
社会主义市场经济	socialist market economy
依照	pursuant to
经营自主权	autonomy of business operation
平等互利	equality and mutual benefit
缔约方	contracting party
参加方	participating party
最惠国待遇	most-favored-nation treatment
国民待遇	national treatment
自负盈亏	be responsible for one's own profits and losses
委托	entrust
委托方	principal
市场行情	market situation
商品价格	commodity price
客户情况	client position

Notes

1. 此句应译作被动句，主干是"制定本法"，"为了……"之后的部分应作为目的状语跟在其后。这里的"为了"不应该用 in order to 或是 for 等略显不正式的短语，而应译作 with a view to。这是为了与商务英语自身正式、严肃的文体风格相一致。

2. 这里的"是指"不应该直接翻译成 refer to，实际上它的隐含意思是"包括……贸易"，所以用 cover，cover 在这里的意思跟 include 类似，但是比 include 更加正式。

3. "国务院对外经济贸易主管部门"应该翻译成 the authority responsible for foreign trade and economic relations under the State Council；"依照本法"这里译作 pursuant to this Law，相似的表达还有 in accordance with this Law 或 under this Law。

4. "根据所缔结或者参加的国际条约、协定"的意思等同于中国是这些国际条约和协定的缔约方和参加方，所以译者应当翻译成 under international treaties or agreements to which the People's Republic of China is a contracting party or a participating party，这样也同之后的 other contracting parties or participating parties（其他缔约方和参加方）在行文上更加连贯。

5. 此句实际上是一个条件句，所以应该翻译成 in the event of…。

6. "信守合同，保证商品质量，完善售后服务"分别对应的是 honor their contracts, ensure the quality of the commodity and perfect the after-sale services。

7. "委托"可以翻译成 entrust。同 entrust 有关的短语包括 entrust sb with sth 和 entrust sth to sb 等。

8. "保守商业秘密"等同于"不公开商业秘密"，所以可译为 shall not disclose the business proprietary information。

 参考译文

FOREIGN TRADE LAW OF THE PEOPLE'S REPUBLIC OF CHINA (1994)

Chapter I   Principles

Article 1
This Law is formulated with a view to developing the foreign trade, maintaining the foreign trade order and promoting a healthy development of the socialist market economy.

Article 2
Foreign trade as mentioned in this Law shall cover the import and export of goods, technologies and the international trade in services.

Article 3
The authority responsible for foreign trade and economic relations under the State Council is in charge of the administration of the foreign trade of the entire country pursuant to this Law.

Article 4
The State shall apply the foreign trade system on a uniform basis and maintain a fair and free foreign trade order in accordance with law.

The State encourages the development of its foreign trade, exercises the initiative of localities and safeguards the autonomy of business operation of the foreign trade dealers.

Article 5

The People's Republic of China promotes and develops trade ties with other countries and regions on the principles of equality and mutual benefit.

Article 6

The People's Republic of China shall, under international treaties or agreements to which the People's Republic of China is a contracting party or a participating party, grant the other contracting parties or participating parties, or on the principles of mutual advantage and reciprocity, grant the other party most-favored-nation treatment or national treatment within the field of foreign trade.

Article 7

In the event that any country or region applies discriminatory prohibition, restriction or other like measures against the People's Republic of China in respect of trade, the People's Republic of China may, as the case may be, take counter-measures against the country or region in question.

…

Article 10

The establishment and operation of enterprises and organizations engaged in international trade in services shall be in compliance with the provisions of this Law and other relevant laws and administrative regulations.

Article 11

Foreign trade dealers shall enjoy full autonomy in their business operation and be responsible for their own profits and losses in accordance with law.

Article 12

In foreign trade activities foreign trade dealers should honor their contracts, ensure the quality of the commodity and perfect the after-sale services.

Article 13

Any organization or individual without foreign trade operation permit may entrust a foreign trade dealer located in China as its agent to conduct its foreign trade business within the business scope of the latter.

The entrusted foreign trade dealer shall provide the principal with actual business information such as market situation, commodity prices and client position. The agent and the principal shall conclude and sign an agency agreement, in which the rights and obligations of both parties should be specified.

Article 14

Foreign trade dealers are obligated to provide documents and information in relation to their foreign trade dealings to the relevant authorities pursuant to the regulations of the authority responsible for foreign trade and economic relations under the State Council. The relevant authorities shall not disclose the business proprietary information provided by the dealers.

Section 3 实践总结

一、翻译技巧

（一）国际商法的语言特点

与一般文体相比，国际商法语言十分正式，用词讲究、逻辑严密，多用长句和复合句。尤其是一些具有规范、约束力等公文性质的商务文书，更是充分体现出此特点。鉴于国际商法所特有的语言风格，它的翻译也有其特有的方法和要求。

1. 词汇特点

1）专门法律术语

国际商法中存在大量的法律术语和专有词汇。这些法律术语和专有词汇词义单一、语意精炼、严谨规范，有其特有的适用条件和范围，在任何情况下都需要对其有统一的解释，例如：claim（索赔）、arbitration award（仲裁裁决）、termination（终止）、infringement（侵权），等等。还有一些专业词汇如 obligee（债权人）、obligor（债务人）、tort（侵权行为）等专业法律语言，不能随意地引申或者用其他词汇来替代。

2）普通词汇的特殊意义

国际商法语言的一个重要特征就是其使用的很多普通词汇往往都具有特定的含义，在进行翻译时，必须要遵照其特定的含义才能正确翻译，否则很容易出现偏差，甚至是错译。例如：article 的基本含义有"文章""物品"，但是在法律英语中，它指的是"条款"；principal 的意思有"首要的""校长"等，在法律英语中它还有另外一个含义，指"委托人"；claim 通常是"声称"的意思，在商务文件中其指的是"索赔"。因此，要正确译出普通词汇在法律文书中所代表的特殊意义，要求译者对普通词语的法律含义有一定的积累。

3）古体词和外来词

为体现法律文本行文正式、庄重的文体特征，国际商法中常使用一些古体词。这些词主要来源于古英语和中古英语，不常用于日常交流，但是却保留在英文商务文本中。古体词精练、直观，其使用显示出法律语言的权威性、简洁性和严密性。常见的古体词主要是由 here、there 和 where 分别加上 after、as、by、from、in、of、to、under、upon、with 等一个或几个介词共同构成的复合副词，在这些复合副词中，here 表示 this, there 表示 that, where 表示 what 或 which。例如：hereafter（此后，今后）、hereby（特此，兹）、herein（此中，于此，本合同中）、hereinafter（以下，此后，在下文）、hereof（于此，在本合同中）、hereto（于此）、hereunder（在下文，据此，根据本合同）、herewith（与此一道）、thereafter（此后，后来）、thereby（因此，由此，在那方面）、herefrom（由此，从此）、therein（其中，在其中）、thereinafter（在下文）、thereof（关于，由此，其中）、thereto（此外，附随）、thereunder（在其下，据此，依据）、whereas（鉴于），等等。

此外，国际商法用词正式、保守还体现在外来词的使用上。它所使用的外来词主要来自拉丁语和法语。例如：status quo（现状）、as per（按照）、de facto（事实上的）、force majeure（不可抗力），等等。

4）同义词和并列词

国际商法用语的正式性还体现在它经常使用成对的同义词或并列相关的词语。同义词和并列词的使用看似重复却可以使内容更加完整和准确，避免出现歧义。例如：furnish and provide（供应）、by and between（由……和……间）、null and void（无效的）、terms and conditions（条款）、losses and damages（损失），等等。这类叠词的使用充分彰显了国际商法的正式性和专业性，有力地避免了含糊不清和模棱两可的状况。

5）书面用语

国际商法的正式性和专业性还体现在它常使用书面用语，不使用俚语、口语和方言。例如："认为"用 deem，而不用 think 或者 believe；"如果"用 in the event of 或 in case of 或 should，而不用 if；"在……之前"用 prior to，而不用 before；"因为"用 by virtue of，而不用 because of；"为了"用 in the view of，而不用 in order to；"关于"常用 with regard to 或 with reference to，而不用 about。同后者相比，前者用法更加正式，因此经常用在国际商法中。

6）模糊语

模糊语作为一种弹性语言，是指外延不确定、内涵无定指的特性语言。与精确语言相比，模糊语具有更大的概括性和灵活性。虽然说法律语言强调准确性，但使用模糊语并不会从根本上同法律语言产生冲突。相反，适当使用模糊语能使所列内容更符合客观实际，使表意更加充分、完整。国际商法中常见的模糊语有 about、serious、reasonable、appropriate、more than、less than、not less than 等。

2. 句法特点

1）长句

为了保持法律语言精确和平实的特点，准确地表达复杂的逻辑关系，法律英语经常大量使用长句。同普通英语句子相比，长句的句子结构、长度和使用从句的连贯性要复杂得多，因此可以有效涵盖所有相关信息，减少被曲解、误解和产生歧义的可能性。例如：

原文：Where, as a result of the operation of a risk covered by this insurance, the insured transit is terminated at a port or place other than that to which the subject matter is covered under this insurance, the underwriters will reimburse the assured for any extra charges properly and reasonably incurred in unloading, storing and forwarding the subject matter to the destination to which it is insured hereunder.

译文：如果由于本保险承保范围内的某项风险，导致承保运输终止于某一港口或地点，且该港口和地点并非保险标的在本保险承保下所应运达的目的地，保险人应就投保人因卸货、储存和续运保险标的至承保目的地而发生的额外费用，对投保人进行适当和合理的赔偿。

2）被动句

国际商法旨在调整各国商事组织在跨国经营中所形成的商事关系，这要求其文本语言必须庄严、客观、公正，因此被动句常用于国际商法文体中，用以规定行为人的权利、义务和相关法律后果，传递主动语态无法表达的信息。例如：

原文：由于一方过失，致使不能履行或不能完全履行本合同及其附件时，由违约方承担违约责任。

译文：Should all or part of the contract and its appendices be unable to be fulfilled owing to the fault of one party, the breaching party shall bear the responsibilities thus caused.

3）名词化结构

国际商法中另一频繁出现的句式结构就是名词化结构。名词化就是把句子中的动词或形容词转换为名词或名词词组，从而使名词或名词词组获得动词或形容词的意义但具有名词的语法功能，从而使原来的句子转换为名词词组。国际商法的名词化结构用以表明抽象思维的逻辑性和概念化，可使行文更加简洁，使语体更加庄重。例如：

原文：订立技术合同，应当有利于科学技术的进步，加速科学技术成果的转化、应用和推广。

译文：The conclusion of a technology contract shall be conducive to the advancement of science and technology, and expedite the conversion, application and dissemination of scientific and technological achievement.

（二）国际商法的翻译原则

1. 准确性原则

国际商法在术语、条款、篇章结构、类型上的专业性越来越强，这就要求我们在翻译国际商法时必须把准确性作为其首要翻译原则来遵守。准确性是国际商法翻译的根本，忠实于原文内容，力求准确无误是法律文本翻译区别于其他文体翻译的一个重要特征。这里的准确性是指译者在将原文内容转换到译文时要尽最大可能地再现原文本的所有信息，不遗漏、添加、篡改原文内容，不令译文读者产生误解和困惑。国际商法翻译时的任何一个漏译、错译，甚至一个词语自身语义的模糊不清都可能造成巨大的损失，带来严重的后果，因此准确性无疑是国际商法翻译的第一标准。

2. 一致性原则

一致性原则是指在同一份文件中，译者在处理两次或者多次出现的同一个词语时，应该始终坚持用同一个术语表述同一个概念，以避免产生歧义，对各方造成不必要的经济损失。此外，在法律翻译过程中，那些看似同义或近义的词却可能表达不同的概念。如果遇到这种情况，译者应该意识到它们并非同义词，应尽力分辨它们，用最准确的词语表达它们的意思。例如：contract 一词，可以译为"合同"，也可以译为"契约"。但是如果第一次翻译为"合同"的话，以后的行文中也应该翻译为"合同"，而不能翻译成"契约"。

3. 规范性原则

中英文的国际商法术语都有其特定的意义与规范。译者在翻译时一定要遵照专业术语的表达规则，不能随意增字、减字，也不可盲目对译。例如："不可抗力"可以译成 force beyond human power 或是 force controlled by God 或是 irresistible force，但正确规范的译法应当是 force majeure。由于国际商法中存在一个词语有多种译法的可能性，译者应当积累统一规范的术语表达，力求在翻译时保持原文的格式风貌。

（三）国际商法的翻译技巧

1. 转换法

转换法是翻译常见的技巧之一，它是指一个词在源语中的词性与目的语中未必就是同一个词性，如将中文的动词转化成英语的名词。例如：

① 原文：订立劳动合同，应当遵循合法、公平、平等自愿、协商一致、诚实信用的原则。

译文：The conclusion of employment contract shall comply with the principles of lawfulness, fairness, equality, free well, negotiated consensus and good faith.

② 原文：A rejection or other refusal by the buyer to receive or retain the goods, whether or not justified, or a justified revocation of acceptance revests title to the goods in the seller. Such revesting occurs by operation of law and is not a "sale".

译文：当买方不论有无正当理由以任何形式拒绝接收或保留货物时，或当买方正当地撤销对货物的接收时，所有权重新转移至卖方。所有权的此种重新转移系有法律规定，不构成一次"买卖"行为。

以上两个句子都涉及了翻译时的词性转换问题。在例（1）中，中文的动词"订立"翻译成英文的名词conclusion，这符合英文国际商法善用名词化结构的特点。汉语动词的造句功能很强，有一种动态趋势。因此在将英文翻译成中文时，例（2）中的rejection和refusal会翻译成中文的动词"拒绝"。

2. 增减法

汉语重意合，句子之间常靠内部的逻辑关系联系在一起，所谓"形散而神聚"；而英语重形合，句与句之间往往靠各种语言形式紧密结合。因此，相较于英语严谨、冗长的句子，中文更加简洁明了，这也就会涉及两种语言在互译时的增减问题。例如：

① 原文：外国企业在中国境内未设立机构、场所，而有取得的来源于中国境内的利润、利息、租金、特许权使用费和其他所得，或者虽设立机构、场所，但上述所得与其机构、场所没有实际联系的，都应当缴纳百分之二十的所得税。

译文：In case a foreign enterprise does not have an organization or site in the territory of China but has profits, interests, rental, royalty and income originating in China, or has an organization or a site in the territory of China but the above-said income does not have any actual connection with organization or site, a 20 percent income tax shall be charged on all above-said income.

② 原文："Delivery time" shall mean the delivery period beginning from the effective date and ending on the date by which the goods have been delivered, in accordance with the terms and conditions of the contract.

译文："交货时间"指根据合同条款从生效期起至货物送达结束的交货期。

例①实质上是一个条件状语从句，但是由于中文注重"意合"，因此并没有把引导词写出来。在翻译成英文时，需要把隐形的逻辑用显性的引导词表示出来。翻译时根据逻辑结构，增加了in case，使得译文逻辑更加通顺，更便于英文读者理解。英语的国际商法中有很多同义词或近义词，译者在翻译过程中要学会取舍，如例②中的terms and conditions都有"条款"和"条件"的意思，但是译者在翻译时只需要译出"条款"即可。

3. 调整语序法

英汉对比研究表明，英汉两种语言在语序上有相同的地方，也有不同之处。一般而言，中英文句子的主语、谓语、宾语的位置基本保持一致，但是状语和定语的位置却有很大差别。

英语的状语和定语在句中的排列更加灵活，可置于修饰词前，也可放在修饰词之后，而中文状语和定语的位置则相对稳定。因此，中英文两种句子语序有时相差甚远。在翻译国际商法时，译者需要根据目的语语序调整原文语序，使译文更加顺畅、可读。例如：

① 原文：A treaty shall be interpreted in good faith in accordance with the ordinary meaning to be given to the terms of the treaty in their context and in the lights of its object and purpose.

译文：条款应依其用语按其上下文并参照条约之目的及宗旨所具有之通常意义，善意解释之。

② 原文：缔约方均须依照法律准则采取必要措施，确立法人行贿外国公职人员应承担的责任。

译文：Each party shall take such measures as may be necessary, in accordance with its legal principles, to establish the liability of legal persons for the bribery of a foreign public official.

在例①中，动词 interpreted 之后跟着一个由 in accordance with 引导的方式状语，在翻译成中文时，根据中文的表达习惯，可以把动词调整至状语之后再翻译。例②则恰恰相反，中文的"依照法律准则采取必要措施"在翻译时要先译出谓语成分，再译出状语成分，这符合英文的表达习惯。

二、常用术语和表达

（一）常用术语

会计法	accounting law
税法	tax law
公司法	company law
出资	contribution
注册资本	registered capital
公司章程	articles of association/articles of incorporation
公司存续	existence of company
公司合并分立	merger and split of company
公司并购	corporate merger and acquisition
公司清算	company liquidation
股本	stock capital
股东	shareholder
表决权	voting right
监事会	board of supervisors
股息	dividend
红股	bonus stock/dividend stock
法定公积金	legal accumulation fund
资本公积金	capital accumulation fund
公司犯罪	corporate crime
证券法	securities law

证券发行	issuance of securities
披露制度	disclosure system
交割日	settlement day
风险投资基金	venture capital fund
票据法	law of negotiable instrument
票据	note/bill
商业票据	commercial instrument
追索权	right of recourse
海商法	maritime law
船舶检验	register of ship
船舶进港费	groundage
船舶抵押	ship mortgage
船舶租赁	ship chartering
船舶遇难	maritime distress
船舶扣押	detention of ship
海事报告	sea protest
海事法院	maritime court
保险法	insurance law
商业保险	commercial insurance
财产保险	property insurance
人身保险	personal insurance
意外保险	accident insurance
社会保险	social insurance
养老保险	endowment insurance
医疗保险	medical insurance
保险人	insurer/ underwriter
被保险人	the insured
保险费	premium
保险赔偿	insurance indemnity
索赔	claim
理赔	settlement of claim
委付	abandonment
退保	cancellation/discharging of insurance

(二) 常用表达

① This law is formulated with a view to…
为了……制定本法。

② No reservations are permitted except those expressly authorized in this convention.
除本公约明文许可的保留外，不得作任何保留。

③ This convention is subject to ratification, acceptance or approval by the signatory states.
本公约须经签字国批准、接受或核准。

④ Declarations made under this convention at the time of signature are subject to confirmation upon ratification, acceptance or approval.
根据本公约规定，在签字时做出的声明，须在批准、接受或核准时加以确认。

⑤ This convention applies to contracts of sale of goods between parties whose places of business are in different states.
本公约适用于营业地在不同国家的当事人之间所订立的货物。

⑥ The parties may exclude the application of this convention or, subject to article 12, derogate from or vary the effect of any of its provisions.
双方当事人可以不适用本公约，或在第十二条的条件下，减损本公约的任何规定或改变其效力。

⑦ The parties are bound by any usage to which they have agreed and by any practices which they have established between themselves.
双方当事人业已同意的任何惯例和他们之间确立的任何习惯做法，对双方当事人均有约束力。

⑧ Anyone who imports or exports technologies that are subject to import or export prohibitions or restrictions in violation of this law and commits criminal offenses, shall be subject to criminal prosecutions in the light of the supplementary decision on the punishment of smuggling.
违反本法规定，进口或者出口禁止进出口或者限制进出口的技术，构成犯罪的，按照惩治走私罪的补充规定追究刑事责任。

Section 4 巩 固 练 习

一、翻译以下短语。

1. antidumping
2. business model
3. common law
4. currency exchange
5. government guarantee
6. 国际商法
7. 国际商事仲裁
8. 民法法系
9. 司法不公
10. 征收

二、翻译以下句子。

1. 本法所称不可抗力，是指不能预见、不能避免且不能克服的客观情况。

2. 申请设立的外资企业，其产品涉及出口许可证、出口配额、进口许可证或者属于国家限制进口的，应当依照有关管理权限事先征得对外经济贸易部门的同意。

3. "发货人"是指其本人或以其名义或其代表同多式联运经营人订立多式联运合同的任何人，或指其本人、或以其名义、或其代表将货物实际交给多式联运经营人的任何人。

4. 进出口商会应当遵守法律、行政法规，依照章程对其会员的对外贸易经营活动进行协调指导，提供咨询服务，向政府有关部门反映会员有关对外贸易促进方面的建议，并积极开展对外贸易促进活动。

5. 除非公约本部分另有明文规定，当事人按照本部分的规定，以适合情况的方法发出任何通知、要求或其他通知后，这种通知如在传递上发生耽搁或错误，或者未能到达，并不使该当事人丧失依靠该项通知的权利。

6. The charterer shall pay the hire as stipulated in the contract. In default of payment by the charterer for seven consecutive days or more after the time as agreed in the contract for such payment, the shipowner is entitled to cancel the contract without prejudice to any claim for the loss arising from the charterer's default.

7. If the offeree dispatched its acceptance within the period for acceptance, and the acceptance, which would otherwise have reached the offeror in due time under normal circumstances, reaches the offeror after expiration of the period for acceptance due to any other reason, the acceptance is valid, unless the offeror timely advises the offeree that the acceptance has been rejected on grounds of the delay.

8. After the approval of the application for the establishment of a foreign-capital enterprise by the examining and approving organ, the foreign investor shall, within 30 days after receiving the certificate of approval, file an application with the relevant administrative department for industrial and commercial registration, and obtain a business license. The date on which the business license is issued shall be the date of the establishment of the said enterprise.

9. Where the performance of the carriage or part thereof has been entrusted to an actual carrier, whether or not in pursuance of a liberty under the contract of carriage by sea to do so, the carrier nevertheless remains responsible for the entire carriage according to the provisions of this convention. The carrier is responsible, in relation to the carriage performed by the actual carrier, for the acts and omissions of the actual carrier and of his servants and agents acting within the scope of their employment.

10. Where the parties do not wish to, or are unable to, resolve such dispute through settlement or mediation, the dispute may be submitted to the relevant arbitration institution for arbitration in accordance with the arbitration agreement between the parties. Parties to a foreign related contract may apply to a Chinese arbitration institution or another arbitration institution for arbitration. Where the parties did not conclude an arbitration agreement, or the arbitration agreement is invalid, either party may bring a suit to the People's Court. The parties shall perform any judgment, arbitral award or mediation agreement which has taken legal effect; if a party refuses to perform, the other party may apply to the People's Court for enforcement.

Keys to Exercises

Chapter 1 商务广告

一、翻译以下英文广告。

1. 给电脑一颗奔腾的"芯"。(奔腾)

2. 分分秒秒欢聚欢笑。(麦当劳)

3. 身在35 000英尺的纽约上空,巴黎的浪漫仍系心中,唯有你的劳力士可以两地相容。(劳力士)

4. 她是周围最轻捷聪慧的女子,轻捷是她的举止特点,而轻巧面包是她的钟爱,松软,味美,轻巧。(Nimble)

5. 专注完美,近乎苛求。(雷克萨斯)

6. 旅行不是一段路程,也不是一种假期。它是一种过程,一种发现,一段发现自己的过程。旅行让我们面对面与自己交流。旅行带给我们的不仅是这个世界,还有我们如何在这个世界上生活。是人们创造了旅行,还是旅行造就了我们?旅行其实就是生活本身。生活将会带你去哪里呢?问一问路易威登。(路易威登)

7. 隆重推出有史以来第一台涡轮启动式复印机——新型Toshiba 2230 Turbo。在精秀的机壳下,是一套业已授予专利的先进复印系统。拥有它,你一分钟能复印22份材料。如果按下涡轮键,则一分钟可复印30份。现在你可以提高40%的工效,同时节约33%的增色剂。更具创新精神的是,我们并没有因此而提高价格。如需安排免费的示范表演,只需拨打1-800转Toshiba。(东芝)

二、翻译以下中文广告。

1. Behind that healthy smile, there's a Crest kid. (Crest)

2. Fresh-up with Seven-up. (Seven-up)

3. The world smiles with Reader's Digest. (Reader's Digest)

4. Fair skin now? Dabao knows how. (Dabao)

5. Good milk is an integration of love and wisdom. Milk Deluxe, rich in good quality natural lacto protein, drops all happiness into your cup and your heart. From the base of milk source to packaging, everything experiences every test, forming a model that the entire world should follow. The advanced technology guarantees the milk to be mellow. This best taste only comes from Milk Deluxe. Noble life is an integration of mental and material enjoyment. Work with my heart, enjoy with my soul. A gold-brand demand for myself brings me a gold-brand life, just as I drink Milk Deluxe. I indulge myself in this greenness and let my soul be totally free. This is Milk Deluxe and life deluxe. (Milk Deluxe)

6. Suzhou Gardens are widely reputed in the unique styles. Their towers, gazeboes, terraces,

winding corridors and water-side pavilions are so artistically laid out among ponds, rockeries, trees and grottoes that visitors are impressed by the depth they create, and find a different vista at every turn. (Suzhou Gardens)

Chapter 2 产品说明书

一、翻译以下短语。

1. net weight
2. maintenance
3. wear-resisting
4. energy consumption
5. edible after opened

6. 蒸馏水
7. 药草
8. 调味品，调料
9. 美白精华
10. 制造商

二、翻译以下句子。

1. 专为严重受损发质设计的修护洗发水，含神经酰胺。可使头发重获健康亮泽与活力，并可帮助抵御紫外线对头发的伤害。

2. 偶尔可能对口腔黏膜有麻醉作用，但若不嚼碎药片，而以水送服，上述作用可以避免。

3. 安装或使用本机如遇问题，请先阅读本疑难解决之说明，再致电客服部。请在左栏中查找问题，在右栏查看所建议的解决方法。

4. 一般不会发生副作用。有些患者可能出现常见的、并无害处的"硝酸盐性头痛"。如遇此种情况，可酌情减剂量。因为患者对这种硝酸盐作用易产生快速耐受性，所以不必停药。本品可在8~10小时内保护心绞痛患者安全。严重患者咀嚼本品可立即缓解。

5. 奇宝轻怡巧克力架选用上乘原料，由独特秘方精制而成，如此轻巧松脆，带给您全家奇宝特有的新鲜美味。全球饼干及小食领袖——联合饼干集团专注于烘制最优质的饼干及小食，产品遍及全球90多个国家。

6. After cleaning face, take out a piece of mask, put it on face and keep it 10 to 20 minutes, then take it off. And massage gently to absorb it. Two or three times a week. It will be more effective if you use it once a day.

7. Connect the USB under power on state, pull down the notification bar, select USB connection, and then select "Open USB Storage Device", then you can operate a computer for data transfer between phone and computer; at the same time, you can also charge the phone through USB connecting with the computer.

8. Products of this kind feature safe-use, weather-resistance, abrasion-resistance, high mechanical intensity and low line loss. They are widely used in the power network reconstruction of cities and forest areas and can improve the safety and reliability of power network.

9. This air conditioner is suitable for hotels, restaurants, hospitals, nurseries, houses, creating a comfortable environment with ideal temperature.

10. In case of a reaction during the application such as intense stinging, rash or a burning sensation on the scalp, rinse immediately with lukewarm water.

Chapter 3　企业宣传材料

一、翻译以下短语。

1. business scope
2. corporate philosophy
3. enjoy a good reputation
4. registered capital
5. attract investment
6. 求真务实
7. 旗舰店
8. 不遗余力
9. 服务至上
10. 平等互利

二、翻译以下句子。

1. 今天，强生公司在中国已经拥有 6 家子公司和机构，员工 3 000 多名，生产的产品遍及消费品、药品和医疗器械等领域，并且始终致力于促进中国人民健康事业的发展。

2. 渣打银行在全球 56 个国家共招募了 4 万多名员工。他们分别带来了不同的企业文化。去年我们又增加了 1 万名雇员，其中包括我们去年收购的韩国第一银行（现易名为渣打第一银行）而增加的 5 000 多名韩国员工。

3. 我们培养创造和开拓能力，吸收新信息、新知识、新观念，转换思维角度，突破成规局限，采用超前方式和措施，建立先进理念和体系，创造最好的技术和工艺，开创一流业绩和局面。

4. 杜邦是一家以科研为基础的全球性企业。公司致力于创造可持续的解决方案，让全球各地的人们生活得更美好、更安全和更健康。杜邦公司的业务遍及全球 70 个国家和地区，公司的创新产品与服务现已广泛运用于农业、食品与营养、电子产品、通信、安全防护、家具与建筑、交通运输、服装等众多领域。

5. 康菲石油相信无论是个人还是公司，都要积极投身社会才能成为好公民，秉承这样的信念，我们长久以来一直致力于回馈社会——运用我们的想象力和专业的技能，投入时间或提供经济支持。无论是公司还是员工，康菲中国都在积极回馈公司业务所在的社区，包括发展教育、保护环境、确保员工安全和进行技术转让。康菲石油的表现得到了社会各界的肯定。

6. We are planning to create three multinational companies in Asia, Europe and the Americas. They will be entirely independent units responsible for their own profits and losses.

7. Dishes served at Cuihualou Restaurant require fine material, meticulous cooking, adept skills and strict cooking time. All of them are pleasant to your eyes, your tongue and above all, your health.

8. As a large state-owned listed developer with national first class qualification, we have been standing out as a leading brand in China's real estate sector for 5 consecutive years. Since we got listed in the Shanghai Stock Exchange in July 2006, our preliminary contracts signed had reached RMB 136.676 billion by the end of 2015, with more than RMB 360 billion of total assets.

9. As a trusted partner dedicated to China's economic and social development, Siemens has been actively engaged in corporate social responsibility programs and activities to promote access to technology and access to education, and contribute to sustainable community. Founded in 2012, the Siemens Employee Volunteer Association (SEVA) has organized volunteering activities in 15 cities and benefited tens of thousands of people across China.

10. Making Suning a century brand relies on talents. Suning has taken human resources as the core competitiveness and strategic capital for its long-term development, and has established the systems of recruitment, training, cultivation, motivation and career planning. Insisting on the HR policy of internal cultivation and promotion, Suning emphasizes the excellent character, moderate capability, great devotion and strong team spirit, and has initiated 10 plus training programs such as "1200 Project", "General Manager Team", "Purchasing Manager Team", "Store Manager Team", "Supervisor Team", "Sales Team", and "Blue Collar Project" for the further development of both the employees and the company.

Chapter 4　商务会议报告

一、翻译以下短语。

1. present market trend
2. priority
3. loss of profit
4. questionnaire
5. open tendering
6. 前言部分
7. 可行性报告
8. 售后服务
9. 总的来说
10. 例会

二、翻译以下句子。

1. 本报告根据家电制造企业的销量对前 50 名进行排名。

2. 尽管中国人口众多，中国果汁饮料消费量很低。2009 年，人均果汁消费量不到 10 升。

3. 根据目前中国服装产业的状况，未来相当长一段时间内，下列八大发展趋势在中国服装市场占主导地位。

4. 我们的调研结果表明：虽然大体上说两家公司在（待遇）条件方面有许多共同点，但在对待当地和国外管理人员方面，跨太平洋海运和国际空运还是有一些小小的区别。

5. 报告中所分析的公司，其总营业额大约为 5 870 亿欧元，包括本报告中涉及价值 1 250 亿欧元的常用电器：冰箱、冷柜、洗衣机、烘干机、洗碗机、烹饪器具、微波炉、空调和吸尘器。

6. Thirty-five foreign ministers from the Group of 77 developing nations will be present and other member countries are expected to be represented by high-level non-ministerial delegations at the two-day meeting.

7. The digital and transportation network, as a secure and neutrally operated low cost common infrastructure, can act as a conduit to streamline data communications among the many players in the trade and logistics community both locally and internationally and so significantly improve the flow of both goods and information.

8. We would like to extend our warm welcome to friends, old and new, from various circles who come to our fair, and we sincerely hope that buyers and sellers will enter into pleasant cooperation and enjoy prosperity in their business.

9. The 20th China Carpet Fair will be the largest of its kind in scale. Foreign trade

corporations specialized in carpet business, other various foreign trade companies authorized to export carpets as well as 108 carpet factories from all over the country are to take an active part in the exhibition. Moreover, over 200 companies and firms from more than 30 countries and regions around the world have gladly accepted the invitation to the Carpet Fair.

10. With China's entrance into the World Trade Organization, it has embarked on a historic program of market-opening reforms that will affect all Chinese regions and all segments of society.

Chapter 5 商务谈判

一、翻译以下短语。

1. selling rate
2. processing on giving materials
3. invitation for tender
4. more or less clause
5. price indication
6. 有效期限
7. 港口税
8. 报关
9. 回佣
10. 即期装运

二、翻译以下句子。

1. I would like you to complete the payment in 2 years if it's not too difficult for you.

2. We hope for you to provide us with the necessary technique used in assembling the parts.

3. Would you like to tell me the rate of processing and assembling charges, and also the method of payment?

4. After the delivery, we pay off the rest of it in four payments in accordance with the progress of the project installation.

5. Technical specifications of the goods offered by bidders must comply with the requirements set forth in the attached specification sheet for each item.

6. 我们要求你方提供的设备和技术应达到世界先进水准，价格合理，适合我方生产情形。

7. 为了掌握你方提供的设备的全部技术，我方要求对设备的操作和维修人员进行技术培训。

8. 我们所关心的是开户银行何时能支付这笔款项。

9. 我们希望得知你方提议的要点，以便我们对你方建议的经济可行性做出初步的估计。

10. 全部材料由你方提供，我公司只负责加工，对此我们需要收取加工费。

Chapter 6 代 理 合 同

一、翻译以下英文代理合同。

独家代理协议

本协议系于_____年_____月_____日，由当事人一方 ABC 公司，按中国法律组建并存在的公司，其主营业地在_____（以下简称卖方）与他方当事人 XYZ 公司，按_____国法律组建并存在的公司，其主营业地在_____（以下简称代理商）所签订。双方一致同意约定如下：

第一条　委任

在本协议有效期内，卖方指定代理商为本协议第四条项下商品的独家代理商，在第三条所规定的区域内招揽顾客的订单。代理商同意并接受上述委任。

第二条　代理商的义务

代理商应严格遵守卖方随时给予的任何指令，而且不得代表卖方作出任何担保、承诺，以及订立契约、合同或做出其他对卖方有约束力的行为。对于代理商违反卖方指令或超出指令范围的一切作为或不作为，卖方将不承担任何责任。

第三条　代理区域

本协议所指的代理区域是_____（以下简称区域）。

第四条　代理商品

本协议所指的代理商品是_____（以下简称商品）。

第五条　独家代理权

基于本协议授予的独家代理权，卖方不得在代理区域内，直接或间接地通过其他渠道销售或出口代理商品。代理商也不得在代理区域内经销、分销或促销与代理商品相似或有竞争性的商品，也不能招揽或接受以到区域外销售为目的的订单。在本协议有效期内，对来自于区域内其他顾客有关代理商品的订单、询价，卖方都应将其转交给代理商。

第六条　最低代理额和价格

在本协议有效期内，如果卖方通过代理商每年（12 个月）从顾客处收到的货款总金额低于_____，则卖方有权提前 30 天书面通知代理商解除本协议。

卖方应经常向代理商提供最低的价格表及商品可以成交的条款、条件。

第七条　订单的处理

在招揽订单时，代理商应将卖方成交的条件、合同的一般条款充分通知顾客，也应告知顾客任何合同的订立都须经卖方确认。代理商应将其收到的订单立即转交给卖方，以供卖方选择是否接受订单。卖方有权拒绝或接受代理商所获得的订单或订单的一部分，而代理商对于被拒绝的订单或其中的一部分，无任何佣金请求权。

第八条　费用

除另有约定外，所有的费用和开支，如通信费、差旅费及其他有关商品销售的费用，都应由代理商承担。除此以外，代理商还应承担维持其办公场所、销售人员及用于执行卖方指令的任何或全部有关代理商的义务而发生的费用。

第九条 佣金

卖方接受代理商直接获得的所有订单后,就应按商品净销售额的百分之＿＿＿＿,以＿＿＿＿（货币）支付给代理商佣金。佣金只有在卖方收到顾客的全部货款后,每6个月支付一次,以汇付方式支付。

第十条 商情报告

卖方和代理商都应按季度或按对方要求提供有关市场信息的报告,以尽可能促进商品的销售。

第十一条 商品的推销

在代理区域内,代理商应积极、充分地进行广告宣传以促进商品的销售。卖方应向代理商提供一定数量的广告印刷品、商品样本、小册子及代理商合理要求的其他材料。

第十二条 工业产权保护

在本协议有效期内,代理商可使用卖方的商标,但仅限于代理商品的销售。如果在本协议终止后,代理商在销售库存代理商品时,仍可使用卖方的商标。代理商须承认使用于或包含于代理商品中的任何专利、商标、版权及其他工业产权,都属于卖方所有,并且不得以任何方式提出异议。一旦发现侵权,代理商应及时通知卖方并协助卖方采取措施保护卖方产权利益。

第十三条 协议期限

本协议经双方签字生效。在本协议终止前至少3个月,卖方与代理商应共同协商协议的续延。如果双方一致同意续延,在上述规定的条款、条件下,附上补充文件,本协议将继续有效至另外＿＿＿＿年。如果不发生续延,本协议将于＿＿＿＿年＿＿＿＿月＿＿＿＿日终止。

第十四条 协议的中止

在本协议有效期内,任何一方当事人不履行协议或违反本协议的条款,如第五、六、十一条,双方当事人应争取及时解决争议的问题以期双方满意。如果在违约方接到书面通知后3日内问题仍不能解决,非违约方将有权中止本协议。此外,如遇一方当事人破产、无力偿付债务、清算、死亡及/或被第三人兼并,另一方当事人可提出中止本协议,且无须书面通知对方。

第十五条 不可抗力

任何一方对由于下列原因而导致不能或暂时不能履行全部或部分协议义务的,不负责任:自然灾害、政府采购或禁令及其他任何双方在签约时不能预料、无法控制且不能避免和克服的事件。但受不可抗力影响的一方,应尽快将发生的事件书面通知对方,并附上证明材料。

第十六条 准据法

本协议有关的贸易条款应按 Incoterms 1990 解释。本协议的有效性、组成及履行受中华人民共和国法律管辖。

第十七条 仲裁

对于因履行本合同发生的一切争议,双方应友好协商解决,如协商无法解决争议,则应提交中国国际经济贸易仲裁委员会（北京）,依据其仲裁规则,仲裁费应由败诉一方承担,仲裁委员会另有规定的除外。

本合同由双方代表签字后生效,一式两份,双方各执一份。

ABC 公司　　　　　　　　　　　　　　XYZ 公司

代表＿＿＿＿＿＿　　　　　　　　　　代表＿＿＿＿＿＿

二、翻译以下中文代理合同。

AGREEMENT OF EXCLUSIVE SELLING AGENT

Manufacturer:

Agent:

The two parties sign this agency agreement on the basis of equality, free will and mutual consultation. Both sides must comply.

Article 1 Exclusive Selling Agent

The manufacturer appoints the agent to act as its exclusive selling agent in China to sell the following products of the manufacturer:

Products: _____

Article 2 Responsibility of the Agent

The agent shall make all efforts to promote the sale of the products of the manufacturer using the agent's marketing organization. The agent shall send all enquiries and orders received to the manufacturer and have no rights to sign any binding agreement on behalf of the manufacturer. The agent shall explain to the customers all the technical parameters and commercial terms stated by the manufacturer and take all steps to coordinate between the manufacturer and the customers to secure the orders.

The agent, in relation to the products covered by this agency agreement, shall describe them only as "sales and service agent" for the products and not hold themselves out or permit any person to hold himself out as being authorized to bind the manufacturer in any way or to do any act which might reasonably create an impression that the agent is so authorized. The offers given and orders received will always include a clause "Subject to approval/acceptance of the order by M/s Veejay Lakshmi Engineering Works Limited." The right to receive/accept the orders and make the invoices for the products is expressly reserved to the manufacturer.

The agent shall not make or give promises, warranties or guarantees or representations concerning the products other than those authorized by the manufacturer in writing.

The agent shall not use any advertising, promotional or selling materials in relation to the products except those supplied or approved by the manufacturer.

The agent shall obtain all the permissions required by them for carrying the business as agents for sales and service and shall also keep the manufacturer informed of the import duty rates and conditions for any concessions, the laws and regulations in China relating to method of manufacturing, labeling or sale of the products and will also notify the manufacturer in the event the agent is aware that any of the products of the manufacturer is in breach of any such laws or regulations.

Article 3 Training

In order to understand the technical characteristic of the products, the manufacturer agrees to assign technicians to train the sales personnel of the agent in China. The number of persons to be trained and the place of training shall be discussed and finalized on mutual consent from time to time.

In order to provide after-sales service like erection, commissioning and attending service calls during the warranty period, the manufacturer agrees to train two technicians of the agent (one is mechanical technician, the other is electrical technician). If it is necessary for these two technicians to be trained in India, the boarding and lodging and their local travel expenses in India will be borne by the manufacturer. Air fare to & from China will be borne by the agent. Similarly if the manufacturer deputes their engineers for training in China, air fare will be borne by the manufacturer and all expenses for boarding and lodging and local travel expenses in China for the manufacturer's engineers will be borne by the agent. The after-sales service fee within guarantee period should be charged by the manufacturer. If out the guarantee period, the after-sales service fee should be charged by the agent to the customers, which will be negotiated and finalized separately.

Article 4 Advertisement and Exhibition

Both the manufacturer and the agent will discuss and finalize the budget for the sales promotion activities like advertisements in newspapers, road shows, seminars, participation in exhibitions, etc. and the expenses will be shared by both sides. The sharing pattern will be on mutual consent after discussions. The manufacturer at its own expense will provide the catalogues for all products printed in local language. The agent will provide all assistance for translation and printing.

Article 5 Financial Responsibility

The agent is responsible for all activities relating to collection of payment for the goods sold with the customers for opening of letters of credit and collection of payment as per the terms of the order. The agent shall also adopt appropriate measures to inquire upon the customers' credit worthiness and paying capacity whenever the order is secured on credit terms. In the unlikely event of any litigation for collection of payment, the agent will provide all assistance required for such litigation. However, all expenses relating to the litigation will be borne by the manufacturer.

The agent has no rights to accept payment on behalf of the manufacturer without permission.

Article 6 Users' Opinion

The agent has rights to heed and accept the customers' advice and complaints. The agent shall inform the manufacturer immediately and pay attention to the manufacturer's vital interests.

Article 7 Providing Information

The agent shall forward once every three months to the manufacturer detailed reports on current market conditions and competition. The agent shall periodically visit all customers or potential customers in the territory for the purpose of promoting the products as the agent thinks fit and maintain an updated list of customers and potential customers for the products in the territory and supply the manufacturer a copy of such list whenever required by the manufacturer. The agent shall also notify the manufacturer of all enquiries received and offers submitted for the products to prospective customers.

Article 8 Fair Competition

The agent undertakes the following.

(1) not to compete or help others compete with the manufacturer;

(2) not to manufacture the products covered by this agreement or similar products;

(3) not to get any benefits from the manufacturer's competitors and opponents;

(4) not to take agency or sell products similar to the products covered by this agreement.

As soon as this agreement comes into effect, the agent shall inform the manufacturer of all their signed binding agreements with others. And all agreements signed in future shall be informed to the manufacturer. During the period when the agent is engaging in other business activities, the agent shall not ignore their obligations to the manufacturer under this agreement.

Article 9　Secrecy

The agent should not expose the business secrets of the manufacturer, and should not use confidential information exceeding the scope of the agreement.

All the product designs and specifications belong to the manufacturer, and the agent shall return them to the manufacturer when the agreement is terminated.

Article 10　Sub-contract Agent

The agent can use sub-contract agent if agreed by the manufacturer. The agent shall take full responsibility for the activities of the sub-contract agent.

Article 11　Protection of Industrial Property Rights

If the agent finds any third party whose behavior is detrimental to the manufacturer's industrial property rights and benefits, he shall report the truth to the manufacturer. The agent, in consultation with the manufacturer shall take all steps to prevent such illegal action by third parties, and the relevant expenses shall be borne by the manufacturer. This will be subject to manufacturer's prior acceptance, in writing, regarding quantum of expenses.

Article 12　Scope of Exclusive Selling Right

This is an exclusive selling agency agreement for the territories mentioned. The manufacturer, during the currency of this agreement, shall not appoint any other person, firm or company as agent for the promotion, sale or service of the products in the territory. However, the manufacturer can utilize the services of third parties for sale of the products provided the same is approved by the agent in writing. The manufacturer also retains the right to utilize the services of third parties in China who are already involved in the promotion of the products for such further periods the manufacturer and the agent discuss and agree. When such third parties are involved, the commission will be shared with such third parties in such proportion as mutually agreed by all the parties: the manufacturer, the agent and the third parties.

Article 13　Technical Assistance

The manufacturer shall help the agent to train the agent's employees to obtain knowledge of the products covered by this agreement.

Article 14　Amount of the Commission

The manufacturer shall pay to the agent 5% of the FOB value of the goods invoiced as commission to the agent. This commission will become payable only after the goods are invoiced and the payment is realized in full by the manufacturer. If the customers have not given the whole payment of the goods due to the reason of the products' quality, the agent shall get commission in accordance with the manufacturer's actual received payment.

Article 15　Commission on a fifty-fifty basis

If two agents of different areas have made massive efforts to get one order or if the delivery against an order is made to a customer's plant located in another agent's territory, then the commission will be shared on a fifty-fifty basis between the two agents involved.

Article 16 Failure in business, or termination of the agreement

The agent cannot get commission if the manufacturer didn't accept the order; the agent cannot get the commission if the contract introduced by the agent is terminated. This is not applicable when the termination of the contract is caused by the manufacturer.

Article 17 Calculation of the Commission

The commission will be calculated on net realized value. Net realized value will be FOB value of the goods invoiced minus payments, if any, due to third parties.

Article 18 Date of Paying Commission

The commission will be paid to the agent within 30 days of receipt of payment for the goods. For sales made on credit/deferred payment terms, if the credit is fully secured by letters of credit/bank guarantees, the payment of commission will be made within 30 days of delivery of the goods. If the transfer of currency abroad for payment of commission requires any permission from the government of India, payment shall be made after such permission is received.

While making the commission payment, the manufacturer shall also send a credit note giving the details of the workings for the commission with the details of the total invoice value, FOB value and the commission amount. In addition, the manufacturer shall send to the agent a quarterly statement giving the details of the sales made in the territory, the details of the credit notes sent and payments due/made during the quarter. This statement will be sent within 30 days of the end of a quarter.

Article 19 Currency for Commission

The commission is calculated and paid in the same currency in which the goods have been invoiced to the customer.

Article 20 Period of the Agreement

The agreement will become effective after being signed by both parties and will have duration of three years and can be renewed by giving three months' notice before date of expiry subject to acceptance to the other party. If no such notice is given by either one of the parties the agreement will expire on the date of expiry.

Article 21 Premature Termination

The agreement can be terminated earlier only if there is any breach of the duties and obligations under this agreement and one party is acting against the interest of the other party. The agreement also can be terminated earlier, before the expiry, if sufficient sales volumes are not achieved and if both the parties mutually come to a conclusion that it is not viable to continue the efforts for marketing the products in China.

Article 22 Return of the Stock

When the agreement is terminated, the agent shall return the products and spare parts on stock according to the manufacturer's instruction, and the relevant expenses shall be borne by the manufacturer.

Article 23 Unfinished Business Affair

The agent is eligible for full 5% commission for all orders received and pending to be executed at the time of expiry of the agreement and also for orders received with advance or letters of credit within 60 days of expiry of the agreement for offers made prior to the expiry of the agreement. This will be only for orders supported by letters of credit or advance payments and accepted by manufacturer in writing.

Article 24　Compensation

Unless the agreement is terminated due to the reason of breach of terms by the other party, both sides shall not make any claim for any compensation/loss if the agreement is terminated on its expiry.

Article 25　Modification

The modification and additional clauses of this agreement shall be based on the written form.

Article 26　Prohibition on Transfer

This agreement shall not be transferred without negotiation in advance.

Article 27　Lien

The agent has no lien on the manufacturer's property.

Article 28　Application of Law

The execution and performance of this agreement is governed by Chinese law.

Article 29　Arbitration

All disputes arising from the execution of this a greement shall be settled through friendly consultations. In case no settlement can be reached, the case in dispute shall then be submitted to the relevant arbitration commission for arbitration in accordance with its provisional rules of procedure. The decision made by this commission shall be regarded as final and binding upon both parties. Arbitration fees shall be borne by the losing party.

Manufacturer:　　　　　　　　　　　　　　Agent:
Representative:　　　　　　　　　　　　　Representative:
Date:　　　　　　　　　　　　　　　　　　Date:

Chapter 7　国际贸易合同

一、翻译以下英文合同。

加工装配合同

合同号：_____

签约日期：_____

签约地：_____

甲方（加工装配方）：_____公司

地址：_____

电话：_____　传真：_____　电子邮箱：_____

乙方（来料、来件方）：_____公司

地址：_____

电话：_____ 传真：_____ 电子邮箱：_____

　　双方在遵守中华人民共和国法律、法规的前提下，本着平等互利的原则，就来料加工_____进行了充分协商，一致达成如下合同条款：
　　一、双方责任
　　1. 甲方责任：
　　（1）提供有上盖之厂房_____平方米，无上盖场地_____平方米，工厂管理人员_____名，生产工人_____名。生产工人在开业后12个月增至_____名。在合同期内代乙方加工生产上述产品，加工成品后交回乙方复出口至_____。
　　（2）提供现有水、电设备供加工生产之用，如需新安装水、电设施，其费用由乙方支付。
　　（3）办理来料加工、装配有关业务的进出口手续及对工厂实行行政、财务等管理，不得把工作以任何形式承包给任何单位和个人经营。
　　2. 乙方责任：
　　（1）提供设备总值约_____万元。
　　（2）提供加工上述产品所需的原料、辅料和包装物料，具体数量、规格在各份具体生产加工合同中订明。
　　（3）工作人员如因工作不力（含工厂管理人员），经教育无效者，乙方有权向甲方提出调换，但禁止非法搜查甲方工厂工人的身体。
　　二、加工数量
　　第一年加工上述产品，加工费约_____万元，从第二年开始的产量，应在前一年的基础上有所增加，具体数量应在生产合同中订明。
　　三、工资
　　1. 试产（培训）期为_____个月，在试产期内，工人每人每月工资为_____元，每月工作_____日，每天工作_____小时。
　　2. 试产期满后，采取按件计酬方式，在坚持互利原则的基础上，双方应根据加工的品种、规格、款式和工艺繁简不同进行定价，并在生产加工合同中订明为确保工人的合理收入，工资平均每人每月不低于_____元。需要加班时，加班费另计，但每个工人每天加班时间最长不得超过_____小时。
　　3. 甲方工人生产消耗的水、电费由乙方负责。
　　4. 乙方每月支付甲方_____元作为工作管理费。
　　四、损耗率
　　1. 试产期内的损耗率，实报实销。
　　2. 试产期后的损耗率，由双方商定，并在生产加工合同中订明。
　　五、来料和交货期
　　1. 乙方按生产合同的加工量，按月提供足够数量的原材料和包装物料。为使甲方工厂能正常生产，乙方必须在每批产品开始加工前_____天，将所需的原材料和包装物料运抵甲方工厂。除因人力不可抗拒之原因外，甲方工厂每月生产至少_____天。如乙方来料不足，导致甲方停工_____天，乙方应按在厂工人以停工天数计，每人每天补助生活费_____元，支付给甲方工厂。
　　2. 为使乙方能开展正常的业务活动，甲方应向乙方按商定的交货期，按时、按质、按量交货。如非人力不可抗拒原因，甲方不按时、按质、按量交货，造成乙方的经济损失，甲方应负赔偿之责任，赔偿数额可在具体的生产加工合同中订明。

3. 由乙方提供的机械、通风、照明等设备及原材料、包装物料，在甲方工厂由双方进行交收登记，建立账册。甲方工厂加工后的成品，在甲方工厂经乙方验收起运后，甲方不负产品规格、质量、短缺等任何责任。

六、支付条款

工人工资及管理费每月以付款交单形式结算一次，由甲方工厂会同（____政府授权的处理来料加工事务并具有外贸经营权的）_____贸易公司（以下简称"授权贸易公司"）开具发票后，通过中国银行（深圳分行）向乙方在香港开户的银行（____银行，账号_____）办理。如乙方超过_____天仍未付款给甲方，则按逾期天数，承担支付当时银行利率所发生的利息。如乙方连续_____月不结汇，甲方有权停止出货或采取其他措施。

七、劳动保护及保险

1. 工厂应做好劳动保护及安全工作，完善防尘、防烟、防毒设施，厂房保持通风明亮，内外环境卫生整洁，对有污染性的项目，须经市环保部门批准，方能立项经营。

2. 乙方提供的机械、通风、照明设备、原材料、包装物料及甲方工厂加工后的成品运输费用，均由乙方负责。

3. 原材料、包装物料的运进，成品运出及加工期间存放的机械设备、原料和包装物料及操作机械的工人，均由乙方向_____保险公司投保。

八、技术交流

在设备运抵甲方工厂后，乙方应尽快派出人员进行安装，甲方派出人员进行协助。从试产期开始，乙方应派出技术人员到甲方工厂进行技术培训，直到工人能基本掌握生产技术，进行正常生产为止。乙方技术人员的工资及一切费用由乙方负责，甲方提供生活上的方便。

九、有效期限

本合同经批准签订后，乙方须将商业登记及银行资信证明书交由甲方办理营业执照和海关登记。本合同有效期为____年，即从____年__月__日至____年__月__日。如要提前终止或延长本合同，须提前三个月通知对方，并经双方协商处理终止或延长合同事宜。如某方单独提前终止合同，需负责补偿对方的经济损失。补偿办法以终止合同前半年内的月平均工资为准，补偿_____个月的工资总额给对方。

合同期满后，不动资产（如厂房、宿舍）归甲方所有，机械、车辆、通风设备归乙方所有，并按海关和有关规定及时办理核销手续。

双方同意，在本合同经批准签订后_____天内，乙方向甲方预付_____元作为履约保证金，从甲方收到履约保证金之日起_____个月内，乙方仍不投产开业，履约保证金即无条件归甲方所有，同时，甲方有权终止合同。如乙方能按时投产开业，该履约保证金可作工资抵付给甲方。

十、仲裁

凡因本合同引起的或与本合同有关（包括任一生产加工合同）的任何争议，应通过友好协商解决，如协商不能解决，均应提交中国国际经济贸易仲裁委员会深圳分会，按照申请仲裁时该会施行有效的仲裁规则进行仲裁。仲裁裁决是终局的，对双方均有约束力。

十一、语言

本合同以英文和中文书就，两种文本具有同等效力。但在对其解释产生异议时，以中文文本为准。

十二、合同的份数和修订

本合同正本一式五份，甲乙双方、海关、车管所、政府授权的处理来料加工事务并有外贸经营权的_____公司各一份，均具有同等效力。

本合同如有未尽事宜，双方可随时补充或修改，并报政府有关部门批准实施。

甲方：_____　　　　　　乙方：_____
授权代表：_____　　　　　　授权代表：_____
代表（签字）：_____　　　　　代表（签字）：_____
授权贸易公司：_____

二、翻译以下中文合同。

Import Contract

Contract No.:_____
Date:_____
Signed at:_____

The Buyer:_____
Address:_____
Tel:_____ Fax:_____
E-mail:_____

The Seller:_____
Address:_____
Tel:_____ Fax:_____
E-mail:_____

The seller and the buyer agree to conclude this contract subject to the terms and conditions stated below:

1. Name, specifications and quality of commodity:_____

2. Quantity (_____% more or less allowed):_____

3. Unit price:_____

4. Total amount:_____

5. Terms of delivery (FOB/CFR/CIF):_____

6. Country of origin and manufacturers:_____

7. Packing: The packing of the goods shall be preventive from dampness, rust, moisture, erosion and shock, and shall be suitable for ocean transportation/ multiple transportation. The seller shall be liable for any damage and loss of the goods attributable to the inadequate or improper packing. The measurement, gross weight, net weight and the cautions such as "Do Not Stack Upside Down" "Keep Away From Moisture" "Handle With Care"

shall be stenciled on the surface of each package with fadeless pigment.

8. Shipping marks: _____

9. Time of shipment: _____

10. Port of loading: _____

11. Port of destination: _____

12. Insurance:

Insurance shall be covered by the ____ for 110% of the invoice value against _____ Risks and _____ Additional Risks.

13. Terms of payment:

(1) Letter of credit: The buyer shall in _____ days prior to the time of shipment /after this contract comes into effect, open an irrevocable letter of credit in favor of the seller. The letter of credit shall expire ____ days after the completion of loading of the shipment as stipulated.

(2) Documents against payment: After shipment, the seller shall draw a sight bill of exchange on the buyer and deliver the documents through the seller's bank and _____ Bank to the buyer against payment, i.e. D/P. The Buyer shall effect the payment immediately upon the first presentation of the bill(s) of exchange.

(3) Documents against acceptance: after shipment, the seller shall draw a sight bill of exchange, payable _____ days after the buyer delivers the documents through the seller's bank and _____ Bank to the buyer against acceptance (D/A _____ days). The buyer shall make the payment on date of the bill of exchange.

(4) Cash on delivery (COD): The buyer shall pay to the seller total amount within _____ days after the receipt of the goods (This clause is not applied to the terms of FOB, CFR and CIF).

14. Documents required:

The seller shall present the following documents required to the bank for negotiation/ collection:

(1) Full set of clean on board ocean/combined transportation/land bills of lading and blank endorsed marked freight prepaid/ to collect;

(2) Signed commercial invoice in _____ copies indicating Contract No., L/C No. (terms of L/C) and shipping marks;

(3) Packing list/weight memo in _____ copies issued by ____;

(4) Certificate of quality in _____ copies issued by _____;

(5) Certificate of quantity in _____ copies issued by _____;

(6) Insurance policy/certificate in _____ copies (terms of CIF);

(7) Certificate of origin in _____ copies issued by _____;

(8) The seller shall, within ____ hours after shipment effected, send by courier each copy of the above-mentioned documents No. ____.

15. Terms of Shipment:

(1) FOB: The seller shall, 30 days before the shipment date specified in the contract, advise the buyer by _____ of the contract No., commodity, quantity, amount, packages, gross weight, measurement, and the date of shipment in order that the buyer can charter a vessel. In the event of the seller's failure to effect loading when the vessel arrives duly at the loading port, all expenses including dead freight and/or demurrage charges thus incurred shall be for the seller's account.

(2) CIF/CFR: The seller shall ship the goods duly within the shipping duration from the port of loading to the port of destination. Under CFR terms, the seller shall advise the buyer by _____ of the contract No., commodity, invoice value and the date of dispatch two days before the shipment for the buyer to arrange insurance in time.

16. Shipping advice:

The seller shall, immediately upon the completion of the loading of the goods, advise the buyer of the contract No., commodity, quantity, invoice value, gross weight, name of vessel and shipment date by _____ within _____ hours.

17. Quality guarantee:

The seller shall guarantee that the commodity must be in conformity with the quality, specifications and quantity specified in this contract and letter of quality guarantee. The guarantee period shall be _____ months after the arrival of the goods at the port of destination, and during the period the seller shall be responsible for the damage due to the defects in designing and manufacturing of the manufacturer.

18. Inspection:

(1) The seller shall have the goods inspected by _____ days before the shipment and have the inspection certificate issued by _____. The buyer may have the goods reinspected by _____ after the goods arrival at the destination.

(2) The manufacturers shall, before delivery, make a precise and comprehensive inspection of the goods with regard to its quality, specifications, performance and quantity/weight, and issue inspection certificates certifying the technical data and conclusion of the inspection. After arrival of the goods at the port of destination, the buyer shall apply to China Commodity Inspection Bureau (hereinafter referred to as CCIB) for a further inspection as to the specifications and quantity/weight of the goods. If damages of the goods are found, or the specifications and/or quantity are not in conformity with the stipulations in this contract, except when the responsibilities lie with insurance company or shipping company, the buyer shall, within _____ days after arrival of the goods at the port of destination, claim against the seller, or reject the goods according to the inspection certificate issued by CCIB. In case of damage of the goods incurred due to the design or manufacture defects and/or in case the quality and performance are not in conformity with the contract, the buyer shall, during the guarantee period, request CCIB to make a survey.

19. Claim:

The buyer shall make a claim against the seller (including replacement of the goods) by the further inspection certificate and all the expenses incurred thereafter shall be borne by the seller. The claims mentioned above shall be regarded as being accepted if the seller fails to reply within _____ days after the seller receives the buyer's claim.

20. Late delivery and penalty:

Should the seller fail to make delivery on time as stipulated in the contract, with the exception of force majeure causes specified in Clause 21 of this contract, the buyer shall agree to postpone the delivery on the condition that the seller agrees to pay a penalty which shall be deducted by the paying bank from the payment under negotiation. The rate of penalty is charged at _____% for every _____ days, odd days less than _____ days should be counted as _____ days. But the penalty, however, shall not exceed _____% of the total value of the goods involved in the delayed delivery. In case the seller fails to make delivery _____ days later than the time of shipment stipulated in the contract, the buyer shall have the right to cancel the contract and the seller, in spite of the cancellation, shall nevertheless pay the aforesaid penalty to the buyer without delay.

The buyer shall have the right to lodge a claim against the seller for the losses sustained if any.

21. Force majeure:

The seller shall not be responsible for the delay of shipment or non-delivery of the goods due to force majeure, which might occur during the process of manufacturing or in the course of loading or transit. The seller shall advise the buyer immediately of the occurrence mentioned above and within _____ days. Thereafter the seller shall send a notice by courier to the buyer for their acceptance of a certificate of the accident issued by the competent government authorities under whose jurisdiction the accident occurs as evidence thereof. Under such circumstances the seller, however, is still under the obligation to take all necessary measures to hasten the delivery of the goods. In case the accident lasts for more than _____ days the buyer shall have the right to cancel the contract.

22. Arbitration:

Any dispute arising from or in connection with the contract shall be settled through friendly negotiation. In case no settlement is reached, the dispute shall be submitted to China International Economic and Trade Arbitration Commission (CIETAC), for arbitration in accordance with its rules in effect at the time of applying for arbitration. The place of arbitration is in _____, China. The award is final and binding upon both parties.

23. Notice:

All notice shall be written in _____ and served to both parties by fax/courier according to the following addresses. If any changes of the addresses occur, one party shall inform the other party of the change of address within _____ days after the change.

24. The terms in the contract are based on INCOTERMS 2000 of the International Chamber of Commerce.

25. Additional clause:

If any conflicts between contract clause here above and this additional clause occur, it is subject to this additional clause.

26. This contract is executed in two counterparts each in Chinese and English, each of which shall be deemed equally authentic. This contract is in _____ copies, effective since being signed/sealed by both parties.

Representative of the Buyer
(Authorized signature):_____

Representative of the Seller
(Authorized signature):_____

Chapter 8　国际贸易单证

一、翻译以下短语。

1. documents against payment
2. documents against acceptance
3. telegraphic transfer
4. documentary collection
5. terms of payment
6. 航运提单
7. 净重
8. 海运船只
9. 关税壁垒
10. 成本加运费价

二、翻译以下句子。

1. 以下规定的每项款额须用美元支付。

2. 我们同意采用开立以你方为受益人的跟单即期汇票来代替信用证的支付方式。

3. 全套整洁已装船的海运提单，凭船方指令签发，空白背书，并标明"通知XYZ公司，运费到付"。

4. 由承运的运输公司所开具的收据的日期即被视为交货日期。

5. 货物的相关议付单据现存我行，请接本通知后前来收取。

6. Packets of biscuits with a guarantee period of two or three weeks.

7. All master cartons must bear the name of country of origin.

8. 30% advance payment paid against stand by L/C and the remaining paid by T/T against B/L before shipment.

9. We declare that the goods will not be sent by a ship which is included on the black list.

10. The bearer shall present the draft to the payer for acceptance before the date of maturity.

Chapter 9　信　用　证

一、翻译以下短语。

1. 电汇
2. 善意持票人
3. 开证行
4. 承兑
5. 光票信用证
6. 提示/交单
7. 即期汇票
8. 提单
9. 担保书
10. 有效期
11. documentary L/C
12. packing list
13. collection
14. consignee
15. remittance
16. insurance policy
17. negotiation bank
18. commercial invoice
19. clean on board bill of lading
20. certificate of origin

二、翻译以下句子。

1. 已签署的商业发票一式三份，且该发票中规定的货物须与形式发票中提及的货物保持严格一致。

2. 全套清洁已装船提单，凭指示空白背书。

3. 保兑的不可撤销的无追索权的以中国远洋运输公司为受益人的信用证，合同货物全部货款为美元，凭即期汇票并附运输单据向装运港的中国银行议付。

4. 由出口国商会出具的原产地证书须与运输单据正本一起提交。

5. 合同签订后7天内，买方以电汇方式预付全部货款的10%作为定金，余款（90%）采用不可撤销即期跟单信用证方式结算。

6. In accordance with the negotiation, payment is by 100% confirmed and irrevocable L/C at sight in favor of us. This credit must be issued and sent to the seller one month before shipment, and it is valid to be negotiated in Hong Kong 15 days after the date of shipment.

7. Beneficiary's original signed commercial invoices at least in 8 copies issued in the name of the buyer indicating the merchandise, country of origin and any other relevant information.

8. A reimbursing bank's charges are for the account of the issuing bank. However, if the charges are for the account of the beneficiary, it is the responsibility of an issuing bank to indicate in the credit and in the reimbursement authorization. If a reimbursing bank's charges are for the account of the beneficiary, they shall be deducted from the amount due to a claiming bank when reimbursement is made.

9. In documents other than the commercial invoice, the description of the goods, services or performance, if stated, may be in general terms not conflicting with their description in the credit.

10. Payment is to be made by confirmed, irrevocable letter of credit, without recourse, available by 60 days sight draft upon presentation of shipping documents to the negotiating bank in Nanjing. Party B shall pay Party A 2% of invoice value as interest charges for the 60 days delayed payment. The letter of credit for each order shall reach Party A 45 days before the date of shipment.

三、翻译以下两段话。

1.
自发出信用证修改书之时起，开证行就不可撤销地受其发出修改的约束。保兑行可将其保兑承诺扩展至修改内容，且自其通知该修改之时起，即不可撤销地受到该修改的约束。然而，保兑行可选择仅将修改通知受益人而不对其加具保兑，但必须不延误地将此情况通知开证行和受益人。在受益人向通知修改的银行表示接受该修改内容之前，原信用证（或包含先前已被接受修改的信用证）的条款和条件对受益人仍然有效。受益人应发出接受或拒绝接受修改的通知。如受益人未提供上述通知，当其提交至被指定银行或开证行的单据与信用证以及尚未表示接受的修改的要求一致时，则该事实即视为受益人已作出接受修改的通知，并从此时起，该信用证已被修改。

2.
Provided that the stipulated documents are presented to the nominated bank or to the issuing bank and that they constitute a complying presentation, the issuing bank must honor if the credit is available by:

(1) sight payment, deferred payment or acceptance with the issuing bank;

(2) sight payment with a nominated bank and that nominated bank does not pay;

(3) deferred payment with a nominated bank and that nominated bank does not incur its

deferred payment undertaking or, having incurred its deferred payment undertaking, does not pay at maturity;

(4) acceptance with a nominated bank and that nominated bank does not accept a draft drawn on it or, having accepted a draft drawn on it, does not pay at maturity;

(5) negotiation with a nominated bank and that nominated bank does not negotiate.

An issuing bank is irrevocably bound to honour as of the time it issues the credit.

An issuing bank undertakes to reimburse a nominated bank that has honored or negotiated a complying presentation and forwarded the documents to the issuing bank. Reimbursement for the amount of a complying presentation under a credit available by acceptance or deferred payment is due at maturity, whether or not the nominated bank prepaid or purchased before maturity. An issuing bank's undertaking to reimburse a nominated bank is independent of the issuing bank's undertaking to the beneficiary.

Chapter 10 商 务 索 赔

一、翻译以下短语。

1. 到货重量
2. 错误包装
3. 质量低劣
4. 向某人索赔
5. 由……支配
6. short weight
7. rough handling
8. delay shipment
9. in view of
10. go into

二、翻译以下句子。

1. 我们很惊奇地发现货物的质量低于样品的质量。
2. 8 日送达时有 5 箱货物严重损坏。
3. 我们就上批船货的全部损失向你方提出 1 000 英镑的索赔。
4. 根据合同第 18 款，我方向你方提出如下索赔。
5. 兹附一份检验报告作为我们索赔的根据。

6. About one third of the glassware has been broken owing to improper packing, with which our clients are much unsatisfied.

7. Much to our regret, the size and shape of the goods we received are not in conformity with what we ordered. We, therefore, must ask for replacement by the correct goods as soon as possible.

8. As the quality of your shipment for our order No.586 is not in compliance with the agreed specifications, we cannot but file a claim against you.

9. We are sending you documentary proofs to back up our claim.

10. We shall lodge a claim for all the loss incurred as a consequence of your failure to ship our order in time.

三、翻译以下两封信函。

1.

敬启者：

我们写信通知贵方，第519号订单玩具已经收到，但货物状况很不令人满意，故我们不得不提出索赔。经检查，我们发现有10%的货物破损，而且有一些有严重破损现象。很明显，这是由于包装不妥造成的。因此我们无法以原价售出货物。建议贵方依照发票金额给予20%的折扣，这是我们所建议降低的售价额度。如果贵方无法接受，我们将不得不退货，并要求替换新货。

谨上

2.

Dear Sirs,

Re: Claim on Short Weight

The shipment of 1,500 cartons of canned mushroom under the contract No. FA7708 has arrived per "YONGFENG" steamer on 10th April. Unfortunately we have found 145 cartons missing. The shipping company told us that only 1,355 cartons had been shipped on the steamer.

As the weight is short in large quantities, could you make up for the 145 cartons of missing goods when you deliver the last three items? You are kindly requested to check whether these 1,500 cartons of mushroom were loaded on ship in whole at the port of shipment.

We await your early reply.

Sincerely yours,

Chapter 11　商 务 仲 裁

一、翻译以下短语。

1. 涉外民事案件
2. 仲裁员
3. 公证行为
4. 口头裁定
5. 总则
6. commercial arbitration
7. arbitration award
8. final ruling
9. damages
10. appeal

二、翻译以下句子。

1. 为保证公正、及时地仲裁经济纠纷,保护当事人的合法权益,保障社会主义市场经济健康发展,制定本法。

2. 若前述裁决或协定所用文字非援引裁决地所在国之正式文字,申请承认并执行裁决的一方应具备该文件之此项文字译本。

3. 任何国家在签署、批准或加入本公约时,或于本公约第十条通知扩展适用时,应本着互惠原则声明,本国只对另一缔约国领域内作出的仲裁裁决的承认及执行适用本公约。

4. 在这种情况下,买方在合理的期限内已对货物作过检查,因为在货物抵达之前,一位专家曾被请去检查过装船。买方也应被认定在合理的期限内,即在专家报告公布后的8天内,就产品瑕疵作过通报。

5. 仲裁庭有权根据案件的具体情况在裁决书中裁定败诉方应补偿胜诉方因办理案件而支出的合理费用。仲裁庭裁定败诉方补偿胜诉方因办理案件而支出的费用是否合理时,应具体考虑案件的裁决结果、复杂程度、胜诉方当事人及/或代理人的实际工作量及案件的争议金额等因素。

6. The tribunal awarded the seller the full amount of its claim and set it off against part of the counterclaim filed by the buyer.

7. The parties adopting arbitration for dispute settlement shall reach an arbitration agreement on a mutually voluntary basis. An arbitration commission shall not accept an application for arbitration submitted by one of the parties in the absence of an arbitration agreement.

8. The respondent shall submit its statement of defense, evidence and other supporting documents within twenty (20) days of its receipt of the notice of arbitration. Counterclaim, if any, shall also be filed with evidence and supporting documents within such time period.

9. Where the arbitral tribunal considers it necessary, or where a party so requests and the arbitral tribunal agrees, the arbitral tribunal may first render a partial award on any part of the claim before rendering the final award. A partial award is final and binding upon both parties.

10. For a case examined by way of an oral hearing, after the arbitral tribunal has fixed a date for the first oral hearing, the parties shall be notified of the date at least fifteen (15) days in advance of the oral hearing. A party having justified reasons may request a postponement of the oral hearing. However, the party shall communicate such request in writing to the arbitral tribunal within three (3) days of its receipt of the notice of the oral hearing. The arbitral tribunal shall decide whether or not to postpone the oral hearing.

Chapter 12　国 际 商 法

一、翻译以下短语。

1. 反倾销
2. 商业模式
3. 普通法系

6. International Business Law
7. international commercial arbitration
8. civil law

4. 货币兑换
5. 政府担保
9. denial of justice
10. expropriation

二、翻译以下句子。

1. For purposes of this Law, force majeure means any objective circumstance which is unforeseeable, unavoidable and insurmountable.

2. With respect to a foreign-capital enterprise, the establishment of which has been applied for, if its products are subject to export license, export quota, or import license, or are under restrictions by the State, prior consent of the department of foreign economic relations and trade shall be obtained in accordance with the limits of powers for administration.

3. "Consignor" means any person by whom or in whose name or on whose behalf a multimodal transport contract has been conducted with the multimodal transport operator, or any person by whom or in whose name or on whose behalf the goods are actually delivered to the multimodal transport operator in relation to the multimodal transport contract.

4. Chambers of Commerce for Importers and Exporters shall abide by relevant laws and administrative regulations, coordinate and guide the foreign trade activities of their members under their articles of association, provide advisory services, report to the relevant authorities of the government the suggestions of their members with respect to foreign trade promotion, and actively promote foreign trade.

5. Unless otherwise expressly provided in this part of the Convention, if any notice, request or other communication is given or made by a party in accordance with this part and by means appropriate in the circumstances, a delay or error in the transmission of the communication or its failure to arrive does not deprive that party of the right to rely on the communication.

6. 承租人应当按照合同约定支付租金。承租人未按照合同约定的时间支付租金连续超过七日的，出租人有权解除合同，并有权要求赔偿因此遭受的损失。

7. 受要约人在承诺期限内发出承诺，按照通常情形能够及时到达要约人，但因其他原因承诺到达要约人时超过承诺期限的，除要约人及时通知受要约人因承诺超过期限不接受该承诺的以外，该承诺有效。

8. 设立外资企业的申请经审批机关批准后，外国投资者应当在收到批准证书之日起三十天内向工商行政管理机关申请登记，领取营业执照。外资企业的管理执照签发日期，为该企业的成立日期。

9. 如果将运输或部分运输委托给实际承运人执行时，不管根据海上运输合同是否可以这样做，承运人仍须按照本公约的规定对全部运输负责。关于实际承运人所履行的运输，承运人应对实际承运人及其受雇人和代理人在他们的受雇范围内的作为和不作为负责。

10. 当事人不愿和解、调解或者和解、调解不成的，可以根据仲裁协议向仲裁机构申请仲裁。涉外合同的当事人可以根据仲裁协议向中国仲裁机构或者其他仲裁机构申请仲裁。当事人没有订立仲裁协议或者仲裁协议无效的，可以向人民法院起诉。当事人应当履行发生法律效力的判决、仲裁裁决、调解书；拒不履行的，对方可以请求人民法院执行。

参考文献

[1] NEWMARK P. 翻译问题探讨[M]. 上海：上海外语教育出版社，2001.
[2] 董金玲，郝景亚，郑凌霄. 国际商务函电双语教程[M]. 北京：机械工业出版社，2011.
[3] 董晓波. 国际贸易英语函电[M]. 北京：北京交通大学出版社，2010.
[4] 董晓波. 商务英语翻译[M]. 北京：对外经济贸易大学出版社，2011.
[5] 车丽娟，贾秀海. 商务英语翻译教程[M]. 北京：对外经济贸易大学出版社，2007.
[6] 陈广，符兴新. 国际贸易制单实务[M]. 北京：中国经济出版社，2005.
[7] 陈孙笙. 商务会议报告汉英翻译探析：以吴仪副总理在中美知识产权圆桌会议上的讲话为例[J]. 金田，2011（8）.
[8] 何恩. 外贸"索赔、理赔"信函结构浅析及常用表达小结[J]. 广西大学梧州分校学报，2001（3）.
[9] 胡克. 承包工程中的商务索赔[J]. 国际经济合作，1988（9）.
[10] 黄赟琳. 商务往来写译模板 All-in-One[M]. 重庆：重庆大学出版社，2011.
[11] 李永红. 目的论视角下的企业外宣资料英译[J]. 文教资料，2007（4）.
[12] 梁法丽，黄宏. 产品说明书及其翻译[J]. 天津市经理学院学报，2012（3）.
[13] 廖英. 实用外贸英语函电、译文、练习答案及常见错误辨析[M]. 武汉：华中科技大学出版社，2003.
[14] 林巧莉. 解读科技英语中的名词化结构[J]. 科研英语学习，1988（1）.
[15] 刘白玉，高新华. 国际海运提单英语术语的特点及其翻译[J]. 湖北经济学院学报（人文社会科学版），2009（5）.
[16] 刘克，张琦. 银行国际业务英语[M]. 北京：首都经济贸易大学出版社，2013.
[17] 刘文义. 商务谈判中的翻译技巧的运用[J]. 黑龙江史志，2007（5）.
[18] 陆丹，黄琦. 国际商务英语中信用证的语言和翻译[J]. 湖南科技学院院报，2005（8）.
[19] 栾颖，韩立华，贯丽丽. 商务英语翻译[M]. 北京：世界图书出版公司，2012.
[20] 马庆林，孟超，周朝伟. 英汉法律文本翻译：理论与实践[M]. 北京：中国人民大学出版社，2012.
[21] 马会娟. 商务英语翻译教程[M]. 北京：中国商务出版社，2007.
[22] 梅德明. 新编商务英语翻译[M]. 北京：高等教育出版社，2005.
[23] 彭萍. 实用商务文体翻译[M]. 北京：中央编译出版社，2008.
[24] 任月花. 商务翻译概论[M]. 广州：暨南大学出版社，2010.
[25] 陶全胜. 从翻译目的论看企业外宣资料汉英翻译原则[J]. 合肥工业大学学报（社会科学版），2005（4）.
[26] 滕超，孔飞燕. 英汉法律互译：理论与实践[M]. 杭州：浙江大学出版社，2008.

[27] 王春玉. 商务谈判英语[M]. 北京：中国纺织出版社，2002.
[28] 王磊，贾玉. 功能目的论指导下的产品说明书翻译[J]. 湖北经济学院学报（人文社会科学版），2013（1）.
[29] 王建国. 当代商务英语翻译教程[M]. 北京：中国对外翻译出版公司，2009.
[30] 王盈秋，张莉. 商务英语翻译教程[M]. 北京：北京理工大学出版社，2010.
[31] 吴国新. 国际贸易单证实务[M]. 3版. 北京：清华大学出版社，2012.
[32] 吴磊. 外贸单证的词句特点及翻译方法[J]. 外语教学与研究，2009（63）.
[33] 严平. 对外经济贸易业务知识大全[M]. 太原：山西人民出版社，1987.
[34] 易露霞，方玲玲，陈原. 国际贸易实务[M]. 3版. 北京：清华大学出版社，2011.
[35] 尹诗文. 从商业广告的文体特点看商务广告翻译[J]. 赤峰学院学报，2010（2）.
[36] 苑春鸣，姜丽. 商务英语翻译[M]. 北京：外语教学与研究出版社，2013.
[37] 袁洪，王济华. 商务翻译实务[M]. 北京：对外经济贸易大学出版社，2011.
[38] 张长明，平洪. 法律英语的句法特点及其汉英翻译策略[J]. 广东外语外贸大学学报，2005（4）.
[39] 张法连. 法律英语翻译[M]. 济南：山东大学出版社，2009.
[40] 郑欢. 商务英语 谈判技巧与句型[M]. 成都：西南交通大学出版社，2000.